The Gardener's Guide
to Growing
DAHLIAS

The Gardener's Guide to Growing

DAHLIAS

Gareth Rowlands

DAVID & CHARLES
Newton Abbot

TIMBER PRESS
Portland, Oregon

ACKNOWLEDGEMENTS

We are grateful to Roger Aylett, of Aylett's Nurseries, and to Richard Ayres, Head Gardener of Anglesey Abbey, for assistance with photographic locations and the provision of blooms to be photographed.

PICTURE CREDITS

Karl Adamson pages 20, 24, 32, 52–53, 62–63, 71, 74–75, 106–107, 124–125, 140–141; Derek Hewlett page 147; Clive Nichols pages 2 (The Priory, Kemerton, Worcestershire), 42 (Hadspen Garden, Somerset), 44 (RHS Gardens, Wisley), 45 (The Priory, as before); Gareth Rowlands pages 10, 11, 51, 66, 80, 89, 109, 112, 115, 119, 126, 128, 144; all other photographs by Justyn Willsmore.

NOTE

Throughout the book the time of year is given as a season to make the reference applicable to readers all over the world. In the northern hemisphere the seasons may be translated into months as follows:

Early winter	December	*Early spring*	March	*Early summer*	June	*Early autumn*	September
Midwinter	January	*Mid-spring*	April	*Midsummer*	July	*Mid-autumn*	October
Late winter	February	*Late spring*	May	*Late summer*	August	*Late autumn*	November

First published in the UK in 1999 by David & Charles Publishers, Brunel House, Newton Abbot, Devon
ISBN 0 7153 0858 0

First published in North America in 1999 by Timber Press Inc., 133 SW Second Avenue, Suite 450, Portland, Oregon 97204, USA
ISBN 0-88192-434-2

A catalog record of this book is available from the Library of Congress

Designed by Jo Weeks
Illustrated by Coral Mula
Printed in Italy by Lego SpA

page 1   'Dana Frank' (p.105) is a modern pompon variety with exhibition-quality blooms.

page 2   The red border at The Priory, Hereford and Worcester with dahlias 'Bishop of Llandaff' and 'Blazdon Red' along with nicotianas and sedums (see p.44).

page 3   'Tender Moon' (p.130) is a fine dahlia for garden display.

CONTENTS

Introduction		7
1.	Origin and History	8
2.	Botany	14
3.	Dahlia Types	23
4.	Dahlia Species	37
5.	Dahlias in the Garden	43
6.	Cultivation *including Pests and Diseases*	47
7.	Propagation	70
8.	Raising New Varieties	79
9.	Exhibiting Dahlias	87
10.	A-Z of Dahlias in Cultivation	97
11.	Dahlias in North America *by Martin Kral*	135
12.	Dahlia Societies and Trials	145

Appendices
   I   Glossary 149
   II Where to Buy Dahlias 150
   III Where to See Dahlias 152
   IV Dahlias on the Internet 152
   V Selected British Varieties 153
   VI Selected American Varieties 154
   VII Reading about Dahlias 157

Index   158

INTRODUCTION

The dahlia has fans all over the world. This is a tribute to its adaptability as well as to the enthusiasts who have worked to make it so popular. After its arrival in Europe from Central America, towards the end of the eighteenth century, its development proceeded apace in Britain, France, Germany and the Netherlands. It was popular in Britain during the Victorian era, and as the British Empire spread it was taken to the colonies.

Few public parks and gardens are without a dahlia border, and from stately home to council house, dahlias contribute to many and varied magnificent floral displays. They also make an eye-catching focus in any horticultural show and are ideal for flower arrangements. For variety of form and colour, dahlias are difficult to beat, and they are remarkably easy to grow.

Following its popularity as a garden plant, the dahlia rapidly became an exhibition flower in Britain, and later in America, Australia and New Zealand. Thus most of the dahlias available in these countries today are show varieties. In most of Continental Europe, in contrast, dahlias are still primarily garden flowers, and any show or trial focuses on massed beds of them in parks or exhibition gardens.

SHOW CAMARADERIE

Over thirty years of growing and showing dahlias has brought me into contact with many dahlia growers, and has made me many firm friends. One of my earliest memories of the dahlia world was being introduced to the legendary A.T. Barnes at a Bedford Dahlia Society

Anemone-flowered 'Scarlet Comet' is a good variety for growing in gardens.

show in the early 1960s. As a novice grower I was interested to find out where I could get some plants of the varieties that had won on the show bench. Mr Barnes invited me to visit him and I duly called at his house on an agreed Sunday morning. Over the next few hours I learned a tremendous amount about growing dahlias *and* returned home with a collection of plants. Among them was a giant decorative that he had raised called 'Lavengro', which gained worldwide recognition.

Although there has been a great deal written about the dahlia, much of it has been in the journals of specialist dahlia societies, which are not widely available to the average gardener. Likewise there have been several monographs on dahlias, but most of these are now out of date and unobtainable. Among the popular books on dahlias, those by the late Philip Damp, a past Secretary of the National Dahlia Society, are outstanding. His love of dahlias was evident in his writing.

To Philip and my many dahlia friends I am forever grateful for the knowledge and experience that is embodied in this book. I am grateful for the generosity of 'Bertie' Barnes and the many other dahlia enthusiasts who helped me to get started, and to whom this book is dedicated. First and foremost is Ernest Pitt who was chairman of the local dahlia society and a writer for *Amateur Gardening* for over thirty years. I am indebted to him for his help and encouragement over the years and much of the content of this book has been gleaned from him and other colleagues in the dahlia world. More recently, I have gained many dahlia friends from the four corners of the world over the 'dahlia-net'. This has served to reinforce my belief in the worldwide appeal of the genus.

1
ORIGIN AND HISTORY

The garden dahlia, *Dahlia × variabilis*, is a plant of cultivation, derived from wild relatives found growing in Mexico.

In 1651 reports of flowers bigger than asters, with double or multiple whorls of ray florets, and of many colours (red, yellow, blackish and white), were published in Rome. These reports originated from Francisco Hernandez, a Spaniard who had spent seven years in Mexico from 1570–1577 sponsored by Phillip II of Spain. The initial report was written in Latin with illustrations drawn by another Spaniard, Francisco Dominguez. Later, a Madrid edition appeared and this was translated at the beginning of the twentieth century by an American, W.E. Safford. He added further notes to the original and his translation was published in the *Journal of the Washington Academy of Science* in 1919. In the United States at this time, interest was being shown in the dahlia, with the American Dahlia Society being established in 1913, but it is clear that, in Europe, dahlias were a popular flower nearly one hundred years earlier.

CHRONOLOGY

For many years it was confidently believed that the dahlia had been introduced into England in 1789. However, the record was put straight in 1916 by a horticulturalist called C. Harman Payne FRS. His paper to the Royal Horticultural Society, the result of a number of years studying the early records, reads like a detective story. It began in 1889 when the National Dahlia Society celebrated the centenary of the introduction of the dahlia into England with the Centenary Show and Conference at the Crystal Palace. At the conference, a Mr Shirley Hibberd read a paper entitled *The History of*

the Dahlia in which he stated that Lady Bute, wife of the then Ambassador from England to the Court of Spain, had acquired some seeds of the dahlia and sent them to England in 1789, but had failed to keep the plants for more than two or three years. Mr Harman Payne, unhappy with this statement, decided to investigate.

The reason for the confusion about the date can be traced to the first reference to the dahlia in English horticultural literature, namely in a volume of that classical reference, *Hortus Kewensis*, which is a catalogue of the plants cultivated in the Royal Botanic Garden at Kew. The volume in question was published in 1813. It noted the date of the introduction of dahlia plants by Lady Bute (sometimes referred to as the Marchioness of Bute) as being in 1789. However, this date was a printer's error. Despite an update in 1814 in *Epitome of the second edition of the Hortus Kewensis* where the date was corrected to 1798, the original error was perpetuated for over a hundred years, the correction going unnoticed until Harman Payne made his study. All the horticultural reference works in the intervening period quoted the original date (and some still do so!) and hence the NDS Centenary Show and Conference was held in 1889.

The early history of the dahlia in Europe makes sense once the correct chronology of events is established: dahlia seeds only reached Spain in 1789 and were not successfully flowered until the autumn of 1790. Thus they could not have been sent on to England in 1789.

THE FIRST THREE SPECIES

The first seeds to arrive in Spain were sent from Mexico by Vicente de Cervantes, Director of the Mexican Botanical Gardens, and were grown in Madrid by the

Abbé Cavanilles. (Cavanilles was not the Director of the Madrid Botanic Gardens, as is asserted by some authors, but simply worked there. The Director at the time was Casimiro Gomes de Ortega, see below.) In *Icones et Descriptiones Plantarum* published in 1791, Cavanilles described and illustrated the growing plants. The drawing was not in colour, but showed a plant with single flowers, which Cavanilles named *Dahlia pinnata* in honour of the Swedish botanist Andreas Dahl (a pupil of Linnaeus). The Abbé published further volumes, and in the third in 1793 he described two other species, which he called *Dahlia rosea* and *Dahlia coccinea*. The descriptions of these new exotic flowers caused great interest among horticulturalists and led to correspondence and requests for seeds, largely without success.

Kew Gardens were keen to obtain seeds, and their records show that they enlisted the help of Lady Bute, wife of John Stuart, the Viscount Montstuart. She was a very keen gardener and had close links with Kew. The early record books, which list exchanges of plants and seeds, include a 'List of plants in the Hort. Madrid and wanted for Kew Gardens', marked with the name of

'Kathleen's Alliance' is a small cactus variety excellent for exhibition, garden display and cutting.

Lady Bute. The list names the three species described by Cavanilles in his books. These three must have been received at Kew and grown there, since dried specimens of them found their way into Sir Joseph Banks's herbarium at Kew and were later transferred to the Natural History Museum in London. The three specimens are labelled *D. pinnata*, *D. rosea* and *D. coccinea* 'C.G. Ortega (Lady Bute)'. Lady Bute had been able to help get the material to Kew via her connections with Spain, made while her husband was Ambassador in Madrid from 1795 to 1797. C.G. Ortega was Director of the Botanic Garden, Madrid, from 1771–1801.

The same three dahlia species were introduced into France in 1802 and grown in the Botanic Garden in Paris. André Thouin provided descriptions of them, together with coloured illustrations, for the *Annales* of the garden's museum in 1804. Dahlias arrived in Germany about the same time and were described by Professor Willdenow in 1803. However, the Professor changed the genus name to *Georgina*, in honour of a

Russian botanist Professor Georgi, and this was to cause endless confusion in the horticultural world; dahlias are still often referred to under this name in Eastern Europe.

CULTIVATION IN BRITAIN

In 1802, John Fraser of Sloane Square in Chelsea obtained *D. coccinea* from France and it flowered there in the following year. A coloured figure and description of this plant appears in the *Curtis's Botanical Magazine* of 1804 (plate 762).

The next record of the dahlia in British horticultural literature is found in a paper presented to the Horticultural Society (which became the Royal Horticultural Society in 1861) in 1808 by Richard Anthony Salisbury FRS, an eminent botanist and horticulturalist. He described plants that he had grown in his garden at Hampstead in 1806 from seeds obtained from the Right Honourable Lady Holland's gardener, Mr Buonaiuti, who had, in turn, grown plants from seed received by Lady Holland from Madrid in May 1804.

Richard Salisbury acquired the seeds in April 1806. He sowed them in rich potting soil on May 5th. The subsequent plants were planted out into good soil in the garden, but the first flower was not seen until October 7th. The tubers were lifted and overwintered in pots under cover, being planted out again on April 27th 1807, when Richard Salisbury considered that the risk of frost in his garden was over. One plant was grown in poor stony ground and first flowered on August 19th. A second plant was grown against the south-east side of the house in rich soil and made a very large plant but had not flowered by October 14th. From this Mr Salisbury concluded that in order to flower dahlias successfully they should be planted in poor soil, otherwise they made too much growth.

Seeds were passed on to other horticulturalists; those that were received by Messers Lee & Kennedy's nursery at Hammersmith had successfully flowered in 1806. Richard Salisbury also referred to a Mr E.J.A. Woodford having flowered *D. rosea* in his garden at Vauxhall in 1803, these plants having been received from Paris.

The remarkable thing about this paper is that there is no mention of Lady Bute and the plants she had supplied to Kew Gardens ten years earlier. This suggests a lack of communication between the Horticultural Society and Kew Gardens. A later letter to the

One of the show and fancy dahlias of the nineteenth century 'Royal Adelaide' would be classified as a ball today.

Horticultural Society from Mr J. Wedgwood describes dahlias flowered at Etruria in the Midlands. (Mr Wedgwood was the famous pottery magnate.)

SINGLE AND DOUBLE FLOWERS

A notable feature of the early history of the dahlia in Europe is that most of the illustrations are of plants that have single flowers. The exception is that of *D. superflua* (now regarded as *D. pinnata*) in *Curtis's Botanical Magazine* (plate 1885B) which shows a purple semi-double form. The sister illustration (plate 1885A) is clearly a single-flowered dahlia with eight crimson ray petals and a large disc.

Both illustrations were of plants received from the Comtes de Vandes 'who imported these with several other varieties from France, where these plants have been cultivated for some years with great assiduity, particularly by M. Lelieur at Sevre, near Paris'.

So how did the fully double dahlias of today arise? Some indication is given in Mr W.J.C. Lawrence's article in the *NDS Dahlia Annual*, 1970. He says that the explorer Alexander von Humbolt sent seeds of dahlias from Mexico to Paris and Berlin in 1804. From this date onwards, a dramatic increase in the variability of the dahlia took place. Lawrence suggests that the seed was naturally cross-pollinated in its native Mexico and must have come from a wide range of types. According to Lawrence, there is no evidence that von Humbolt collected the seed from the wild; as he was no botanist, Lawrence concludes that he probably obtained the seed from a gardener. Professor Paul D. Sorensen, an American authority on the genus, points out that in Hernandez's original work, one of the illustrations shows semi-double dahlias, similar to those of modern cultivars. Professor Sorensen states that during his extensive travels in Mexico studying natural populations, all of the wild dahlias he has observed have single flowers with eight ray petals. In contrast, garden populations in Mexico are typically double or semi-double.

It is well documented that the Aztecs were great gardeners, and that Montezuma had created a spectacular tropical garden at Huaxtepec. Moreover, Hernandez spent the bulk of his time devoted to writing at the Convent of Huaxtepec. Although there is no direct evidence that the plants he described came from gardens, Hernandez must have been familiar with these garden dahlias. It is also likely that the seeds that were obtained by von Humbolt in 1804 were collected from garden plants with double or semi-double flowers. Hence it can be assumed that von Humbolt is the original source of our double dahlias of today, rather than those seeds obtained by Cavanilles in Madrid in 1789.

DEVELOPMENT OF FLOWER FORMS

Regular consignments of tubers were arriving in England from France during the early part of the nineteenth century, and English nurserymen had started developing new types. Mr J. Lee of Lee & Kennedy's nursery, Hammersmith, is credited with developing the first ball type of dahlia in 1818. By 1836 the Horticultural Society of London (now the Royal Horticultural Society) published the *Dahlia Register* listing more than 700 varieties. These were intended for show purposes and the *Dahlia Register* referred to 45 dahlia shows being held throughout England during 1835.

The dahlia was becoming a rich man's flower with tubers of new varieties changing hands at a guinea a time – a great deal of money in those days. In 1833 at a tavern in Hackney Road, London, a challenge was issued to a show of 12 'pans' containing 12 blooms for a wager of £24, and a new variety called 'Yellow Defiance' was sold for £200 in 1835, obviously in anticipation of considerable prize money in the future. In September 1858, a Grand National Dahlia Show was advertised in St James's Hall, London, with total prize money amounting to 100 guineas.

Such prize money stimulated great interest in dahlias and nurserymen responded to the demand for new varieties. Raisers such as Inwood, Lyne, Bartlett, Brown Bros, Cooe Bros, Harris, Heale & Son, Skillman, Glenny and Wheeler proceeded to release new types.

Inwood released a ball dahlia called 'Springwood Rival' in 1832; this was followed by a slightly different form also called 'Springwood Rival' from Lyne in 1834. Both were perfect ball dahlias with 'cupped' florets.

'Commander-in Chief' is an early example of an decorative-type dahlia. It was grown in the nineteenth century.

Bicolour and picotee forms also emerged. For example Harris's 'Inimitable' was a clear-cut bicolour while their 'Acme of Perfection' was a laced or picotee variety. Wheeler's 'Warminster Rival' and Skilman's 'Hebe' were improved forms of 'Springwood Rival' and gave rise to the popular show and fancy types which dominated the dahlia show scene for a hundred years.

The obsession with show and fancy dahlias meant that other forms were ignored by growers and nurserymen, and this restricted the development of the dahlia in Britain for many decades. Other flower types that appeared in the seed beds of English raisers were ruthlessly eradicated.

LILLIPUT OR POMPON DAHLIAS

The lilliput or pompon dahlia was developed in Germany. Johann Sieckmann announced in 1850 that he had developed a range of these little dahlias and they were described in Regel's *Gartenflora* in 1852. They varied in petal formation from tight, quill-petalled forms to loose, wide-petalled forms. Raisers in France took over the breeding of these forms and eventually produced the tight forms typical of today's poms. (The name pompon arose through the resemblance of the flowerheads to the red button worn on the caps of French sailors.) The pompon types were offered in England during the 1860s; a catalogue of 1864 offered thirty varieties, divided into two groups: those growing 1.5–2m (5–6ft) tall and shorter varieties of about 60–90cm (2–3ft) tall. The first pompon dahlias are believed to have arrived in North America in 1861.

CACTUS DAHLIAS

The cactus-form is believed to have arisen from *D. juarezii*, which arrived in the Netherlands in 1872, the same year as the cactus form appeared. At the time, all dahlias on the showbench in Britain were still of decorative and ball formation. It is thought that the name 'cactus' was bestowed on this form because of the similarity to the flowers of *Cereus* cactus.

The original cactus-form plant was thought to be sterile, but in 1887, an English raiser, J.T. West, found one seed which gave rise to a variety named 'Beauty of Brentwood'. Other seedlings derived from *D. juarezii* soon followed. Initially they were mainly purple or red, but later, pinks and mauves appeared and, finally, a white variety, 'Keynes' White'. The cactus blood

spread into more formal decorative stocks giving rise to many larger varieties with strap-like petals and to peony-flowered varieties.

PEONY-FLOWERED DAHLIAS

Peony-flowered dahlias, which have been around from very early days, often appear from single-flowered dahlias. The very large peony-flowered dahlias were developed by Wilhelm Pfitzer of Germany and taken up by M.H. Hornsveld of Baarn in the Netherlands who eventually produced a range of large peony types in the late nineteenth century. Giant-flowered decoratives seem to have developed from these types and were introduced into France where Rivoire in Lyons popularized them.

New giant informal dahlias were exported from the Netherlands around the world at the turn of the nineteenth century. English raisers took up the challenge and matched the Dutch breeders with excellent giant decorative dahlias at the beginning of the twentieth.

DECORATIVE DAHLIAS

The origin of the decorative type of dahlia grown today is not clear. The name was coined in Britain to provide a convenient grouping for those types that did not fall into any other clearly defined group, and includes formal and less formal types. It is most likely that the peony-flowered dahlia was the source of this type.

The development of the more formal decorative dahlias is relatively recent and is driven by the desire of English exhibitors and judges to see 'more perfect' blooms on the showbench.

COLLERETTE DAHLIAS

The collerette dahlia originated as a sport in the municipal gardens of the Parc de la Tête d'Or at Lyons, France in 1899 and soon became very popular in France and Germany. Two single-flowered varieties had produced blooms with a second row of abnormal florets, that resembled a ruffled collar, around the disc. These sports were fixed and propagated and finally released by Messers Rivoire and Sons of Lyons. The collerettes they raised produced seed, some of which came true to type.

It was 1901 before collerettes came to Britain and British breeders started developing the range. Like the French and the Germans, British gardeners were attracted to these dahlias and they were soon in wide-spread cultivation; however, their use declined with the coming of the First World War.

STAR AND ORCHID

Other dahlias that appeared around this time include the star form, which was like a single cactus, and the orchid form, again a modified cactus type. The development of these dahlias was taken up by, among others, Dobbie and Co of Edinburgh in the 1930s, but it was not until 1948 that the double orchid form 'Giraffe' was released in the Netherlands.

DWARF DAHLIAS

Dwarf dahlias were found in 1750 growing on the semi-wooded lower slopes of the Sierra del Ajusca mountains, Mexico, and in 1803 von Humbolt described similar types found at 2100m (7000ft). These species, which were named *D. dissecta*, *D. pubescens* and *D. tenuis*, all grew to a height of 38–45cm (15–18in) and had finely divided leaves. Using them as a base, French and Belgian breeders began to develop dwarf varieties. Rivoire of Lyons raised a number of seedlings, among them 'Lucifer', which had very dark, almost black, leaves and subsequently gave rise to a stream of new types, named collectively, *D. 'laciniata purpurea'*, which had finely divided, black or bronze foliage. This spread to England and was taken up by Mr J. Cheal of Crawley who produced a wide range of colours and types released under the title of Tom Thumbs, later changed to Mignons. Bedding features in public parks and gardens were soon planted up with these popular plants. As seed from these varieties produced very variable results, they were propagated vegetatively.

Reports from 1873 state that *D. gracilis* had been used as the parent of dwarf bushy singles that were then introduced by Benedict Roezl.

During the 1930s, some varieties were found to come relatively true to type from seed and they were released as the Coltness Gem Hybrids. Charles W.J. Unwin of Histon developed a race of dwarf Charm dahlias. Easy from seed, these gave rise to a range of singles and semi-doubles in most colours, and are still popular today.

WATERLILY DAHLIAS

Waterlily types of dahlia are believed to have arisen from a sport found growing in a garden in New Jersey by a Mr Peacock, and the first named variety of this type was released by him in 1893.

Chapter 3 Dahlia Types gives details of the modern system of classifying dahlias.

MODERN DAHLIAS

Since the early days of its cultivation the dahlia has gone from being available only to the rich, to being a plant to be enjoyed by almost any gardener. Following the end of the Second World War, the dahlia scene was dominated by a group of Dutch nurserymen – Ballego, Lammerse, Geerling, Bruidegom, Maarse, Bakker, Topsvoort and Hoek – who developed a huge export business, selling small tubers in plastic bags, each bag with a large colourful picture of the dahlia inside. Of these, only Geerling survives. The English nurserymen of the post-war period suffered a similar fate with only Halls of Heddon and Oscroft surviving from the immediate post-war period. A similar picture exists in North America and in Australia and New Zealand where gifted amateur raisers dominate the scene. While the early development of dahlias was in the hands of nurserymen feeding the demands of keen exhibitors, who were prepared to pay large sums for the newest varieties, more recently the keen exhibitor has found that raising new forms is quite feasible for an amateur. This has led to a flood of new varieties on the market and, hence, the disappearance of many of the old nurseries.

The drawback of this new development is that very little thought is given to the performance of these types in comparison to existing ones. Many of them are seen for one season on the show bench and then disappear and, in any case, the average gardener has difficulty in finding them for sale, as much of the trade is simply between the raiser and a limited circle of exhibitors. Because most exhibitors are interested in raising varieties suitable for exhibition, rather than garden display, only a limited genetic pool (based on exhibition varieties) is being exploited and a conscious effort will be required to maintain a wider variety of genetic material. More positively, some exhibitors are now offering lists of varieties that they are willing to sell, and the distinction between amateurs and professionals, once important in leading shows, has gone. Many amateurs are now able to sell plants without prejudicing their amateur status. This can only be good for the future of the dahlia.

2

BOTANY

*D*ahlia belongs to the Compositae family, which is now often called Asteraceae. The most obvious characteristic of this family is the composite structure of its 'flowers'. Each 'flower' consists of a group of florets arranged on a more or less flat or domed disc, the receptacle, at the top of a common stem. Each floret is actually a true flower, with individual reproductive organs; for this reason flowers of plants of the Compositae are usually called flowerheads. A daisy flowerhead is typical of the Compositae: the centre of the flowerhead consists of disc florets, each a tiny flower, and these are encircled by ray florets, which have long, petal-like structures radiating outwards. Other genera that belong to the Compositae are *Aster*, *Helianthus* (sunflower) and *Chrysanthemum*.

Compositae is the largest family of flowering plants with over 14,000 species throughout the world. It comprises examples of almost all known types, from large trees and shrubs, to tiny desert plants, aquatics and alpines. Many species are valuable garden flowers; there are also vegetables, such as lettuce, endive, artichoke and salsify.

Within Compositae there are tribes, consisting of smaller, more closely related genera. The tribe to which the dahlia belongs is called Heliantheae and also includes *Helianthus*, *Rudbeckia*, *Coreopsis* and *Cosmos*. Among these, the dahlia is distinguished by producing root tubers and having bracts between the florets (although some perennial *Helianthus* species have tubers). Under natural conditions, it dies back to the root tubers in the autumn and regenerates in early summer. The flowerheads are insect-pollinated which, in cultivated plants, leads to seedlings that can vary considerably from the parents.

DAHLIA SYSTEMATICS

The genus *Dahlia* is thought to contain 27 species that grow in the wild, mainly in Mexico and Guatemala.

The systematics of the genus were extensively revised by Professor Paul Sorensen in 1969 on the basis of studies of many of the species growing in the wild in Mexico, and of herbarium specimens, together with previously published descriptions. The cultivated dahlia is believed to be the result of hybridization between two wild species. One of these is agreed by all to be *D. coccinea*, while the other is believed to be a purple-flowered species. Of the two purple-flowered species known to produce semi-double flowerheads, *D. imperialis*, the tree dahlia, is unlikely to have been involved because of its size and habit, so the other, *D. pinnata* is the most likely second parent. However, hybrids between *D. coccinea* and *D. pinnata* have not been recorded in the wild, even though these species co-exist in one part of southern Mexico.

It is interesting to note that the dramatic increase in the variability of the 'cultivated' dahlia took place in Europe during the early part of the nineteenth century. There was only very limited variation in the original population of *D. pinnata* and *D. coccinea* grown from seed in the Madrid Botanical Garden by Cavanilles in 1791 (*D. rosea* described by Cavanilles is now generally considered to be a slightly different form of *D. pinnata*, while others attribute it to *D. merckii*). However, the plants of seeds sent by Alexander von Humbolt to the Paris and Berlin Botanical Gardens in 1804 showed a great deal of variability. As stated in Chapter 1, von Humbolt probably obtained seeds from one or more botanical gardens in Mexico. These gardens may have contained plants that originated with the Aztecs, who

The single-flowered dahlia 'Moonfire' is classified as a dwarf bedding variety, but usually grows to nearer 1m (3ft).

were great gardeners, and it may be that the cultivated dahlia of today arose centuries ago in those Aztec gardens. However, it is more likely that the addition of a new source of variability from von Humbolt to the existing pool of variability already expressed by *D. pinnata* and *D. coccinea*, growing alongside each other in the botanical gardens of Europe, gave rise to the modern cultivated dahlia.

In 1809 Professor Willdenow of Berlin, faced with the bewildering array of cultivated dahlias, coined the epithet *variabilis* to include all cultivated forms. Unfortunately, he also used the generic name *Georgina* instead of *Dahlia* and thus caused furore in the botanical world. In 1829 Desfontaines published a catalogue of the plants in the Paris Botanical Garden and gave the name *Dahlia variabilis* to all the cultivated forms. This was immediately accepted and persists to this day as *Dahlia × variabilis* (Willd.) Desf. This name is used here as it is the one that is most familiar in horticulture for the garden dahlia (the correct name may be *D. × hortensis* Guillaum.).

THE TYPICAL GARDEN DAHLIA

The garden dahlia, *Dahlia × variabilis*, is described as an herbaceous perennial that is usually 1–2m (3–6ft) tall. The stems are 8–12mm (⅜–½in) in diameter and unbranched except in the flowering portion. They are hollow and scabrous (rough), often red or maroon, and have internodes 9–16cm (3½–6in) long. The leaves are simple or pinnatisect to bipinnate and their surfaces are slightly hairy. Their petioles have a broadly winged midrib, which is crescent-shaped in cross-section.

There are 2–8 flowerheads per plant. These vary from 'single' blooms, with an outer ring of ray florets surrounding a central disc, to fully double blooms containing 200–300 ray florets and a reduced central disc only visible as the blooms fade. The ray florets are in various shades: white, whitish-lavender to deep purple, or yellow to various shades of orange to deep blackish-scarlet. They are female or sterile. The disc florets are tubular and yellow, yellow with purple tips, or purple throughout. They are hermaphrodite and fertile.

Achenes (seeds) are 10–15mm (½in) long and 2–4mm (1/16–1/8in) wide. Greyish-black to black when mature, they are more or less linear and flattened, capped with a small tan disc.

Named after a friend by the raiser Terry Clarke, 'Ernie Pitt' is a small decorative dahia that is ideal for exhibition.

The foregoing description applies to plants in their first year of growth from seed. The juvenile plant typically dies back in the autumn and regenerates from underground tubers during the following spring or early summer. Plants grown from tubers (ie more than a year old) exhibit sturdier growth, thicker stems, more pinnately divided leaves, and more and larger blooms.

ROOTS

Young dahlia seedlings develop a mass of fibrous roots, some of which thicken up and eventually become the tubers that overwinter. These thicker roots tend to descend deeper in a good loamy soil to seek out water and to anchor the plant. A mass of fibrous roots also spreads out below the surface of the soil. These are the main feeding roots and are easily damaged by cultivation or by drying out of the soil. Buds develop where the tuberous roots join the main stem. These will form the next season's stems. Some dahlia varieties produce only a few tuberous roots while others typically make a tight clump of tubers.

The Connecticut Agricultural Experiment Station has investigated the yield and chemical composition of dahlia tubers. It found between eight and 15 tons per acre. About fifty per cent of the storage material in the tubers is inulin, a material similar to but not the same

as starch as found in plants such as the potato. In this respect the dahlia is like the Jerusalem artichoke. The great French botanist de Candolle tried the tubers as a food, both boiled and baked, but said he could not develop a taste for them. Cattle and horses also rejected them, but the Connecticut Agricultural Station has suggested that grated in salads their pungent flavour resembled that of radishes. Dahlia tubers were certainly eaten for food by Mexicans during earlier times, and may have been eaten in the Netherlands as a potato substitute during the Second World War, but they are obviously an acquired taste.

An investigation into the possibilities of growing dahlias as a commercial crop for inulin production has been inconclusive. When inulin is treated with hydrochloric acid it breaks down into a sugar called levulose, which is similar to glucose but much sweeter. In the plant, inulin is broken down by an enzyme, inulase, to provide sugars as a source of energy as the tuber starts back into growth in the spring. Small quantities of other useful chemicals have also been found in dahlia tubers, but not enough to make commercial cultivation an economic proposition.

SHOOTS

When the dahlia starts into growth during spring, the buds that appear where the tubers join the old stem quickly develop into shoots. If removed and rooted in a suitable medium, a new shoot is capable of developing into a complete plant. If left to grow on the parent tuber, it is likely to suppress the development of further shoots. However, the tubers can be individually cut from the old plant, together with some tissue from the old stem, then each separate tuber will probably send up a new shoot. This indicates that apical dominance is very strong in the dahlia, that is, one strong shoot will suppress the growth of side, or secondary, shoots. The mechanism is activated by a powerful plant hormone called auxin, which is produced in the stem apex and stimulates elongation of the stem. Once the shoot starts elongating, the auxin is translocated from the tip and suppresses the development of lateral buds. The effect wears off after some time, more quickly in some varieties than in others. Thus, to allow secondary and side shoots to develop, the primary shoot should be removed.

The young shoots are solid with no central canal, but

after two or three nodes of growth they become hollow. (The Aztec names for dahlia are *acocotli* and *cocoxochitl*, both of which signify a hollow-stemmed plant: *acocotli* means water-pipe and *cocoxochitl* means hollow-stem flower. It is said that the Mexicans used the dried hollow stems to duct water in their irrigation systems.) Although the outer layers have some thickening, the rigidity of the stem is largely due to the water content. During the later part of the growing season, stems cut down near their base release a considerable quantity of water from the hollow centre. When tubers are lifted in the autumn, it is important that they are inverted, allowing all the water to drain away, otherwise they will rot away from the centre and will not keep through the winter.

LEAVES

Dahlia leaves are usually produced in pairs at each node, the next pair up the stem being at right angles to the pair below. Sometimes, in some varieties, three leaves may be found per node on the lower nodes, but this usually reverts to two as new nodes are formed above. A wide range of foliage types is to be found among dahlia varieties – some have finely divided foliage, others have leaves that are almost entire. Generally, juvenile leaves are entire, lobed or divided into three parts – a basal pair of leaflets and a terminal leaflet; occasionally there may be two basal pairs so the leaf consists of five parts. Later leaves tend to be more divided, each basal and terminal leaflet being further divided into three or sometimes five leaflets. Margins also become more toothed.

The petioles are winged in most varieties and have a crescent-shaped cross section. In the axils of each leaf are tiny buds from which side shoots, or laterals, develop. This only occurs when the apical dominance is removed (by pinching out the tip), or as the plant flowers and ages. The leaves on such laterals are usually larger than those produced on the main stem, and they also tend to be more divided and toothed.

This multiple division of the leaves and more pronounced dentation of the margins also occurs when flower buds are formed. However, the uppermost leaf subtending the apical flower bud often reverts to an entire leaf form with little dentation. In most exhibition varieties, laterals are slow to develop unless the growing tip of the main stem is removed; these plants are influenced by the auxin. Branching is more common in dwarf bedding varieties, because dwarfing usually means reduced apical dominance, with less auxin production and hence less suppression of laterals. But even here, branching is accelerated if the growing tip of the main stem is removed.

The function of the leaves is to produce sugars from carbon dioxide in the air and water, which is drawn up through the roots, by the process of photosynthesis. During photosynthesis oxygen is released into the air. Sunlight is essential for photosynthesis and is usually the limiting factor. Sugar provides the energy needed for growth and development; it is transported around the plant in solution, and energy is released when oxygen breaks it down. This is called oxidation and it can take place without light: it is dominant when tubers break into growth during the spring and it also occurs during the hours of darkness. Thus more plant growth tends to take place at night than during the day. During oxidation, carbon dioxide is released into the air, together with water vapour. When the plant is growing vigorously, the water vapour collects in the leaves and seeps out through the pores near the tips, forming large globules. This phenomenon, known as guttation, is a sign of healthy growth.

(For information on leaf disorders see Pests and Diseases pp.59–69.)

FLOWER DEVELOPMENT AND STRUCTURE

By the time the flower buds are clearly visible on the plant, the parts of the flowerhead are already differentiated. Pollen grains and ovules are already formed although they may not yet be fully developed. All that remains is for the flower parts to increase in size. As cell division has virtually ceased in the flowerhead by this time, size is determined by cell enlargement or elongation, and this occurs purely by increased water content. If leaves and stems are growing rapidly at this time, then there can be competition for the available water between flowerheads and leaves. Therefore, if size of bloom is the main objective, one should aim to have built the plant framework before flowering commences. Moreover, flowerheads that are past their peak should be removed, or they will compete with developing ones.

Although flowerheads rarely contain chlorophyll *a* or *b*, carotin and xanthophyll or derivatives are present and provide the pigmentation. Magnesium, iron and other trace elements have an effect on flower pigmentation and adequate trace elements are necessary for brightness and vibrancy of colour.

The flowerhead of a single-flowered dahlia consists of a central disc of short tubular florets from which radiate eight long, strap-shaped ray florets. Each disc floret has a central ovary from which arises a long style that splits into two stigmas at its tip.

Surrounding the style is a tube of anthers. The anthers open to release the pollen, but the tip of the style does not split apart until a day or two later. The florets are thus designed to avoid self-pollination. The oldest florets are on the outer part of the disc, the youngest to the centre; florets open in waves over a period of days.

The shape of the 'petal' of the ray florets varies enormously in garden dahlias, from the broad, strap-shaped petals of single dahlias to the blunt, tubular petals of ball dahlias, and the long, spiky petals of cactus types. The petals can incurve or reflex, they can be split at the ends (fimbriated), or be blunt or pointed. In ball dahlias, the petal margins roll inwards to form a tube (involute), while in cactus dahlias, the margins roll outwards to form a tube (revolute). Petal colour ranges from white through ivory, cream, yellow, pink, orange, red to purple, but never blue. Colour may be uniform, blended, tipped, or streaked; sometimes a faint flush of colour may edge an otherwise uniformly coloured bloom.

Outside the ray florets is a ring of green bracts which protect the florets inside the developing flower bud. The base of the flowerbud is formed by a fleshy receptacle upon which the florets develop.

In fully double flowers, the central disc is not visible and the bloom consists mainly of ray florets, although as it passes its peak, some disc florets can often be seen.

Between the individual florets are short, fleshy bracts which help the bloom to open. When the petals fall after the seed is set, the bracts grow to protect the still-developing seeds and supply nutrients to them. When the seeds are ripe, the bracts dry out and become paper-thin.

'Anniversary Ball' was raised by the author and introduced by Aylett's Nurseries to commemorate their fortieth anniversary.

FLORET ARRANGEMENT

As in other members of the Heliantheae, bloom formation in dahlias is very precisely determined. Looking into the centre of a single-flowered bloom from above, the central disc florets can be seen to be regularly arranged in a spiral. Closer examination reveals that there are two sets of spirals, one shallower than the other. There are eight shallow spirals and five steeper spirals. The outermost floret on each shallow spiral has an expanded petal and is called a ray floret, thus most single-flowered dahlias exhibit eight petals. Occasionally, single-flowered types have thirteen petals, one at the end of both the shallow and the steep spirals.

The arrangement of florets on the capitulum follows the Fibonacci sequence, which is a series of very precise mathematical rules. Each number in the series is constructed by adding together the two previous numbers: 1, 1, 2, 3, 5, 8, 13, 21, 34, 55, 89, 144, 233, 377, 610 and so on. The spatial arrangement of plant parts according

to this series is very common, and in dahlias allows certain conclusions to be drawn. For example, a bloom that has two rows of petals is most likely to have thirteen petals (5 + 8 = 13), in contrast to the eight of most single varieties. Informal decorative types with 160–170 petals will have thirteen or so spirals in two sets (13 x 13=169), and tighter formal types will have 21 or so spirals giving 230 or more petals.

The tight formal flowerhead formations found in pompons and miniature balls show the spiral arrangement of the florets very clearly.

SEEDS

While the ray florets of most dahlias contain a rudimentary ovary, stigmas are rarely visible and seed rarely develops. It is only the disc florets that contain fully developed ovaries and form seed. The size of seeds reflects the size of bloom. Pompon seed is typically 6–7 mm (¼in) long and 1–2 mm (¹⁄₁₆in) wide, whereas seed

from giant blooms can be 15 mm (½in) long and 4–5 mm (⅛–¼in) wide. The number of seeds which set per flowerhead varies from nothing to thirty or so, the most frequent number of seeds per head in a good season being about twenty. Some crosses rarely set seed, even in a good season, while other crosses are more prolific and give rise to good seedlings. Clearly cross-sterility is common in the garden dahlia, and is more likely where related varieties are involved.

There is no record of seed dormancy having been observed in cultivated dahlias. Most seed will germinate as soon as it is ripe, so long as conditions conducive to germination are provided. Seed germination is epigeal, that is the cotyledons (seed leaves) open above ground. Sometimes the seed coat still envelopes the cotyledons after germination and interferes with the development of the young seedling. As the new shoot tries to emerge, the forces involved often break one of the cotyledons, but this seems to cause no permanent damage to the new seedling. Germination usually takes 7–10 days at a temperature of 16°C (60°F) and subsequent growth of the seedling is rapid at this temperature. Seedlings respond well to transplanting at an early stage as fine roots grow quickly from the hypocotyl (the area between the cotyledons and the primary root) and young stem if buried below soil level.

DAYLENGTH AND BLOOM PRODUCTION

Flower initiation is imperfectly understood. Some plants, such as chrysanthemums, bloom only in short daylength, others will flower only when the daylight hours are long, and yet others flower at any daylength. Different dahlias appear to have different requirements. Late-flowering varieties have been shown to require short days before flowerheads are formed, but early-flowering varieties seem to be less susceptible to daylength.

Dr John W. Mastalerz of the Pennsylvania State University experimented on the effect of daylength on dahlias and described the results in the NDS *Dahlia Annual* 1978. He concluded that the flowering of some dahlia varieties can be regulated more precisely than others and that flowerheads are initiated when the daylength is shorter than 14 hours. Continuous exposure to days of only nine hours resulted in short flower stems and flowerheads with open centres and few ray

PLATE I

CROSS SECTION OF A SINGLE-FLOWERED DAHLIA

pollen-containing anthers

ray floret

stigma

disc floret

calyx

Flower is shown at approximately twice life size

florets. Short days for 14 days, followed by long days until buds were visible, produced fully double flowerheads with good flower stems. He used plants that had been grown from rooted cuttings in 8–12 weeks; the flowerheads developed 6–8 weeks after pinching out the growing tip and giving the short day treatments. The stage of growth of the plants did not affect flower initiation in these experiments, as long as the plants had at least 4–5 pairs of leaves. Other studies suggest that very young plants do not respond to photoperiodic effects and that 2–3 pairs of leaves are required before flowering will commence. It is now generally accepted that flower initiation is caused by a plant hormone called florigen which is produced in mature leaves. Unless sufficient mature leaves are present, the hormone concentration is too low for flowering.

The observation that short-day treatment can reduce flower stem length and produce open-centred flowerheads is interesting. Low light intensity could have the same effect; dull and murky conditions for two or three weeks after pinching out could be responsible for open-centred blooms in some varieties.

The time taken from the planting of a dormant tuber to the opening of the first flowerhead varies with the dahlia variety concerned. The earliest flowerers will do so in about 70 days, while the latest may take 120 days. From the appearance of pea-size flower buds to fully open blooms takes between 20 and 45 days: the larger the bloom, the longer it takes to open. In order to achieve blooms before midsummer, tubers need to be started into growth in warmth under cover, and planted out during mid-spring. If young shoots appear above soil level before the beginning of early summer, then they will need protection from frost. However, early planting will not help to speed up the process for those late-flowering varieties that need short days in order to initiate blooming.

At the latitude of London, it is mid-August before the period from sunrise to sunset reduces to 14 hours – the critical daylength. On the longest day, June 21st, the period from sunrise to sunset at this latitude is 16½ hours and daylength reduces very little until mid-July. Thus, as long as the basic framework of the plant has developed by mid-July then, for most varieties, flowering will follow in four or five weeks. It is important to bear in mind possible photoperiodic effects when raising seedlings; new seedlings that have not flowered by mid-August are best consigned to the compost heap, otherwise one may be selecting for photoperiod sensitivity and therefore late flowering.

FLOWER FORM AND FERTILITY

The form of the flowerhead is genetically determined. In 1929, W.J.C. Lawrence of the John Innes Institute (then at Merton in South London) described the inheritance of this and other characters in the garden dahlia. He hybridized a single-flowered variety that had eight ray florets with a fully double variety that had between 160 and 170 florets. From this cross he raised 48 seedlings, and their flowerhead form ranged from single to double, although neither parental form was exactly replicated.

Lawrence also described how the garden dahlia was self-sterile – pollen produced by a flower on a particular plant cannot fertilize flowers on the same plant. In his experiments blooms covered in bags to prevent insect pollination never set seed. Although more recent work suggests that occasional seed can be recovered from protected blooms of some varieties, the general rule is that dahlias are self-sterile. This means that for controlled pollination, pollen simply has to be brushed or shaken from a flower of the pollen parent on to the open stigmas of the seed parent. A temporary cover can be put on the bloom in order to avoid insects introducing different pollen. In practice this is not essential, as the stigmas close up soon after pollen is applied and further pollen has no effect.

During Lawrence's time, even fully double blooms bore only 160–170 florets. Today, fully double blooms can contain over 200 florets (some have up to 300 florets), and so selection for floret number, or petal count as it is usually called, can be effective.

This cross-section of 'Reddy' shows the central disc florets, each of which has a stigma and pollen-bearing anthers.

DAHLIA TYPES

There is such an enormous range of dahlias available that it is difficult to make sense of this diversity. The first real attempt to do this took place during 1904 when the National Dahlia Society (NDS) in conjunction with the Joint Dahlia Committee of the Royal Horticultural Society (RHS) published a *Classification and Description of Dahlias*. Although quite a rudimentary publication, this represented an important step in that the authors recognized that show and fancy types were not the only sort of dahlia, and that horticultural shows throughout the country needed some guidance in designing classes for dahlias. The nursery trade also welcomed the publication as it meant that customers would be able to understand what sort of dahlia they would receive under the various names current at the time.

In 1947 the *Revised Official Classification and Description of Dahlias* was drawn up by the NDS, and approved by the RHS Joint Dahlia Committee. Much more detailed than the first classification, this was published in the 1947 *Dahlia Annual* and identified 13 dahlia types with some subdivided according to size of bloom.

It gradually became clear that some sort of rationalization was required as in North America a different classification system operated, particularly in the case of bloom sizes, and yet another system existed in Australia and New Zealand. At the 16th International Horticultural Congress in Brussels in 1962 discussions took place regarding the appointment of an International Registration Authority for Dahlia Names. At the subsequent congress in Maryland, USA, in 1966,

the RHS was made the International Registration Authority. Its first task was to secure international agreement to a classification system. The national dahlia societies of Britain, the Netherlands and North America were very much involved, and the classification finally agreed upon was based on ten groups. Subdivision, based on the size of blooms, of some of these groups was necessary and it was accepted that the size category would be determined by the country of origin, as size is influenced very much by cultivation, soil and climate. The *Tentative Classified List and International Register of Dahlia Names* was published in 1969 and contained approximately 15,000 names.

The NDS *Classified Directory and Judging Rules* is published every two years. The current edition contains nearly 800 varieties. An indispensible booklet for exhibitors and affiliated societies, it also contains a wealth of information for all dahlia growers. For example, individual varieties are recommended as exhibition standard, for display in the garden or for cut flower production.

The ten groups in the directory are:
Group 1   Single-flowered dahlias
Group 2   Anemone-flowered dahlias
Group 3   Collerette dahlias
Group 4   Waterlily dahlias (previously peony-flowered dahlias
Group 5   Decorative dahlias
Group 6   Ball dahlias
Group 7   Pompon dahlias
Group 8   Cactus dahlias
Group 9   Semi-cactus dahlias
Group 10 Miscellaneous dahlias

The orange-pink 'Shandy' is a small semi-cactus dahlia that is ideal for garden display.

Some groups are subdivided according to the diameter of the blooms. In the British Isles the size of blooms, under normal growing conditions in Britain, is set out in the NDS's classified list and is as follows:
Groups 4, 5, 8 and 9:
    a Giant, usually over 254mm (10in).
    b Large, usually 203–254mm (8–10in).
    c Medium, usually 152–203mm (6–8in).
    d Small, usually 102–152mm (4–6in).
    e Miniature, usually not 102mm (4in).
Group 6:
    a Ball dahlias, usually 102–152mm (4–6in).
    b Miniature ball dahlias, usually not exceeding 102mm (4in).
Group 7 must not exceed 52mm (2in) in diameter.

In countries other than the British Isles, variety classification has diverged from the previously accepted international classification system set up by the Registration Authority. For example, in America, there are 17 groups including Orchid and Laciniated, which are currently grouped under Miscellaneous in Britain, see Appendix 6 and Chapter 11, for more information about the dahlia scene in North America.

Size limits on dahlias are slightly different in America: no additional tolerance is allowed for showing, and miniature ball sizes are 5–9cm (2–3½in) in diameter with ball dahlias over 9cm (3½in) in diameter. Thus most of the current British miniature ball varieties would be classified as small ball dahlias in America.

In the Netherlands, the old group of 'Large Pom' still exists and its size limit is similar to the American miniature ball group.

FLOWER TYPES

The following descriptions of types of dahlias are based upon the British definitions.

SINGLE-FLOWERED DAHLIAS

Single-flowered dahlias have blooms with a single outer ring of florets, which may overlap. The centre of the bloom forms a disc. For exhibition, the number of ray florets may vary from eight upwards. They should be even in shape, size and formation, and should radiate from the central disc in a single, flat plane. The central disc should be flat and circular, and should not contain more than two rows of pollen-bearing stamens

once they have dehisced. The blooms should be poised at an angle of 45 degrees to the flower stem which should be straight and proportionate to the bloom size.

Few shows have classes for single-flowered dahlias, and the vast majority are typically dwarf bedders or lilliputs. They make a fine display when grown close together in beds composed of a single variety, or singly in pots or containers. Peony-flowered dahlias differ from singles in that there are two or more rows of ray florets radiating from a central disc, and today, these are included in Group 10 Miscellaneous in Britain.

ANEMONE-FLOWERED DAHLIAS

Anemone-flowered dahlias have blooms with one or more outer rings of generally flattened ray florets. These surround a dense group of tubular florets that replace the central disc of a single-flowered dahlia. Anemone-flowered dahlias are rarely seen on the showbench; their use is primarily for garden display. There are dwarf bedders, such as 'Honey', which has a yellow central cushion and ray florets with bronze and dark pink blends, as well as taller varieties, such as 'Comet', which has dark red florets in both the central cushion and rays, and its sport 'Scarlet Comet', which has uniformly scarlet florets.

COLLERETTE DAHLIAS

Typically, collerette dahlias have an outer ring of eight or more flat ray florets with an inner ring of smaller florets, often of a different colour. The inner florets should be symmetrical and not less than one-third of the length of the outer florets. Their colour should be even. For exhibition, the central disc should be flat and circular, and should not contain more than two rows of pollen-bearing stamens, once the stamens have dehisced. The flower stems should be straight and proportionate to the size of the bloom, and the blooms should be held at an angle of 45 degrees to the stem.

Collerettes can be used for striking garden decoration. Many shows now also have classes for them, which has stimulated the raising of new varieties. Examples of collerettes include 'Choh', a lilliput with

The petals of cactus dahlias are revolute (folded back lengthways) for more than half their length, while those of semi-cactus types are revolute for less than half their length and have a broad base. The difference between cactus and semi-cactus is one of degree in respect of the revolute petals.

PLATE II

PETALS OF CACTUS AND SEMI-CACTUS DAHLIAS

'Weston
Nuggett'

'Kenora Sunset'

'Lavender Athalie'

'Banker'

'Hamari Accord'

'Jessica'

'Salmon Athalie'

'Kiwi Gloria'

All petals are shown at approximately life size

'Glorie van Heemstede' is a waterlily dahlia with shallow blooms held on good stems. It is ideal for cut flowers.

purple ray florets and an inner ring of white florets, and 'Thais', an old variety raised in the Netherlands by Dirk Maarse. It has a striking combination of dark red outer ray florets and an inner ring of purple-tinged white florets. The latter is difficult to grow to show standard but makes a wonderful display in the garden.

WATERLILY DAHLIAS

Waterlilies were separated from decoratives as a distinct group in Britain in 1985. They have fully double blooms characterized by broad and generally sparse ray florets that are straight or slightly involute or revolute along their length, giving the flowerhead a shallow appearance. The centre of the flowerhead should be firm, circular, closed and in proportion to the size of the bloom. The depth of the bloom should be equal to approximately half its diameter. A straight flower stem, of a length and thickness appropriate to the bloom, is desirable. Most varieties are classified as small, but a few with larger blooms fall into the medium-size class and there are also miniatures.

Waterlily dahlias make excellent cut flowers and also provide good garden display. Since being recognized as a separate group, waterlilies have become a popular show flower. Some of the earlier varieties originated in the Netherlands: 'Gerrie Hoek', a lovely pink, was developed in 1945, and 'Glorie van Heemstede', a yellow of classical form, arrived in 1947. Since then, English breeders have taken up the challenge, among them John Sharp, Jack Kinns and John Crutchfield. The latter won the Supreme Award at the Wisley Trials in 1982 with his variety 'Porcelain', a beauty with blooms of white and lilac blends.

DECORATIVE DAHLIAS

There are probably more decorative-type dahlias grown than any other. They range from varieties capable of producing blooms that are 35cm (14in) in diameter down to those bearing miniature flowerheads of 10–15cm (4–6in) across. Most of the larger bloom types are strictly for the showbench, although a few giant decoratives have gained awards in the trials at Wisley for garden display.

DAHLIA FLOWER TYPES

chrysanthemum

peony

star

pompon

DAHLIA FLOWER TYPES

single flower

anemone

collerette

waterlily

ball

formal decorative

cactus

semi-cactus

Decoratives range in height from dwarf bedders, which usually do not exceed 60cm (24in), to some that grow to 1.8m (6ft) or more.

Older varieties tended to have flowerheads with a more open and loose formation and were classed as informal decoratives. There were some with tighter blooms and these were referred to as formal decoratives. This distinction has been discarded in Britain and all decorative varieties are now described as having fully double blooms showing no disc. The ray florets are broad, generally flat and usually blunt-pointed. More recent varieties tend to have a higher petal count and with this has come a more involute floret formation, bringing such dahlias closer to the ball type. For show purposes, the more formal decorative is regarded as ideal, particularly in the small and miniature sub-groups. On the other hand, most giant decoratives are more informal and are sometimes difficult to distinguish from semi-cactus types.

Giant Of the giant decoratives, the yellow 'Alva's Supreme' has perhaps the best form and this has ensured its success, as it is not as large as some. Raised in New Zealand by V. Frost, it was introduced in 1956 and has been one of the top varieties at the shows in London and Harrogate in recent years, and still wins all over Britain. One of the biggest giants ever raised is 'Bonaventure', bred by B. Simon in North America and introduced in 1982. The sheer size of this bronze-blends giant often carries the day in shows.

Large In the large decorative class only a limited number of varieties of show potential exist, most of them coming from North America or the southern hemisphere. However, one of the older varieties with superb form is the white 'Silver City' raised in Britain by the late Reverend Brother Simplicius and released in 1967. It still wins its class at shows over the country. 'Inca Metropolitan', a formal yellow variety, was raised by George Brookes of Birmingham in the 1970s and remains remarkably successful. Of the more recent varieties, 'Kenora Valentine', raised in North America by Gordon Leroux, is a red bloom with plenty of form. It does well all over Britain.

Medium The medium-sized group used to be the Cinderella in the decoratives. 'Evelyn Foster' used to be

The small decorative, 'Ruskin Diane' has excellent formation and is perhaps the leading dahlia in its class.

the leading show variety of twenty years ago. It still wins on the showbench, but was somewhat overtaken by the yellow 'Rustig' from South Africa, and then by the white 'B.J. Beauty', raised in England by Terry Clarke and introduced in 1976. This latter variety is less formal but its reliability makes it the top exhibition medium decorative of today. However, its position is now threatened by a stream of new medium decorative varieties and it remains to be seen whether or not it will hold its own.

Small The small decorative group really developed during the 1960s in response to the demand for a show dahlia with good formation.

The first of the more formal small decoratives was an orange-red with excellent form named 'Keltie' by its raiser 'Bertie' Barnes and released in 1960. Bertie thought it one of his best raisings and he believed that it would be the forerunner of a new type of formal small decorative dahlias. He used it as a seed parent, but did not live to see its progeny make the grade. It was left to Terry Clarke of Braintris Nurseries in Essex to make the next advance with his lilac 'Dedham',

'Laura Marie' is a miniature ball that is good for both exhibition and garden display.

released in 1962. The 1970s were dominated by 'Frank Hornsey', a variety with orange-yellow blends, and its sports, 'Pink Frank Hornsey' and 'Yellow Frank Hornsey'. The 1980s saw 'Ruskin Diane', a yellow of perfect form, take most of the honours. 'Ruskin Diane' was challenged in 1989 by another yellow, 'Swanvale'. Today, yellows, bronze and pinks dominate the show-bench; reds and purple blooms have a propensity to fade in hot sunshine, so exhibitors tend to avoid them.

Miniature A wider range of colours is evident in the miniature decorative group, probably because the miniatures lend themselves better to garden decoration, cut flowers and especially floral arrangement. One of the most recent varieties, the purple 'Anglian Water', raised by Norman Lewis of Northampton, won the Gold Medal at the NDS Bradford Trials in 1992. 'Jeanette Carter', a yellow and pink miniature, won the AGM at Wisley in 1991. On the show scene, the three varieties most often in the winning exhibits are: 'Abridge Taffy', a white from Jack Kinns of Essex (1978), 'Elizabeth Hammett', a lilac from Keith Hammett of New Zealand (1980), and 'Karenglen', a red from Gerry Woolcock (1990).

BALL DAHLIAS

These were the show and fancy dahlias of yesteryear, renamed ball dahlias in 1966. As their name implies, they are fully double, globular, with tubular petals blunt or rounded at the tips.

Show and fancy dahlias were originally classified as over 7.5cm (3in) in diameter, but when they were renamed as ball dahlias, the size limits were brought into line with those of small and miniature decoratives and cactus and semi-cactus dahlias. At the same time, the original large pompon class, with flowerheads 5–7.5cm (2–3in) in diameter, ceased to be recognized and varieties previously classified as large pompon were lumped in with the miniature balls.

This latter reclassification probably had the most far-reaching effect of all the work done by the International Registration Authority. On the showbench, the 7.5cm (3in) diameter large pompons stood no chance alongside the 10cm (4in) diameter miniature balls, and they soon disappeared from the British show scene and from nursery catalogues. Dutch growers, however, appreciated the reliability and floriferousness of these tiny balls for garden use, and continue to offer them to this day. Although often called poms, they do not meet the size criterion for poms, and should be labelled as miniature balls.

Size is a problem throughout the ball group. There are few varieties capable of making blooms of 15cm (6in) diameter, most clustering around the 10cm (4in) limit. The most successful miniature ball of today, the pink 'Wootton Cupid', was originally released as a small ball by Les Jones (a grower from Leek Wootton) in 1979, and won many prizes in its first season. However, it was classified officially as a miniature ball and, together with its lighter pink sport 'Kathryn's Cupid' and deeper pink 'Candy Cupid', forms the mainstay of the miniature ball show scene. A good contrast is the red 'Laura Marie' from the late Norman Lewis.

Of the small balls, 'Risca Miner' from Terry Clarke has been the leading variety since its introduction in 1977, but some newer releases are beginning to challenge it.

POMPON DAHLIAS

Today's pompons are globular, less than 5cm (2in) in diameter and have tubular florets, blunted at the tip. These little beauties are popular for show, garden decoration and cut flowers. Many of the top show varieties have been around for years. The most widely grown are the purple 'Moor Place', an English-raised seedling released in 1957, and its Australian parent 'Willo's Violet', raised in 1937 by the leading pom breeder Norman Williams. Also raised by Mr Williams are 'Hallmark', a perfect pink released in 1960, and the white 'Small World', dating from 1967, completing a quartet of winning poms.

CACTUS DAHLIAS

True cactus dahlias are fully double with pointed florets that are revolute for more than half their length. Sometimes the florets are incurving, otherwise they are straight. For showing, the ideal bloom is full petalled without overcrowding, with no gaps in formation, and the depth of the bloom should be at least two-thirds of its diameter.

Some of the small-flowered cactus varieties make excellent garden displays; the shorter bedding varieties, such 'Border Princess', 'Park Princess' and 'Park Delight', which originate in the Netherlands, are in great demand for parks and gardens. Varieties with larger blooms are usually grown for show, but the number of good varieties is limited as, on the showbench, prizes are generally won by the more substantial semi-cactus varieties, since classes normally call for cactus and/or semi-cactus blooms.

Giant The only true giant cactus variety listed in the NDS classified directory is the white 'Polar Sight' from Maarse in the Netherlands, released in 1960.

Large There are two dahlias in the large group, 'Pride of Holland' (1946) and 'Light Music' (1966). Again both are old varieties, this time from Bruidegom of the Netherlands.

Medium More medium cactus varieties are listed because many of them can provide spectacular garden displays. The older ones are dominated by Dutch dahlias like 'Raiser's Pride', 'Orfeo' and 'Banker', but more recently English breeders have taken an interest in this group. 'Shy Princess', a white variety from Keith Fleckney, came in 1981, and 'Hillcrest Royal', a purple from Les Jackson, emerged in 1992 and was awarded the AGM at Wisley in the same year.

Small The small-flowered cactuses, besides being excellent for garden display, have also been foremost on the showbench. The classic small cactus is epitomized by the Dutch 'Klankstad Kerkrade'. This has yellow flowerheads of perfect form. It was released by Bruidegom in 1954 and is still winning medals today. 'KK' (as 'Klankstad Kerkrade' was commonly called) gave rise to a number of sports, such as 'White Klankstad', which are still among the winners. Its supremacy was challenged in 1974 by an English-bred dahlia named 'Athalie', a robust grower with excellent blooms in pink and bronze blends, held on good flower stems. This variety has provided a stream of colour sports that complement each other well in multi-vase classes. More recently, a new variety, the lilac 'Kiwi Gloria', has swept the prizes on the showbench. Raised by Eddie Durrant and introduced in 1988, 'Kiwi Gloria' has proved to have tremendous form in the right hands. It is not easy to grow well and does not have impact in the garden, but has won the Best in Show at London and Harrogate.

Miniature True miniature cactus varieties are few, but the best known is the white 'Rokesley Mini', released in 1971, which received the AM at Wisley in 1975. It is superb for garden display.

Probably still the best pompon for showing, 'Willo's Violet' was introduced in 1937 by Norman Williams of New Zealand.

PLATE III

PETALS OF DECORATIVE, BALL, POMPON,
WATERLILY AND COLLERETTE DAHLIAS

'Phoenix'

'Gala Parade'

'Kotari Magic'

'Charlie Kenwood'

'Ruskin Diane'

'Kidd's Climax'

'Pensford Marion'

'Willo's Violet'

'Hamari Sunshine'

'Hallmark'

'Chimborazo'

'Duet'

'Red Balloon'

'Downham Royal'

'Cornel'

'Red Velvet'

'Edinburgh'

'Hamari Rose'

'Peace Pact'

'Riisa'

All petals are shown at approximately life size

SEMI-CACTUS DAHLIAS

The distinction between true cactus and semi-cactus varieties is that the latter have broader florets, revolute for half their length or less. This is a quantitative distinction and many varieties lie on the borderline. Moreover, under some growing conditions and on some soils, dahlias classified as cactus can tend towards semi-cactus and vice versa. However, semi-cactus flowerheads tend to have heavier florets and are more substantial. This inevitably gives them the advantage in competition over true cactus varieties shown in the same class, particularly in the larger size ranges.

Giant During the 1950s, the giant semi-cactus scene was dominated by 'Arab Queen', an orange and yellow variety from Australia. This was followed by two from Dutch raisers: 'Respectable', a yellow from Ballego in 1962, and 'Bizet', a pink and yellow released in 1971. American breeders Phil Traff and Jack Almand had winners with the yellow 'Vantage' (1972) and the orange and bronze 'Alfred C.' (1974), respectively. English raisers got into the frame with George Brookes producing the yellow 'Inca Dambuster' in 1975, followed, in 1979, by the late George Krzywicki's 'Daleko Jupiter'. This red and yellow variety quickly came to dominate the giant semi-cactus classes, and together with its pink and rose sports, continues to play a prominent role today. However, a stream of new giant semi-cactus varieties has emerged in the last few years and the choice of show varieties is now wide open.

Large The large semi-cactus group was somewhat on the fringe until 'Nantenan', a yellow-flowered dahlia, was released by the Dutch firm Bruidegom in 1961. It gained an AM at Wisley in 1962 and held sway until 1972 when 'Hamari Katrina' (AM 1976), which was also yellow, came from the top English breeder Pi Ensum. Another winner appeared in 1974. It was 'Reginald Keene', an orange and red semi-cactus raised by Geoff Flood. It too gained an AM and has given rise to a number of sports, including 'Candy Keene', 'Salmon Keene' and 'Cryfield Keene', all of which are winners. More recently, a Canadian variety has come

Waterlily petals are flat. Decorative petals are flat or partly involute (folded inwards lengthways). Ball dahlia petals are involute for more than ⅔ of their length, while pompons are mostly involute. Collerettes have petaloids attached to the rays.

to the fore. This is the white 'Kenora Challenger' from Gordon Leroux. Released in 1991, it was awarded a Gold Medal at the NDS Bradford trials in 1993. Another Gold Medal winner at Bradford in the same year was 'Starlight Keene', a new yellow sport of 'Reginald Keene'. The large semi-cactus group is now one of the strongest groups on the showbench.

Medium The medium semi-cactus group has been strong since the end of the Second World War when Dutch raisers released a stream of excellent varieties. Perhaps the best known of these was the orange and bronze 'Symbol', released by Bruidegom in 1958. It still wins prizes. Another Bruidegom variety, released in 1961, was 'Rotterdam'. This had bright red flowerheads that caught the eye in garden displays. Although it did well on the showbench, 'Rotterdam' tended to fade in bright sunlight. In 1968, Terry Clarke from Braintris in Essex released another red, the darker 'Othello', which was less liable to lose colour than 'Rotterdam', but like all reds, it did show some fading. Also in 1968, Pi Ensum released the white 'Hamari Bride' and it became an instant success, receiving an FCC in 1982; in 1992 it was given the AGM at Wisley.

In the meantime, 'Symbol' had thrown up a range of sports, some quite distinct from the original. No less than six are listed in the NDS *Classified Directory and Judging Rules* of 1993. In 1975, a strong yellow of perfect form was released by John Sharp of Essex. Named 'Eastwood Moonlight', it is still one of the leading varieties, and has produced a white sport, 'White Moonlight' that is every bit as good as its parent, and more recently further sports have appeared.

In 1984 a bronze-flowered medium semi-cactus was released by Les Jones. Called 'Wootton Impact', it is another excellent show variety, and has started to produce sports like 'Golden Impact'. The latest variety to take this class by storm was the light pink and yellow 'Grenidor Pastelle' from John Carrington, Essex, in 1988. 'Grenidor Pastelle' is vying for supremacy with 'Eastwood Moonlight', and has again started producing sports. One such, 'Pink Pastelle', is already in the NDS directory and others are reaching the showbench.

Small Small semi-cactus varieties figure strongly in garden display and for cutting. They rarely have the refinement of bloom to compete on the showbench with the true cactus varieties. 'Pipers Pink' is a well-known bedding variety frequently found in parks, and although classified as a dwarf bedder it tends to be taller than most of the other bedders.

Three eye-catching dahlias in this group are the bicolour, white tipped with purple varieties: 'Match' from South Africa, 'Hayley Jane' from England and 'Jura' from the Netherlands. On the showbench, 'Cryfield Bryn', a yellow, dominated the 1970s while a recent introduction from Geerlings, 'Lemon Elegans', another yellow, is threatening to take over. The dark pink variety 'Conway', released by Neville Weekes in 1986, can do well on the showbench, but it received the AGM in 1993 for garden display.

Miniature In the miniature semi-cactus group, 'Andries Orange', an old Dutch-bred dahlia, is still one of the best for garden use, and although slightly taller than a dwarf bedder, does extremely well in mid-border. It is also useful as a cut flower and its bright orange colour makes it good in floral arrangement. 'So Dainty', a bronze miniature from the late Jock Richards of Bedford, is another excellent bedding variety. Raised in the 1970s, it received an FCC in 1976 and in 1992 it was awarded the AGM at Wisley.

MISCELLANEOUS DAHLIAS

Any dahlia that does not fall into one of the above groups is classified as miscellaneous. 'Bishop of Llandaff', a peony type with red florets, now comes into this group. Although it has seen a revival in recent years, it was first released in 1928 by Treseders of Cardiff and was very popular in parks and gardens before the war. Taller than many bedders, it gives a great show when mass-planted as demonstrated in the Ebbw Vale Garden Festival in 1992.

Also included in the miscellaneous group are the orchid-flowered dahlias favoured by flower arrangers. The best-known is 'Giraffe', a yellow and bronze variety from Hoek, Holland in 1948. Its pink sport goes well with it. An English variety, 'Jescot Julie', released in 1974, is also popular. A recent introduction from Japan is the pink and white 'Tohsuikyoh'. With larger blooms than the older double orchid types, this is set to become popular with flower arrangers. An unusual variety is the red and orange 'Akita', which looks more like a chrysanthemum than a dahlia.

RULES FOR EXHIBITION
SIZE

In Britain, the rules for exhibition of dahlias in competitions state that varieties must be qualified for the classes in which they are shown by classification, formation and size. Size has always been a contentious issue since many top exhibitors are capable of producing blooms that exceed the upper size limit of the class. Until 1973, although pompons that exceeded the size limit were always disqualified, some latitude was allowed for other groups. However, it reached the point where judges persistently did not penalize oversize blooms, and this led to the introduction of firm size limits in 1973; blooms exceeding these were disqualified. The NDS *Classified Directory and Judging Rules* XIVth Edition (1976) was at pains to set out the problem and the solution adopted by the NDS for its shows and those of its Affiliated Societies:

'The sizes shown in the internationally recognised Group Classification, Formation and Sizes are an indication for garden purposes of the size of blooms obtainable from dahlias grown under reasonably good conditions, and dahlia cultivars are classified accordingly.

Well cultivated plants grown for exhibition, with superior culture or grown in more favourable soil or climatic conditions, may produce larger blooms and it is not intended that cultivation for exhibition purposes should be discouraged or that larger blooms be penalised solely because of their size, but it is considered essential, to ensure fair competition and standardisation that size limits be set for each class of dahlia.

Exhibition standards have, therefore, been adopted and blooms exceeding the maximum sizes for the class in which they are exhibited must be disqualified. This applies equally to classified and unclassified cultivars.'

To ensure size limits were adhered to, it was recommended that judges use NDS approved rings, through which the florets of blooms exhibited must pass cleanly, without touching. The disqualification limits for exhibition dahlias in Britain are:

Large-flowered dahlias exceeding 260mm (10¼in)
Medium-flowered dahlias exceeding 220mm (8¾in)

Small-flowered dahlias exceeding 170mm (6¾in)
Miniature-flowered dahlias exceeding 115mm (4½in)
Pompon dahlias exceeding 52mm (2in)

FORM

Form has also caused controversy over the years. On the one hand there are the cactus dahlias, which are easily recognizable with pointed florets, narrow and revolute for half their length or more, while on the other hand there are the ball dahlias with florets that have blunt or rounded tips, involute along their length for more than half their length. (Pompon dahlias are similar to ball dahlias, the florets being involute for the whole of their length.) In between the two extremes of cactus and ball dahlias there is a continuous range of forms, and the definition of where one group ends and another begins is not very clear. Moreover, the formation of the florets can be modified by growing conditions and climate.

In the past, the distinction between decorative dahlias and ball dahlias was clearer than it is today. The development of newer decorative varieties, which have a formation closer to that of the ball dahlia, has made classification much more difficult. The ideal form of a decorative dahlia, particularly at the small and miniature end of the size range, seems to be that of a formal decorative. This is more evident now that the shallow blooms of the waterlily type have been recognized in Britain as a distinct type.

The waterlily type was reclassified in 1985 as Group 4, the peony type having been relegated to the miscellaneous Group 10. Formal decoratives and informal decoratives are not recognized as separate forms in Britain although they are in some other countries (such as North America).

In the giant decorative group, some varieties have a very loose formation. Their florets have a tendency to be revolute, thus making them hard to distinguish from semi-cactus types. This is unfortunate from the classification point of view, but is to be expected as the garden dahlia is still evolving.

'Trelyn Kiwi' is a recent white or pale pink sport from the top exhibition small cactus 'Kiwi Gloria' (p.117).

4
DAHLIA SPECIES

The cultivated dahlia of today bears little resemblance to the wild dahlia species, which are found mainly in Mexico, but with some also introduced into other Central American countries. These wild species are generally straggling, 'weedy' plants with small single flowers. They are not at all attractive as garden plants, as most have a restricted range of flower form and their colours are usually in lilac-pink or red-orange.

Over the past 200 years some of the wild species have been introduced into many countries outside the Americas, particularly to Europe. They were originally grown in botanic gardens where it seems that they probably interbred and gave rise to variants, some of which were subsequently described as distinct species and erroneously given taxonomic rank. From the often sketchy descriptions published, it is virtually impossible to relate these dahlias to the modern wild species that are still found in Mexico. Moreover, the cultivated dahlia of today is generally accepted to be the result of interspecific hybridization of a complex nature. At least two wild species are believed to have been involved in this hybridization, namely *D. pinnata* and *D. coccinea*, and possibly others also played a part, but the precise origin of the garden dahlia has not been established.

Chromosome numbers can often be important in pinpointing the origins of species and related species, but in dahlias chromosome numbers are difficult to establish with any certainty, as the chromosomes are very small and numerous (64 in the cultivated dahlia).

'Margaret Anne' is a miniature decorative that is suitable for both garden display and exhibition.

In 1931, W.J.C. Lawrence, working at the John Innes Institute in England, published the initial work on the genetics of the dahlia. He showed that the basic number of chromosomes in the dahlia was n=8 (n is the gametic number, found in the pollen and ovules, while 2n is the somatic number, found in the adult plant). However, no dahlia has ever been discovered with this basic number, but many with a number of n=16 are known. According to Lawrence this makes them tetraploid.

The evidence of chromosome numbers in those species that have been examined is conflicting (for example, numbers of n=17 and n=18 are anomalous, see list overleaf), and, if confirmed as valid, indicate an instability in the genus which suggests that taxonomic decisions based on morphological descriptions may be open to question. The cultivated dahlia has a chromosome number of 64 (i.e. n=32) and is thus an octoploid, with eight times the basic number. This is rare in the plant kingdom and denotes a highly complex cultivated plant that has the ability to be very unstable when reproduced by seed as there are so many possible genetic variations arising from such a large number of chromosomes.

The concept of a taxonomic species in a genus such as *Dahlia* is particularly problematical as unstable variants may survive through vegetative reproduction. It is, therefore, not surprising that many horticulturalists and gardeners have tended to ignore the finer scientific basis of species differences and, instead, have concentrated on the garden value of the various types. Raisers of new varieties, on the other hand, need to understand something of the genetics of dahlias in order to make sense of the results of hybridization.

DAHLIA SPECIES AND THEIR CHROMOSOME NUMBERS

Sorensen classifies the 27 species into four sections: Pseudodendron (tree dahlias), Epiphytum, Entemophyllon and Pinnatum.

Section Pseudodendron
1 *D. excelsa* Benth.
2 *D. imperialis* Roezl ex Ortgies (n = 16)
3 *D. tenuicaulis* Sorensen (n = 16)

Section Epiphytum
4 *D. macdougallii* Sherff

Section Entemophyllon
5 *D. scapigeroides* Sherff
6 *D. foeniculifolia* Sherff
7 *D. linearis* Sherff (n = 17)
8 *D. rupicola* Sorensen (n = 17)
9 *D. dissecta* S. Wats (n = 17)

Section Pinnatum
10 *D. merckii* Lehm (n = 18)
11 *D. apiculata* (Sherff) Sorensen
12 *D. cardiophylla* Blake & Sherff (n = 16)
13 *D. purpusii* Brandg.
14 *D. pinnata* Cav. (n = 32)
15 *D. pteropoda* Sherff
16 *D. brevis* Sorensen (n = 16)
17 *D. rudis* Sorensen
18 *D. moorei* Sherff
19 *D. hintonii* Sherff
20 *D. mollis* Sorensen (n = 16)
21 *D. atropurpurea* Sorensen (n = 32)
22 *D. australis* (Sherff) Sorensen (n = 16 and 32)
23 *D. sherffii* Sorensen (n = 32)
24 *D. scapigera* (A. Dietr.) Know & Westc. (n = 16)
25 *D. barkerae* Knowles & Westc. (n = 32)
26 *D. tenuis* Robinson & Greenman (n = 16)
27 *D. coccinea* Cav. (n = 16 and 32)

Historically, supposed 'species' have been crossed with the cultivated dahlia to produce new forms, but detailed information about the precise 'species' involved is not available. Occasionally, seed of dahlia species or of interspecific hybrids is offered commercially, but precisely what plants will be produced from such seed is open to question for the reasons given above. Sometimes, too, plants are offered for sale whose origin and nomenclature is not validated. Thus many plant descriptions reported in the past must be viewed with suspicion. An intensive genetic study of such hybrids is needed to establish what exactly has been achieved. However, all this uncertainty should not discourage the gardener from trying out new variants. A multiplicity of forms can clearly arise from interspecific hybridization, and this is of great potential in the future. I have hybridized *D. merckii* with *D.* × *variablis*, and *D. coccinea* with *D.* × *variablis*, and, in both cases, forms with double flowers were selected from the progeny. These can be propagated and show no differences from established cultivated dahlias. Nori Pope at Hadspen House Gardens has hybridized *D. sherffii* (lilac flowers) with *D. coccinea* (red flowers) and produced a hybrid form with yellow flowers.

WILD SPECIES

The most recent review of the wild species of dahlia was published by Professor Paul D. Sorensen, American authority on the genus *Dahlia*, in 1969. This is the latest in the series of studies covering a period of over 200 years, from the original publication by Cavanilles in 1791, through the studies of André Thouin in 1804, and Earl Edward Sherff covering the period of 1930–1966. The treatment of the wild species in this book is based upon the work of Sorensen (see above). Many of the species listed here have featured in literature on dahlias and they have been described as far as is possible under the current understanding of the genus.

Professor Paul D. Sorensen made extensive travels in Mexico studying wild dahlias. He described 27 species which are found mainly in Mexico, but that also spread to other parts of Central America. He believed that those dahlias found in South America were introduced from Central America.

SECTION PSEUDODENDRON

This section consists of three species, including the well-known *D. imperialis*. Whether the three species are sufficiently distinct to warrant specific status is open to question. They range in size from 2m (6ft) to over 6m (20ft) with stems becoming woody. Most individuals produce the current season's growth from the previous year's stems, although occasionally new growth comes from the tuberous roots. The flowerheads are usually single with white or lilac ray petals. However, many specimen plants have been grown under cover in botanic gardens in Europe and America and one specimen in America had blooms that were somewhat like anemone-flowered dahlias.

DAHLIA EXCELSA
Benth. 1838

Sorensen failed to discover this species in the wild in Mexico and it is doubtful whether it can be separated from *D. imperialis* as a distinct species.

DAHLIA IMPERIALIS
Roezl ex Ortgies 1863

The original plants of this species were collected in Mexico by Roezl and cultivated in Zurich. Plants were then cultivated in the Royal Botanic Gardens in Berlin where the species was initially described.

Often called the tree dahlia, in its natural environment from Guatemala to Columbia *D. imperialis* grows to 6m (20ft) tall. Its leaves are 2- or 3-pinnate and 50–90cm (20–36in) long. The flowerheads, which are borne in corymb-like clusters in the leaf axils, consist of white or whitish-lavender to rose-purple ray florets, 3.5–6cm (1½–2½in) long, and yellow or reddish-tipped yellow disc florets.

It is propagated by cuttings or sections of the stem and can be grown outdoors in Europe but is unlikely to flower until late autumn or early winter, by which time plants are usually frosted. Plants at the RHS Garden at Wisley have not flowered in the open. *D. imperialis* grows well and flowers outdoors in California.

DAHLIA TENUICAULIS
Sorensen 1969

This species was described by Sorensen as a separate, but smaller, tree dahlia, but it is doubtful whether it merits separate specific status.

SECTION EPIPHYTUM

This section has only one species, *D. macdougallii*. Confined to rainforest habitats and unknown outside

Mexico, it is unusual in that it clambers over the tops of tall trees, producing aerial roots, up to 20m (70ft) long, that drop down to the ground. The flowerheads are white or whitish with a yellow disc.

SECTION ENTEMOPHYLLON

All five members of this section are very similar. They are characterized by very finely divided leaves and all produce many stems arising from a tuberous rootstock. The stems survive for more than one season and become quite woody so that full-grown plants have a shrubby appearance. Flowers of these species range from lavender and rose-purple to deep purple with a yellow disc. It is considered probable that a number of older cultivars with finely divided leaves and dark purple or blackish foliage were derived from *D. dissecta*, the type species of this group. The very old cultivar 'Lucifer' was one of the first to be developed with this purple foliage, and the more recent 'Bishop of Llandaff' is similar.

DAHLIA DISSECTA
S. Wats. 1891

This is the type species for the section. It is characterized by its very dissected foliage and is a dwarf type only 30–90cm (12–36in) tall. The leaves are pinnate-pinnatisect and 10–19cm (4–7½in) long. The ray florets are pale lavender to light purple and 2–4cm (¾–1½in) long. *D. dissecta* is considered by some to be one of the progenitors of the lilliput or mignon dahlia types.

SECTION PINNATUM

This section contains the remaining postulated species that are not tree dahlias, epiphytic, or dwarf with dissected leaves. *D. pinnata* is regarded as the type species. Its name is based upon the plants grown by Cavanilles in the Madrid Botanic Garden in 1791. The other assumed parent of the cultivated dahlia, *D. coccinea*, is probably the most widespread species in this group. Its name is, again, based upon plants grown by Cavanilles in Madrid from seeds sent from the Mexican Botanic Garden.

Another species that belongs to this group and was described in Europe very early on is *D. merckii*. The original material was grown in the Hamburg Botanic Garden, from seeds collected in Mexico, and was described and illustrated there in 1840.

In 1841 *D. glabrata*, the smooth dwarf dahlia, was illustrated in *Curtis's Botanical Magazine* (plate 3878). The illustration shows a plant with flowerheads consisting of eight deep lilac-purple ray florets and a deep purple disc. This species is now considered to be a dwarf form of *D. merckii*.

D. tenuis is another dwarf species. It has yellow flowerheads and is indigenous to Mexico. It is likely to have been involved in the production of the very dwarf or lilliput cultivars, although whether it is really distinct from *D. coccinea* is not clear.

D. scapigera, *D. australis*, *D. purpurea* (not included in Sorensens list), *D. barkerae* and *D. merckii* form a closely related group. It is doubtful whether they can be given distinct specific status, but more likely that they should be considered as variants of a single species and equated ⟩ *D. merckii*.

DAHLIA MERCKII
Lehm. 1839

This species grows wild in Mexico, where it varies from 45–185cm (1½–6ft) tall. It has hollow stems and leaves that may be pinnate or bipinnate with 5–7 opposite leaflets. The ray florets are white, whitish or pale lavender to purple and the disc florets are yellow or yellow with purple tips. A dwarf form is sometimes described as *D. merckii* (compact) and the white-flowered form as *D. merckii alba*.

D. merckii can be hybridized with the cultivated form *D. × variabilis* (see p.15). Barnes describes it as a dainty cosmea-type (*Cosmos*) flower with lilac blooms and finely cut foliage with many possibilities for use in floral art.

DAHLIA PINNATA
Cav. 1791 (syn. *D. superflua* (DC.) Ait., *D. purpurea* Poir. and *Georgina superflua* DC.)

The species is found wild in Mexico on rocky slopes at 2,100–3,000m (7,000–10,000ft). It was originally described by Cavanilles from plants cultivated in the Royal Botanic Gardens of Madrid from seed collected in Mexico and sent to Spain by Vicente de Cervantes in around 1789.

Although said to have single, light purple to lavender-purple flowerheads with yellow discs, some of Cavanilles's plants were semi-double.

DAHLIA COCCINEA
Cav. 1796

This very variable species is one of those described by Cavanilles from material grown by him from seed obtained from the Botanic Garden of Mexico in 1789.

D. sherffii (left), *D. merckii* 'Alba' (centre) and *D. merckii* (right) are among the very few commercially available dahlia species.

It is indigenous to Mexico, where it is widely found in the wild on rocky slopes, fields and roadsides from 450–3,400m (1,500–11,000ft). It is also found in Guatemala and Peru, and probably occurs in many other South American countries.

Plants can be 45–300cm (1½–10ft) tall. The stems are green to purple with hollow internodes, rarely solid. The extremely variable leaves are usually opposite but may be whorled and there are then 3 leaves per node. The flowerheads are borne in 2s and 3s and are erect or nodding on stems 2–30cm (¾–12in) long. The ovate-elliptic ray florets are 16–40mm (½–1½in) long and 12–18mm (½–¾in) wide. They may be lemon-yellow to orange, orange-scarlet, or deep blackish-scarlet, sometimes variegated yellow and orange. The disc florets are yellow, sometimes scarlet tipped.

A number of variants have been described as separate species in the past, but according to Sorensen are better considered as forms of *D. coccinea*. Among these are *D. crocata* (Sessé 1805), *D. cervantesii* (Lagasca ex Sweet DC. 1836), *D. coronata* (Hort ex Sprague 1929), *D. gentryi* (Sherff. 1942), *D. popenovii* (Safford 1918). *D. coronata* was said to be scented, but few people have been able to find any scent associated with this or any other dahlia.

DAHLIA SHERFFII
Sorensen 1969

This was described as a new species by Sorensen following his detailed study of species both in herbaria and in the wild. It is similar to *D. merckii* with slightly larger flowers.

OTHER DAHLIA SPECIES

The following species names appear in literature about dahlias but the plants have not been identified in the wild.

Dahlia fulgens (Hort. ex Sweet. 1829) This is regarded as a synonym for the form of *D. coccinea* previously distinguished as *D. crocata* (*Georgina crocata* Sessé ex Lagasca) Sweet 1829.

Dahlia juarezii (Van der Berg. 1879) This name has been used to describe forms with the revolute petals characteristic of cactus-type dahlias. It is not now

The brilliant red *D. coccinea* is a wild progenitor of the garden dahlia. It is also commercially available.

regarded as a distinct species but rather as a purple foliage form of *D. × variabilis* (see p.15) or as a form of *D. coccinea*.

Dahlia 'laciniata purpurea' With flowerheads varying from bright scarlet to deep crimson, and purple leaves, this is now regarded as a purple foliage form of *D. × variabilis*. It is believed to be the progenitor of some dwarf purple-foliage dahlias. A.T. Barnes describes using the form as a parent, and all its progeny had purple foliage with red flowerheads.

Dahlia pubescens (Brongn. 1845) This species was described by Brongniart as a segregate of *D. platylepis* but neither can be related to any present-day species.

Dahlia rosea (Cav. 1796) This name was applied by Cavanilles to one of the forms of dahlia derived from the original Mexican seed. Some authors have attributed Cavanilles's description to a form of *D. pinnata* while others ascribe it to *D. merckii*. Sorensen settles for the latter.

Dahlia zimpanii (Roezl 1861) Whether this is actually a dahlia at all is open to question. Some authors attribute it to *Cosmos diversifolius* Otto.

5

DAHLIAS IN THE GARDEN

Although there are dedicated dahlia enthusiasts who are solely committed to the exhibition of perfect blooms, the vast majority of growers are simply interested in producing flowers for display in their gardens, and perhaps for cutting for indoor decoration. Dahlias come in such a wide range of sizes, colour permutations (except blue), flower forms and foliage shades that there is a cultivar suitable for almost anywhere in any garden. Dahlias can be grown *en masse* in dedicated beds or used in mixed plantings with other perennials or with annuals, or both. Of course, the choice is determined by the space available.

The traditional massed beds of bedding dahlias are less common in parks and gardens in Britain these days, although in Continental Europe, they are still the most common way of growing dahlias for display. In some countries, mixed plantings, combining dahlias and other types of plants, such as red or blue salvias, petunias or begonias, are used, and can be very effective.

Public park-style bedding is not very suitable for smaller domestic gardens, but, when looking for inspiration for new ways to grow any plant in your garden, it pays to visit other gardens that are open to the public. There are plenty of National Trust and stately home gardens, as well as smaller private gardens that feature dahlias. These will provide plenty of ideas that can easily be copied on a reduced scale.

At Hadspen House in Somerset, dahlias have been planted in a mixed border that is backed by a wall. This bed features striking red varieties with purplish foliage that set off the helianthus and verbenas. In the

Red-flowered dahlias provide a splash of colour in the walled border at Hadspen House.

foreground, the dwarf bedding dahlia 'Ellen Huston' contrasts with the taller 'Bishop of Llandaff'. The dahlias revel in these protected growing conditions, and clever colour combinations, such as blues with reds and pinks, make the whole display very satisfying. The susceptibility of dahlias to frost makes them difficult to associate with other more hardy herbaceous plants unless they are planted in sheltered locations, or lifted every autumn and replanted each spring.

At Hadspen, the taller dahlias are used to set off the attractive weathered brick wall, but tall types could be planted as a screen to hide an ugly wall or fence, and in large groups can even produce a magnificent, albeit short-lived hedge. Carefully selected dahlias look good with roses and are an effective mask for the often leggy lower limbs of the shrubby types. Obviously care must be taken that the dahlia tubers can be lifted if necessary without damage to the rose roots.

BOLD COLOURS

Borders of dahlias planted in bold blocks of colour are spectacular. Those found at Anglesey Abbey, near Cambridge, or Biddulph Grange Garden in Staffordshire are difficult to establish and maintain but can be copied in more modest forms. Taller varieties (averaging 1.2–1.5m/4–5ft tall) are positioned at the back of the border with shorter varieties (1–1.2m/3–4ft tall) at the front. Alternatively, bedding dahlias (60–90cm/ 2–3ft tall) can be grown together in beds to give a massed colour display that looks particularly effective set off by a closely cropped lawn.

A number of dahlia varieties are described as 'dwarf bedders', but they vary in height depending on conditions. However, all these shorter varieties generally

Foliage and flower colour are combined in this Wisley border, with dahlia 'Tally Ho' playing a major role.

make good garden plants and can be attractive either on their own or in mixed plantings. Even taller ones can do well at the back of a border or as 'spot' plants.

Dahlias also provide a spectacular focus in herbaceous borders where they can be selected to maintain a note of colour throughout the summer and into the autumn. Varieties with very dark foliage and striking blooms can be used to produce vivid contrasts of colour, perfectly setting off more subtle herbaceous plants. 'Hot' borders containing different varieties of red-flowered dahlias along with other fiery-shaded flowers and foliage are very popular and effective. In the red border at The Priory, Kemerton, Worcestershire (see p.2), dahlias dominate the back of the border, where 'Bishop of Llandaff' with its purple foliage contrasts with the paler foliage of 'Blazdon Red'. In front are some complementary dwarf nicotianas and sedums. The main theme in this type of planting may be the colour but the different textures of the foliage also play an important part. A planting on this scale would be overwhelming in an average garden but just a couple of plants of two or three varieties could be selected for a small and attractive group.

Many National Trust properties feature dahlias with purplish foliage, most also with red flowers. It is remarkable how often 'Bishop of Llandaff' is planted. And it is a very worthy candidate with its dual interest of bright red flowers and bronze-purple foliage. At Wisley, dahlias, particularly waterlily types, are frequently used as a focus in borders. In the flower bed shown here, what appears at first sight to be 'Bishop of Llandaff' is actually a new tall, single variety called 'Tally Ho' (of American origin and not to be confused with the old Stredwick variety of the same name, introduced in 1925). In this bed the red dahlia variety has been used with rows of yellow (*Helenium* 'Butterpat') and orange (*Crocosmia*) to produce bold stripes of colour.

SUBTLE COLOURS

Because there is such a wide range of colours in the dahlia tribe, plants can be selected to produce a display of gentle tones as well as more vibrant ones. You can choose to have a decoration of lower tones, allowing darker colours to dominate or, by simply using two different complementary colours, say red and clear mauve or pale pink, you can achieve a more subtle and cooler overall effect. Again at The Priory in Kemerton, Worcestershire, there is an impressive example of this type of planting. Here the pink waterlily dahlia 'Gerrie Hoek' dominates the middle of the border offering a superb foil to the bright yellow of the rudbeckias. At the front of the border the sedums will soon join the display and there are other pink-toned plants such as *Liatris spicata*, which complements the dahlias with its similar colour but contrasting form.

PATIO DAHLIAS

If you have a small garden, dahlias can be grown in pots or containers. The lilliput varieties are exceptionally short and well adapted for this purpose. Some of the shorter dwarf bedding varieties also do well under such conditions. Mixed plantings can work, particularly if varieties of the same height are used in the same container. Care must be taken to provide adequate and regular watering of dahlias grown in pots or containers.

DAHLIAS FOR CUTTING

Dahlias are still an important ingredient for traditional floral decoration, such as in church flower festivals. Many varieties can be used for cut flowers; they also associate well in arrangements with other flowers. The waterlily types in particular are good for cutting as they generally have good strong flower stems and blooms that last well in water. Most collerettes will also make good cut flowers. Even those plants that are not specifically being grown for cutting benefit from having their fully mature blooms cut in order to encourage new buds to develop. (Chapter 10 A–Z of Dahlias in Cultivation gives details of which dahlias are particularly suitable for cutting.)

In all these cases of dahlia growing, there is no substitute for seeing examples being grown and taking notes of successful varieties.

Pale-flowered dahlias enhance a refined planting in this mixed border at The Priory at Kemerton.

6

CULTIVATION
including Pests and Diseases

Dahlias will grow in virtually any soil and situation but, like any plants, they will respond to extra care. As they originated in the volcanic, well-drained soils of Mexican hillsides, it is wise to try to give them such conditions in our gardens if at all possible. So the ideal is a water-retentive soil, but one that drains freely, a position in full sun, so they can flower at their best, and shelter from cold winds. A damp plot on heavy clay is not conducive to the development of a rampant root system, nor will it be possible under such conditions to grow a massive bush 1.8m (6ft) tall and wide from a small cutting in just 10–12 weeks. Plants alongside a high wall, near tall shrubs or under trees will grow and produce blooms despite this, but will have lanky stems and poor flowerheads.

PLANTING

Few gardeners can choose their soil or climate, but whatever the soil and the location, a great deal can be done to improve conditions so that excellent dahlias may be grown. Work on preparing the site should start in the autumn. As soon as the previous year's plants have been lifted, dig the plot over and incorporate as much organic matter as possible into the soil. Some growers use large quantities of farmyard manure, others prefer leafmould or compost; any of these will do. It does not matter what form the organic material takes, nor does it have to be well rotted: its purpose is to improve water retention in the soil. In North America, it is common practice to sow winter rye, or a similar green manure, and dig it under in the spring.

Two dwarf bedding dahlias, 'Ella Britain' and 'Mme. Stappers' in a traditional Victorian bedding display at Anglesey Abbey.

It is not necessary to double dig the plot: a single spit is sufficient, as most of the roots are produced in the top 30cm (12in) of soil. Over time, the level of the plot will be raised through the addition of organic material, and some dahlia growers deliberately develop raised beds with uncultivated paths around them. As access to the dahlias is possible from the paths, this means the soil in the beds remains in good condition and does not become compacted through being walked on.

Spring digging is easy if the groundwork has been put into the plot during the previous autumn. A light forking or a quick run over with a cultivator is all that is necessary. At this time, a dressing of a long-acting fertilizer can be given. Bonemeal is ideal – at 100g (4oz) per square metre/yard – and should be applied at least six weeks before planting out is envisaged.

PLANNING

Before planting out, it is best to have a general plan and mark the position of the plants with canes. Dahlias require plenty of room to develop – ideally at least 60cm (2ft) should be allowed between plants, and giant or large varieties will benefit from 90cm (3ft) spacing. Dwarf bedding dahlias take up less space; 22–30cm (9–12in) between plants will enable them to produce a mass of blooms without the need for stakes. They still benefit from short canes between the plants, but extensive tying up is not necessary. Miniature decorative and ball varieties can be grown at 45cm (18in) spacing, and pompons can be planted 30cm (12in) apart, with 45cm (18in) between the rows.

As well as spacing between plants, remember to leave room for access; before the plants flower, they will make extraordinary growth, and being able to reach

each individual plant for inspection and treatment is vital. If possible, plant in double rows leaving a path of 90cm (3ft), or even more, between each pair of rows.

SETTING OUT

Dahlias should not be planted out until all fear of frost is past. (In most parts of Britain, this is likely to be June 1st, but be guided by local conditions.) Late frosts can occur in most years and it is wise to have newspaper at the ready to cover and protect newly emerging shoots, if frost is forecast and your plot is susceptible.

Harden off plants in a coldframe or in a sheltered spot for a few days. Spraying with a systemic insecticide while they are in the coldframe is easier than waiting until they are planted out. A handful of slug pellets scattered among the waiting plants will keep slugs at bay. Before planting, water the young plants well.

To prepare the site for the plants, dig a hole at the base of each cane. Make it slightly larger than the root ball of the dahlia to be planted, so that when the hole is filled, a depression is left around the plant and when water is applied it does not run away.

Each year, a display of dahlias is grown at Anglesey Abbey. 'Kathleen's Alliance', a small cactus, is in the foreground.

HOW DEEP?

How deep to plant is a question that gives rise to great argument among dahlia growers. Some varieties of dahlias, particularly giant and large types, benefit from deep planting. For example, a plant with five pairs of leaves will have the lowest three pairs of leaves removed and is then planted 20cm (8in) deep in order to cover these three nodes. The growing tip of the plant is also removed. Side shoots will grow from below ground level and will make extra roots, producing a more sturdy plant; any side shoots growing above ground are removed. As well as being more sturdy, it is claimed that such plants will make larger blooms than those more shallowly planted, but the evidence of this claim is conflicting. Some growers regularly plant all their varieties as deep as possible, others say that deep planting does not suit some dahlias. Deep planting on heavy wet soils does cause root rot in some varieties that are prone to such problems, so it may be that this method is only advisable on well-drained, light soils. Clearly the answer is that depth is dependent on soil and growing conditions.

AFTERCARE

Some growers put a handful of balanced fertilizer in the planting hole, but others consider that no feed should be given at planting. Fertilizer against the young roots can cause severe scorching of young plants, so if it is to be applied at planting it is better given as a top dressing. But on balance, application is best delayed until the plants are beginning to grow away (see below). Only water is safe for young plants and this should be liberally provided, as long as it drains away afterwards.

The label from the plant pot should be placed alongside the plant, which should be tied loosely to the cane. Tying up immediately after planting is essential in order to avoid wind damage: it is surprising how frequently strong winds arise around planting time and it is a pity for plants to be broken and damaged after all the care that they have had lavished upon them. Young plants also seem to attract all the slugs in the vicinity, so slug pellets are a must at planting out time.

During the next few weeks after planting, very little work is needed on the dahlia plot. Weeds should be removed by shallow hoeing, which will also keep the soil surface open, and further water is required only if weather conditions are very dry. The young plants must be encouraged to throw out new roots to search for water at deeper soil levels so watering is avoided until the plants are well established and growing rapidly.

Towards the end of early summer, surface roots will begin to spread out from the plant so hoeing should stop. Further weed development from now on has to be prevented by mulching. A wide variety of materials can be used: straw, spent mushroom compost or even old carpets are all suitable. Before laying down the mulch, a handful of organic fertilizer, such as fish, blood and bone, can be applied to each plant, but this should not be overdone or the plant may produce leaves rather than blooms.

CULTIVATION
STOPPING

Sooner or later the plants will need to be stopped. The idea behind stopping is to encourage the plant to produce side shoots. It is done by removing the growing

growing point removed

Stopping (pinching out or cutting away) the main growing shoots is done to encourage side shoots to develop.

tip, either by cutting it with a sharp knife or breaking it away with the fingers. If a knife is used, then it should be disinfected after each plant so that the risk of spreading viruses via the sap is reduced. If blooms are required for garden display only, then the earlier the tip is removed the earlier blooms will develop.

For show purposes, stopping should be done about eight weeks before the desired show date. This is only a rough guide: blooms of giant and large varieties are slower to develop than small blooms, and to make early shows, giant-flowered varieties may have to be stopped when they are planted out, or plants from divided tubers may even have to be allowed to flower on the crown bud (the latter, in which the main shoot is not stopped, results in fewer eventual shoots and, therefore, fewer blooms). In order to spread the flowering dates, not all plants should be stopped on the same day: instead stagger them over two or three weeks.

Removing the growing tip reduces the natural apical dominance (see p.16) and the buds in the axils of all the leaves will be stimulated into growth. If six pairs of leaves are present then 12 side shoots will grow up. With small- or miniature-flowered varieties, all these side shoots may be allowed to develop and bear blooms. However, the number of side shoots allowed to grow on giant and large varieties needs to be restricted if big blooms are desired. For maximum size blooms on giants, only three or four side shoots should be retained; large-flowered varieties can be allowed to develop four or five shoots, while medium-flowered varieties can support between six and eight.

CANING AND TYING

Dwarf bedding varieties, if planted close together, will need little support unless the bed happens to be in a position that is unprotected from prevailing winds. Some twiggy branches pushed into the soil between the plants may be sufficient to prevent them from being blown over.

Taller varieties will require caning or staking. Tying an individual plant to a single cane is rarely satisfactory, as the plant will blow around the cane and may snap at the base. Many growers use three canes per plant, two additional ones being pushed into the ground at an angle to the original cane in order to make an inverted cone. Soft twine, tied around the three canes at intervals as the plants grow, will be sufficient to hold the plant firm.

Some growers prefer to fix chicken wire horizontally along the double rows with extra stakes at each end to pull it taut. Others use elaborate systems of posts and wires to support the plants. In the dahlia trial beds in the RHS gardens at Wisley, wire pig netting is held on four slightly outward-sloping stakes for each block of three plants. As the plants grow, the wire netting is raised up the stakes.

With pompons planted together, a single cane for each plant is usually sufficient as the plants are planted closely, along with extra stakes at each corner of the bed, around which are tied wire or strong twine. The plants thus tend to grow into a hedge-like structure, supporting each other within the outside ties.

Whatever the method used, it should be capable of supporting the considerable weight of plants, particularly when they are wet with rain.

DISBUDDING

At the end of each developing flower stem, a cluster of flower buds will become visible. As the cluster opens out, a central bud with two smaller buds (wing buds) below it will become apparent. If the smaller buds are left to develop, the central bud, or leader, will flower

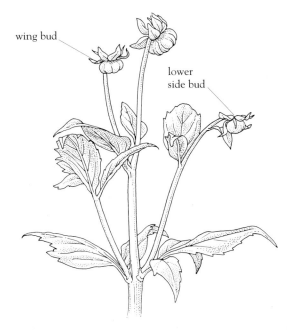

The side buds (wing buds) are removed to enable the crown bud to develop and to encourage the footstalk to elongate.

first, but before it is over, the other two will open, thus forming a cluster of blooms. The central bloom will have to compete with the two wing buds for water and nutrients and will not achieve its full potential.

If the bloom is required for cutting for home decoration or show, then the two wing buds should be pinched out as soon as it is convenient to do so. This enables the central bloom to develop in size and to be borne on a longer stem. If the side shoots immediately below are also removed, then an even longer stem will be available and the leading bloom will increase in size even more.

In order to get the maximum size bloom for show purposes, all the side shoots down the flower stem can be removed. This is known as securing the bloom. However, it is wise to leave at least one side shoot at the base of the flower stem so that when the bloom is cut, a replacement shoot can grow and produce a second flush of flowerheads. Growers should be aware that if the bloom is being produced for show purposes and the side shoots are removed too enthusiastically, the resulting flowerhead may grow oversize and be disqualified on the showbench. Some varieties tend to produce oversize blooms if disbudded too much, while others will not make maximum size unless disbudded heavily. The number of blooms being carried on the plant at any one time will also have an effect and this, in turn, is determined by the number and position of the branches that are allowed to develop.

SUMMER FEEDING

All plants benefit from a summer feed, and dahlias are no exception: growing a bush 1.8m (6ft) high in just a few weeks demands a high nutrient intake, and dahlias are gross feeders. However, it is possible to overfeed them, which can lead to coarse, distorted blooms with loose centres and a mass of lush foliage, which will reduce bloom size. The intention when feeding a dahlia should be to produce an ideal framework on which the blooms can develop. Once this framework has been produced and the flower buds have been formed, there is no advantage in providing further nutrients. On the other hand, as blooms are removed later in the season, replacement stems will need some food. Moreover, trace elements, such as magnesium and iron, can strengthen the colour of blooms and, in this case, foliar feeding is recommended.

When the first buds are beginning to develop, a handful per plant of a high potash feed, such as fish, blood and bone, can be applied, but if the soil is in good heart, this may be unnecessary. Instead, a high potash feed containing trace elements can be applied in a weak solution during late midsummer, and perhaps again two weeks later. No more feeding is needed, except perhaps a top dressing of high potash fertilizer at the end of the season in order to help ripen the tubers. In fact, any extra fertilizer remaining in the soil can be positively harmful; excessive feeding of show dahlias invariably gives rise to soft tubers liable to rot after lifting. This is such a problem with many showmen that they rarely lift field tubers for next year's stock; instead they raise extra pot tubers for propagation (see p.57).

WATERING

Dahlia plants are almost 95% water, and all of this water, and more, has to come from the soil in which they grow. It is water that produces the rigidity to hold up an herbaceous plant, and water carries the nutrients absorbed from the soil and transports food materials to the actively growing parts. Water also forms the basis of

'David Howard' is an excellent variety for garden display, its bronze blooms contrasting well with its dark foliage.

the carbohydrates manufactured in the leaves. Thus, a lack of water will cause the plant to wilt, nutrients will not be taken up from the soil, and carbohydrate cannot be produced. Plenty of water is also needed to develop flowerheads. The flower parts are already laid down in the young flower buds and the individual tissue cells expand through absorbing water, so to achieve their full potential, flowerheads need water: any shortage will reduce bloom size.

Once established, the dahlia is one of the fastest-growing plants and requires vast quantities of water. Over its main growing period – mid-spring to early autumn – its total requirement is equivalent to about 450mm (18in) of rain. Even in the wetter parts of Britain, rainfall is rarely adequate to satisfy this demand. Supplementary water has to be provided and the magnitude of this undertaking should not be underestimated – 25mm (1in) of water on an acre of land is equivalent to approximately 20.5 litres (4½ gallons) per square metre/yard. If the soil starts to become dry, the quantity of water needed to redress the deficit should be applied in one operation otherwise losses from evaporation will reduce its effect. The soil must be able to hold the necessary amount of water without

PLATE IV

BEDDING DAHLIAS

'Reddy'

'Bishop of Llandaff'

D. sherffii

'Brookfield Delight'

'Honey'

'Mignon Silver'

'Sweetheart'

'Bon Esperance'

All flowers are shown at approximately life size

'Weston Nuggett' is a miniature cactus that was specifically raised for showing.

becoming waterlogged, hence the need for good soil preparation and a high organic content.

It is useful to know how much water can be applied to any given soil without causing it to puddle. In an experiment with a 10mm (½in) hosepipe connected to a rotary sprinkler, 1.5mm (⅙in) of water was applied to a 4sq m (12sq ft) area in 10 minutes, without any ill effect. At this rate, it would take 2¾ hours to provide the equivalent of 25mm (1in) of rain. Soil type needs to be taken into account; for example, sandy soil is less likely to puddle than clay, which will retain the water for longer. The rate of application is dependent upon the mains water pressure which can vary considerably during the day. The area in the experiment was about the size of a single dahlia bed; if there were five dahlia beds needing water it would take 14 hours to provide 25mm (1in).

During hot sunny weather the plants transpire water through their leaves at a faster rate than they can take it up through their roots, and some wilting may occur. The larger the root system and the higher the capacity of the soil to hold water, the less this wilting is likely. Applying water during the heat of the day is less effective than applying it in the evening, and water applied at the roots of a plant is better than that applied by an overhead spray. However, although an overhead spray will not redress any water deficit, it may be useful to prevent plants wilting.

Irrigation lines are best laid along the rows of dahlias to provide the water where it is needed and reduce waste. If a mulch is used to prevent water loss, then the irrigation lines must be laid below the mulch. It should be remembered, however, that mulching only reduces evaporation from the soil and that much of the water is released from the plant itself in transpiration.

SPRAYING

In general dahlias are remarkably free from disease and usually suffer only from aphids and earwigs. Massed borders of dahlias in parks and gardens produce magnificent displays without the use of pesticides, even though closer inspection will show the presence of aphids, earwigs and caterpillars. However, to produce top class show blooms without any imperfections, regular spraying is required.

Aphid damage is rarely a problem in itself, the main danger being the spread of viruses by the aphids moving from plant to plant. Under certain weather conditions, aphids can multiply very rapidly and it is important that they are checked. This is why spraying is usually carried out on a regular basis – to prevent the build-up of pests rather than to control an outbreak. Today, there are a number of insecticides available, both contact and systemic, which are safe for use on dahlias. It is wise to use several different insecticides in rotation so that a particular pest does not have the opportunity of developing resistance to a single product. A regular two-week spraying programme is essential, even with systemic products, and the occasional contact insecticide should be used as there is less likelihood of pests developing resistance to these. (For more information on specific pests and diseases see pp.60–69.)

CUTTING BLOOMS

Dahlia flowerheads will wilt very quickly if they are picked during the heat of the day. Instead they should be cut in the evening or early morning. Pick the blooms with as long a stem as possible, making a sloping cut just above a node. Plunge them immediately into cold water and store in cool dark conditions. Blooms that have started to wilt may be revived by cutting a couple of centimetres off the stem while it is still under water. Also under water, pierce the stem above the bottom node with a knife so that any air bubbles remaining in it can be released.

When dahlias are placed in water, all leaves that are below the water level should be removed, but beyond this, nothing more need be done to achieve a long-lasting display. By changing the water every day, blooms can be made to last longer, and an asprin or a flower-arranger's sachet of preservative, dissolved in the water, will prevent fungal growth.

Dahlias make an excellent display on their own or when mixed in with other species and foliage. Floral

'Jessie G', a miniature ball, and 'Cindy', a miniature decorative, growing together in a flower bed.

arrangement classes in horticultural shows are less popular than some years ago, but they still feature in many of the larger ones, and, in late summer, there is little to better dahlias for these.

THE END OF THE SEASON

Dahlias are frost-sensitive, although in mild areas or during less severe winters than are usual in the British Isles, they will overwinter in the ground, given the protection of peat or straw. When left like this the plants soon become unmanageable, so they should be lifted, if only to divide the clumps into more useful pieces.

There is no doubt that a well-grown cutting will produce a far better root system, in a shorter time, than a replanted or divided tuber clump. This is an important factor when growing exhibition blooms, and it is for this reason, as much as any, that all dedicated dahlia growers lift their tubers in the autumn and store them in a protected environment through the winter. (For more information on propagation see pp.70–78.)

LIFTING

There is constant discussion among dahlia growers as to whether or not dahlias should be lifted before the

first frost has occurred. Clearly, once the top growth has been blackened by frost, the sooner the tubers are lifted the better, but in some years frosts do not begin until late autumn by which time the ground may well be unworkable. On the other hand, a premature lifting in early mid-autumn may result in the unripe tubers drying out and shrivelling. The value of a prior frosting lies in the fact that growth is halted and the tuber becomes dormant, all the food reserves are stored in the correct state in the tuber and its skin thickens up so is less prone to damage as it is extracted from the soil. Moreover, the soil comes away from the tuber more easily after a frost, again reducing the likelihood of damage. Even so, some growers lift their tubers every year at the end of mid-autumn, frost or no frost, acting on the belief that in the dahlia's natural habitat of Central America, no frost is necessary for the tubers to ripen successfully.

Whichever course you choose, during early autumn, it is wise to give the plants a high potash dressing to help the tubers plump up and ripen. A handful of potato fertilizer, or its equivalent, to a square metre/yard is ideal.

The first stage in lifting is to decide which plants are to be lifted and to cut their foliage down to a height of 15–20cm (6–8in), provided that frost has not already done the job. Once the dead blooms and foliage have been removed, there will be little indication of what plant it is, so a label with the variety indelibly recorded on it should be tied to the remainder of the stem. Most growers practise stock selection, that is the best plants are marked during the growing season and these are selected for propagation for the subsequent year. Poor plants, those that are diseased and those that have unsatisfactory flowerhead formation, are discarded.

While lifting the tuber, the idea is to extract it with the minimum of damage. As it is difficult to estimate the extent of the tuber spread from the main stem, it is wise to assume that they may have reached up to 30cm (12in) or so away. Some growers advocate using a spade since any roots will be cut cleanly during lifting and the cut ends will heal more quickly. Others prefer a fork and rely on subsequent trimming of the tuber with a sharp knife to minimize damage. Whatever implement is used, a number of insertions around the stem will need to be made and the tuber is then removed with a gentle levering action.

PREPARATION FOR STORAGE

Once it is above ground, as much soil as possible should be scraped from the root using a cane or plastic label, but care is necessary to avoid damaging the skin. Any surface moisture should be allowed to dry off by lying the tubers on the staging of the greenhouse. Large-flowered varieties will have substantial stems which may be full of water. In this case, the tubers should be inverted, with the stems hanging downwards, to enable the water to drain away.

After three or four days, inspect the lifted tubers, remove any loose soil and cut off broken or damaged roots cleanly with a knife. Immature tubers will show signs of drying and shrivelling; to protect them, place them on a layer of peat in a box, with more peat around them. After another week, the more mature tubers should be ready for cleaning up and storing.

Many growers leave as much soil as possible around the tubers after lifting in order to prevent the tubers shrivelling. This way there is less damage to the skin and less likelihood of rots developing. Others wash their tubers after a week or so to remove all the soil, believing that if no soil is left there will be no fungi to set up infections. After washing the tubers, they are dipped into a solution of fungicide or sprayed with the same solution to counter fungal infection. An alternative is to soak the tubers for 15 minutes in a 10 per cent solution of household bleach. This will kill any slugs' eggs and red spider mites as well as the fungi. The bleach solution should be rinsed off with cold water, and a fungicide can be added to the rinsing water to counter subsequent fungal infection.

STORING

There is no single method for storing tubers through the winter. A number of alternative approaches are described here. My advice to growers is: find the one that suits you best, developed and improved by experience over a number of years, and if it proves successful, stick with it.

The key to successful storage is temperature, ideally 5–7°C (41–45°F), and a dry, but not too dry, atmosphere. It is difficult to achieve these conditions except perhaps in a cellar, and few people have access to one. Tubers can be stored in boxes underneath the greenhouse staging, with the greenhouse heater set for frost control. They can be packed in straw, dry peat, sawdust, vermiculite or even newspaper, but whatever method is used, they should be checked over regularly and any rotting cut away, the cut surface being dusted with flowers of sulphur.

Tubers of large bloom varieties, and those with heavy stems, tend to rot around the collar, so some growers cut the stems down to a couple of centimetres (an inch or so) after initial drying off, and bore a hole down the centre with a screwdriver, or even an electric drill, right through the tuber.

An extension of this method is to split the tuber in half through the stem, or even to cut the main clump into separate tubers, each with a tiny piece of stem attached. A grower I know cuts the stems of his plants right down to the collar before lifting the tubers. He then covers the crown with dry sand and leaves the tubers in the ground for the cut end to callus over. This takes about two weeks, by which time the tubers are ready for lifting. They are then easier to divide into separate pieces.

Immature tubers or those that are thin and spindly are best boxed up in peat as soon as possible after lifting. As long as they are kept dry and cool they will survive until the heat is turned on ready for propagation in the spring. Some growers box all their tubers up after lifting and store them in this form until propagation time. I find that this method works well for my conditions. However, tubers can also be stored in clamps or in coldframes, provided they are protected from frost.

For clamping, dig a trench in the garden at least 30cm (12in) deep and line it with straw. Pack the tubers on to the straw and place a layer of straw on top. The whole clamp is then recovered with 30cm (12in) or so of soil and finally topped with a plastic sheet to divert water away from the trench. It is vital to ensure that adequate drainage occurs – it helps if the clamp is on a slope – otherwise the trench may fill with water and the tubers will rot.

If tubers are to be stored in a coldframe, you will need the more substantial type of frame with brick walls. A base of straw is placed in the coldframe and the tubers are heaped on this. Straw is positioned around the frame walls and a thick layer of straw is put over the top. Finally, a layer of sacking or old carpet is placed over the straw and the lights are replaced. During extremely cold spells, more protective material must be added over the top until the worst is over.

POT TUBERS

Some varieties can be very difficult to store successfully. This is particularly so of those that produce fine pencil-like tubers which tend to break off easily from the crown. The tubers of thick-stemmed varieties, especially giant-flowered types, are also difficult to keep. Moreover, such tubers can make enormous clumps which take up a great deal of space on the propagating bench. As a result many growers are tending to rely more and more on pot tubers for overwintering their stocks, as are some commercial raisers.

The basis of pot tuber production is the restriction of tuber growth by keeping the plant in a small pot – usually 10cm (4in) – and planting it out still in the pot. Early-struck cuttings that are too difficult to hold back until planting time, or late-struck cuttings that may be too late to give blooms for the main shows, can also remain in their pots through summer in this way.

These pot-bound plants should be planted up to their rims in shallow drills, close together. Roots may grow through the base of the pot and will help to anchor the plants against the wind. Allow plants to produce a flowerhead on the crown bud to check that the plant is true to type and correctly labelled. Once this is done, the flowerhead is removed and further flowerheads are cut back before they develop. The plant, therefore, devotes its energies to producing foliage and providing nutrients for storage in the tuber.

The growing plants must be sprayed regularly to keep them free from pests, and any virused plants should be removed and destroyed. A foliar feed is recommended during the summer, and a high potash feed will be advantageous during early autumn. In mid-autumn, the foliage is cut back to within 15cm (6in) of the ground and the tubers allowed to ripen for as long as possible. At the first sign of frost, the pots are lifted and placed on their sides under the bench in the greenhouse. Alternatively, they may be stored in a coldframe, so long as frost protection is provided.

The compost in the pots should be allowed to dry out, but the tubers should remain plump until needed for boxing-up in the spring. The success rate for storing pot tubers is normally very good compared with most other methods, the only likely problem being the misplacement of labels, and thus potential misnaming of varieties, as stock is moved. Most of the tubers sold in plastic bags in garden centres are produced this way.

PESTS AND DISEASES

Like most flowering plants, dahlias are subject to a wide range of pests and diseases, but a few precautions can reduce the chances of any problems occurring.

Although during a very hard winter, many pests and diseases will be killed off, usual conditions over most of the British Isles mean that a number of them can survive overwinter in sheltered sites, such as fences, trees, hedges and the soil, and, most importantly, in greenhouses or coldframes. Keeping the greenhouse full of plants over the winter gives little opportunity to have a good clean-out so do this as soon as you can in the spring. Take all the plants out of the greenhouse and give the inside a good wash down with a solution of Jeyes Fluid. This will get rid of all the pests and diseases that have been overwintering inside. It is wise to let the smell of the Jeyes Fluid dissipate completely before putting the plants back in the greenhouse, since some tender plants may be damaged by the fumes.

Fruit trees and ornamental trees and shrubs can be given a good spray with a winter tar oil wash, or a similar compound. This is normal practice for fruit trees, and many ornamentals will benefit from the same treatment. Plant debris lying around the garden will also be a haven for unwanted visitors, and should be cleared up before the spring.

Even if you are careful about keeping your own garden clear, it is impossible to prevent migration of pests and diseases from outside it. Although it is likely that chemicals will be needed as the season progresses, it is also well worth looking to gardening practice to help prevent problems taking hold. Well-grown and vigorous plants will withstand infection better than poor plants. Feed your plants carefully – phosphate is known to reduce infection by fungal and bacterial growth, and chlorosis is a symptom of trace element deficiency, which is often followed by disease in the weakened tissue – but remember, lush growth stimulated by too much nitrogen is more prone to problems, so balanced fertilizer applications are to be preferred.

CHEMICAL PESTICIDES

In my younger days gardeners had an armoury of powerful chemicals to help them against pests and diseases,

'Cornel' (p.105) is a red miniature ball that is suitable for both exhibition and garden display.

and many accidents occurred in their use. Nowadays, all chemicals for domestic (and commercial) gardens have to go through prolonged safety testing programmes before they can be marketed. Modern chemicals have to be relatively harmless to humans while being effective against pests and diseases. Even so, they are all poisons and must be handled with care, and the manufacturer's instructions followed exactly.

Many chemicals kill pests by contact, but there is also a class of chemicals called systemics. These are absorbed into the plant through the leaves or the roots, and travel around it via the sap, retaining their insect- or disease-killing property for many weeks. Although this seems ideal, there is a danger inherent in systemics: if, over time, the dose becomes too small to kill the pest, surviving pests can develop resistance and, thus, greater concentrations are required to kill their descendants. For this reason, a range of chemicals should be employed, including contact pesticides, so that the chances of resistance are reduced.

Systemic insecticides or fungicides have the ability to penetrate the leaf surface. They can also penetrate exposed skin and may be absorbed into the tissue below, so concentrate splashed on skin must be washed away immediately. Even a dilute spray can harm sensitive skin, and washing after use is essential.

'Bishop of Llandaff' (p.101), a peony-type dahlia with contrasting dark foliage, is a favourite in herbaceous borders.

APPLICATION

The application of modern pesticides is a relatively simple affair, since most can be applied in dilute solutions with a sprayer. In a greenhouse, a small hand sprayer is adequate, while a large plot will require a modern pump sprayer with a lance. For even larger areas, a knapsack sprayer may be needed.

The ideal time for spraying is during the early evening when honey bees and bumble bees will have returned to their hive or nest.

Spraying in windy conditions is to be avoided as spray can drift over large distances and cause problems to neighbours, their pets or their fish. Many chemicals are extremely damaging to fish so extra care is essential if a fishpond is in the vicinity.

Avoid spraying in strong sunlight, too, as the agents used to disperse the chemicals can damage the plants. These 'wetting' agents are usually soap, detergent or oil and, within the globules of spray that fall on the leaves, they can act as tiny magnifying glasses concentrating the sun's rays into a fine beam which can burn the plant tissue.

Many sprays start to break down when they are diluted with water, and some of the products formed during this process can damage plants. Moreover, the active ingredient loses effectiveness quite rapidly when exposed to sunlight – this is particularly true of pyrethrum and related chemicals – so dispose of any unused mixture rather than keeping it for another day.

Chemicals in the form of dusts are less convenient to apply than liquids, and can give rise to problems if inhaled. They should only be used for soil treatment or in protected environments such as greenhouses. The cone-shaped 'smokes' that are are available for use in greenhouses have a touch paper, which, when lit, discharges a fine smoke containing the dust particles. Once they are lit, the greenhouse should be vacated quickly and the door closed. Before re-entering the greenhouse, the door should be left open for any chemical fumes to disperse.

BIOLOGICAL CONTROL

In recent years, the use of biological control – using one organism, usually a natural predator or parasite, to control another– for pest infestations has gathered momentum. Initially developed for commercial growers, the technique has now become available for amateur use. Although it is much more effective in a closed environment like a greenhouse, in certain cases it can be used outdoors.

Biological control works by introducing large quantities of a parasite or predator into the pest population, which should also be present in high numbers. This predator or parasite attacks the pest population and reduces its numbers, but as it does so its population falls, too, since it can only live on the pest it is attacking. When the pest has been eliminated, the parasite or predator dies out. This means that any subsequent infection has to be controlled by a new introduction of the controlling organism. Biological control can be expensive, but in some cases, it is the only alternative.

A wide range of glasshouse pests, including whitefly, red spider mite, aphids, vine weevil and thrips, can now be controlled using biological methods. Recently, a nematode (eelworm) control has been launched for slugs. Its manufacturers claim that it controls all species; however, the larger garden snails, which live above ground in drier conditions, are less susceptible.

PESTS

SLUGS AND SNAILS

There are no pests that love dahlias more than slugs or snails. A young plant can be demolished in a single night, leaving no trace. Slugs and snails are nocturnal feeders; during the day, larger ones hide under stones or other debris and the small ones hide in the soil.

The traditional control is metaldehyde mixed with bran. This is sold as compressed pellets treated to make them showerproof. After heavy rain, slugs may recover from metaldehyde and further applications will be necessary. A more effective slug killer in wet conditions are pellets containing the chemical menazon. These are, however, more expensive. The soil can also be treated with a solution of aluminium sulphate which prevents slugs breeding and kills the adults. Keel slugs and other field slugs can be inadvertently brought into the greenhouse when tubers are lifted in the autumn, so it is wise to put down slug pellets when the tubers are boxed-up in the spring. Most slugs have an annual lifecycle, with eggs laid in autumn and spring, each hermaphrodite adult is capable of laying 300 eggs, and in wet conditions, the population can escalate.

The biological control (available by mail-order) uses a nematode that is mixed in a clay powder. A 50g (2oz) pack contains more than 6 million nematodes and treats about 40sq m (48sq yd). It is mixed with water and applied as a drench to the soil. The soil must be kept moist, but not waterlogged, for six weeks after application. The parasite needs temperatures of over 5°C (41°F) to infect and kill slugs and, although overnight frost is not said to affect its performance, prolonged freezing spells will kill it, as will temperatures over 35°C (95°F). It is best applied during spring and early summer when slug populations are high and temperatures are not likely to be too extreme. Once the slug population is killed, the parasite cannot survive so new infestations have to be re-treated.

ANTS, WOODLICE AND WIREWORMS

These pests rarely cause serious problems with dahlias. Ants can disturb the roots of young plants, but more serious is their habit of 'farming' aphids. They will carry wingless aphids up the stems of dahlias and lodge them in the growing tips where they can then 'milk' them of their sugary honeydew. The aphids multiply rapidly and cause a sticky mess which can become infected with fungal spores; they also damage the plant tissue by sucking the sap and can spread viruses in the process.

Although woodlice cause little damage to established dahlia plants, they can eat the tubers in storage, giving rise to fungal infections.

Wireworms are rarely a problem except in heavy infestations when they can damage the root systems of young plants. They are most likely to be problematic where new turf has been turned in and has not properly rotted away before the plants are set.

The recommended treatment for such soil pests is HCH dust (a modern form of benzene hexachloride) or malathion dust. However, liquid malathion or a phenol-based sterilant, such as Jeyes Fluid or Armillatox, can be watered on to the soil.

APHIDS

Many forms of aphids attack dahlia plants. Greenfly, blackfly and those that are red or pink overwinter, usually as eggs, on many plant species and will migrate to dahlias as soon as they are planted out, or even while they are in the coldframe or greenhouse. They can multiply at alarming rates: during the summer they give birth to living young, which, in turn, produce more living young. A single adult is capable of producing millions of young over the summer months. If left alone, they will suck the life-giving sap from the young shoots of dahlias, leaving them crippled and deformed. The most dangerous consequences are the viral diseases they can spread. Some types of virus can multiply in the body of the aphid and are then injected into the plant when it sucks the sap; other viruses are spread by transferring infected sap from one plant to another.

Towards the end of summer, winged females and fertile males are produced. After these mate, eggs are laid and these can overwinter, thus continuing the cycle. In the shelter of a greenhouse or a coldframe, some adults may survive in an active state and continue to breed during the winter months.

Most gardeners apply routine sprays to keep aphids under control, starting as soon as the tubers are boxed-up and continuing throughout the propagating period. Under commercial conditions, some aphids have developed resistance to insecticides based on organophosphorus compounds, and it is important to alternate between chemicals to achieve the best control.

Pirimicarb is a selective aphicide that does not harm bees and other useful insects such as ladybirds, and is a useful chemical for spot treatments, particularly early on in the season. It is absorbed through the leaf and will kill aphids on the underside, as well as by contact.

General insecticides based on permethrin, a man-made insecticide developed from pyrethrum, but more persistent, has a deterrent effect on aphids as well as killing by contact. A different type of insecticide is pirimiphos-methyl (for example ICI's Sybol), which is also effective for controlling a wide range of insect pests, including red spider mite (see p.65). Systemic insecticides based on dimethoate are effective for aphids, and are absorbed into the sap stream where they remain persistent for weeks at a time.

With this wide range of insecticides available, spraying every week or two, with a different one each time, should keep the dahlia plants clear of aphids, as well as a range of other insects as well.

CAPSID BUGS

Unlike the less mobile aphids, capsid bugs can travel quickly from plant to plant. Eggs are laid during the autumn, usually on soft fruits, but also on hedges such as privet and hawthorn. The eggs develop into silvery white nymphs which can cause damage to dahlias by

PLATE V

COLLERETTE DAHLIAS

'Inglebrook Jill'

'Maltby Fanfare'

'Orel'

'Chimborazo'

All flowers are shown at approximately life size

'La Cierva'

'Rita Hill'

burrowing into the young shoot tips and destroying the growing tips. The adults suck sap, causing distortion of the young shoots. Because the adults are so nimble, the best time to control them is during the evening, when the sun is going down. At this time of day, most insects become more lethargic and therefore more likely to be killed by contact sprays. However, systemic insecticides will be more effective. If contact insecticides are to be used as back-up, then spray any hedges near the dahlia plot as well as the plants themselves.

THRIPS

Thrips are more prevalent in hot, thundery weather, hence their common name, thunder flies. They are very small so the damage that they do to the plant is minimal. However, they tend to collect on the flowerheads, to which they are attracted, and their sap sucking activities cause tiny spots on the petals, disfiguring the blooms. They can also transmit some viral diseases. Systemic insecticides are effective in controlling them.

CUTWORMS AND CATERPILLARS

These are generally the larvae of night-flying moths. It is rare for cabbage or common white butterfly to attack dahlias, but some of the smaller butterfly species can lay their eggs on them. The caterpillars that emerge

'Rothsay Reveller' (p.127) is a striking bicoloured medium decorative for gardens.

from the eggs are rarely seen during the day, but they have voracious appetites and can do unbelievable damage to blooms in just one night.

Cutworms are the larvae of the yellow underwing moth, and similar moths, and cause most damage to the young plants in coldframes or after planting out. They overwinter as smooth dull-coloured larvae in the soil and emerge at night to sever the young stems of newly planted dahlias. Later in the season they will also climb the plant and attack the juicy developing blooms.

Caterpillars and cutworm larvae are deterred by strong smells and watering the soil with a strong solution of Jeyes Fluid or Armillatox after planting is effective, but care must be taken to avoid splashing the young plants or they may be damaged. Systemic insecticides are less effective against biting insects as the damage has been done before the pests are killed. Contact insecticides, such as malathion, are a useful control, but more effective is fenitrothion, sprayed during the evening as the caterpillars emerge from their hiding places. Spraying underneath the leaves will also kill the eggs before the caterpillars can emerge.

To attack the bloom, the caterpillars have to climb up to it. They can be prevented from doing this by a smear of vaseline around the flower stem. Beware of adjacent foliage forming a bridge above the vaseline barrier and nullifying its effect. This underlines the value of a good plant habit where the blooms are held up, clear of the foliage, on long flower stems. Remember to wipe vaseline off before staging blooms at a show.

EARWIGS

Earwigs and dahlias are often believed to be an inevitable combination. In reality, earwigs are no more of a pest of dahlias than of most other flowers. They have a legendary resistance to insecticide sprays, epitomized by their impenetrable hard, shell-like body.

The earwig is nocturnal, coming out to feed during the hours of darkness. Some gardens are over-run with earwigs, while other gardens never have any. They breed rapidly during early summer and a second brood appears in late summer, when the young nymphs can play havoc with the blooms.

The key to control is the prevention of build-up in early summer. The overwintering and nesting habitats beloved of earwigs must be cleared in the spring. Rustic and woven fences, rough tree bark and last season's canes all provide winter hiding places. Bundles of canes should be stood in a solution of Jeyes Fluid, or a similar phenolic substance, and fruit trees and fences should be sprayed with a tar oil wash to kill earwigs and any other overwintering insects.

Young plants in the coldframe can be devastated by earwigs but spraying regularly with malathion will at least deter them even if it rarely kills them.

Trapping is the most effective weapon against earwigs, by making use of their love of dark and confined spaces. Fill clay pots with hay or straw and upturn them on short canes in the coldframe or greenhouse, providing convenient nesting places for the earwigs. Inspect the pots each morning, tipping any earwigs out into neat insecticide or paraffin. Small pieces of corrugated cardboard rolled up and tied with string or rubber bands are equally effective, as are half-opened matchboxes containing hay or straw and tied to the canes during the growing season. Some growers seal the ends of their canes with putty or plastic wood, but I prefer to leave mine open as a trap, and I periodically pour paraffin from a washing-up liquid bottle into the open ends. A concentrated solution of malathion has a similar effect but take care to avoid getting it on your skin.

RED SPIDER MITES

Years ago, red spider mite was considered a minor pest of dahlias, being effectively controlled by such chemicals as nicotine-sulphate and organo-chlorine pesticides. These are no longer available, and the current range of insecticides available to the amateur grower is largely ineffective against red spider mites, which have built up resistance to them. There are some new chemicals that can be used by commercial growers, but these are illegal to amateurs.

Glasshouse red spider mite is the form that commonly attacks dahlias and they can be a serious pest, particularly during hot, dry summers. They feed by piercing the leaf surface and sucking the plant sap. The first signs of their presence are pale yellow spots on the upper surface of the leaves. Then the leaves become bronzed and may eventually die; in heavy infestations the whole plant will shrivel and die.

The mites are found on the underside of the leaves. They are generally yellow or green, 0.5mm long, with four pairs of legs. They only become red later in the season and when they overwinter. In heavy infestations,

The pompon dahlias 'Willo's Violet' and 'Pensford Marion', which is flame-red, complement each other in this border.

the fine silk webbing that they spin becomes visible to the naked eye. The female lays up to a hundred eggs on the undersides of the leaves and these hatch in a few days, depending on the temperature. The emerging larvae grow rapidly, moult and transform into adults, which then lay more eggs. In hot, dry conditions it may take only eight days from egg to adult, and this cycle continues until early autumn, when the adults stop feeding and laying eggs, become bright red and seek shelter for hibernation over the winter. When temperatures warm up in early spring, the adults emerge and start a new infestation.

Control rests on a combination of approaches. Disinfection of greenhouses, coldframes and canes or other support materials is essential. All purchased material should be inspected and sprayed before being

'Karenglen' (p.116) is a miniature decorative and one of the best exhibition varieties in Britain.

introduced into the greenhouse. As red spider mite thrives in hot, dry conditions, a cool, moist atmosphere should be maintained as far as possible under the leaf canopy. This can be achieved by spraying the undersides of the plants with water. And, finally, spraying and biological controls can be used to keep numbers down.

Disinfection Red spider mites overwinter in greenhouses, coldframes, in bundles of canes and in dried-out irrigation pipes. It is important to deal with all possible sources of infestation during the spring and a great deal of ingenuity has gone into designing disinfection systems. One method is to dig a trench in the garden, long enough to hold the canes and deep enough to hold the largest bundle. The trench is lined with polythene sheet and filled with water to which is added Jeyes Fluid, Armillatox or domestic bleach. (After use this solution can be allowed to drain away as it breaks down in the soil.) Bundles of canes are allowed to soak in this solution for half an hour or so, and then stood on a path or plastic sheet to drain.

Spraying Pirimiphos-methyl and malathion are effective in controlling adults in spring and early summer but have no effect on the eggs. Later in the season, the silken web that the mites spin insulates the adults from sprays. Some growers dip the plants in a bucket of insecticide at planting-out time so that the plants are clean at the start of the season.

Biological control There is a biological control method that is highly effective in the greenhouse, but less so outdoors. It uses a predatory mite, *Phytoseulius persimilis*, which feeds on all the stages of the red spider mite, killing great quantities, and multiplies rapidly in hot, dry conditions. *Phytoseulius* is killed by insecticides so during control, no spraying for other pests is possible. This method is thus more useful in the greenhouse where other pests can be excluded.

POLLEN BEETLE

Pollen beetle have become a pest since the widespread cultivation of oilseed rape in Britain. The beetles live happily on the developing flowers of the rape during late spring and early summer, but as the flower petals fall, they migrate to other hosts, including dahlias.

Severe infestations cause malformation of the developing blooms, but the effects are usually noticed as marking of the florets, and when the blooms are cut the beetles emerge and crawl all over the displays.

The beetle is a problem in some seasons more than others. Weather conditions and timing of the rape crop have an effect, together with the effectiveness of rape-spraying programmes. If the rape crop has been harvested by late midsummer then flowers of plants like dahlias that open later may escape serious infestation.

Because the beetle hides in open blooms, there is little that can be done in the way of spraying. To avoid problems on the showbench, cut the flowerheads at least a day beforehand and keep them in a cool, dark shed or garage. Any beetles hiding in the blooms will emerge and fly towards a sunlit window, where they can be sprayed without risk to the flowers.

WASPS

This is an occasional pest of dahlias and causes problems only when infestations are severe, such as when there is a nest nearby. Wasps appear to be attracted to certain varieties of dahlias and not others. They gnaw at the stems in order to extract the sweet sap, and may strip off pieces of them for use in their nest building. The weakened stem can break or the bloom will have a reduced water supply and wilt. Slight damage to a stem can be repaired by sticky tape, but more serious damage requires its removal.

If there is a nest nearby the solution is to destroy it. Spraying with insecticide rarely discourages wasps, and the only effective control is by trapping. A simple method of trapping is to half-fill a jam jar with diluted beer or a solution of jam and water and then cover it with a polythene sheet, through which a small hole is made, about the diameter of a pencil.

Wasp traps, baited with proprietary baits or fruit peelings, are available commercially; in North America they are called yellowjacket traps.

DISEASES
FUNGAL DISEASES

Dahlias are less affected by fungal diseases than most plants. However, during propagation, botrytis is a constant threat to young cuttings. Many hormone rooting powders contain an added fungicide to reduce the likelihood of it taking hold, but cold, wet conditions during rooting can often lead to its appearance. Fungal spores are common in rainwater so it should not be used on cuttings. Spores are always present in the atmosphere and can infect cuttings even if tap water is used. The use of Cheshunt Compound in solution for watering cuttings will reduce the chance of infection.

The fungus, *Verticillium dahliae*, that causes wilt disease is common in many soils but rarely infects well-grown plants. It is only when they are subjected to sudden stress or root damage that it gains entry.

Care must be taken that young cuttings have enough water for rapid root growth, but the compost must never become waterlogged as this allows wilt disease to take hold. Some varieties are more prone to this condition than others. The first symptom is a darkening of the foliage followed by wilting of the leaves, despite the compost remaining wet. The young roots become brown or black and the plant quickly collapses. If tackled early enough, the plant can be re-potted into a new compost with extra sharp sand and it sometimes survives, but often the fungus will have invaded the roots and the plant will die. Even older plants can succumb to wilt disease if subjected to prolonged waterlogging.

Fungal rotting is a problem in overwintered tubers. Again, the fungus gains entry when the roots are damaged during the lifting process. If the tubers are given a drying period on the greenhouse staging after lifting, and the broken tubers are cut cleanly, a natural callus will form over the cut surface, preventing fungal growth. This is aided by dusting flowers of sulphur over the cut or dipping it in a fungicide solution. Even so, cold, wet conditions during storage can result in wet rot. Occasionally, the neck of the tuber becomes infected with dry rot (*Fusarium*): the eyes sink and the skin around them becomes papery. Once this has happened, there is little that can be done, even if the tubers themselves remain firm. They rarely survive to give cuttings in the spring and should be destroyed.

Smut disease of dahlias is less common than at one time. It is almost certainly soil-borne, the spores being splashed on to the foliage after heavy rain. The fungus *Entyloma dahliae* causes the problem and, in a wet soil, its spores remain viable for years. Some dahlia varieties appear to be more susceptible to smut than others, and it seems that most modern types are resistant. Infected plants show symptoms on the bottom leaves where small silvery spots turn brown and the dead tissue falls away leaving a small neat hole. Spraying with a fungicide solution appears to control the disease effectively.

In contrast to dahlia smut, which is becoming rare, a new fungal disease, dahlia mildew, has recently become more common. It manifests itself as a white powdery covering on the leaves and stems; in hot, dry seasons it spreads rapidly and, once established, can be difficult to control. During the early stages of infection, the powdery covering can be wiped off, but gradually the underlying cells turn yellow and will then die. Bupirimate + triforine, propiconazole or carbendazim give control if sprayed as soon as the disease is noticed. Dahlia mildew seems to be less of a problem in less highly manured conditions.

BACTERIAL DISEASES

Few bacterial diseases cause problems for dahlia growers. One exception is crown gall, caused by a soil bacterium, *Agrobacterium tumefaciens*. This enters the dahlia through damage at the point where individual tubers join the crown. It then stimulates the infected cells to multiply rapidly, forming cauliflower-like nodules with tiny abortive shoots on the crown.

There is no chemical treatment for this condition and the safest course of action is to burn the infected tuber. Occasionally, a normal shoot appears on an uninfected part of the crown and, if the tuber is especially valuable, this may be cut and rooted. However, this is not recommended unless there is no alternative as the bacteria may still be present in the sap. Sometimes the nodules may be cut away with a sharp knife and new healthy growth may appear. The reason for this is that the bacterium is no longer alive, the nodular growth being the dahlia's resistant reaction to it.

A similar disease is leafy gall (*Corynebacterium fascians*), where the growth on the crown is less nodular and consists largely of a mass of spindly shoots. These are less likely to root successfully if taken as cuttings, and, again, it is best to burn the tuber. Some of the older varieties seem to be more prone to infection than others, and if the disease is present in the soil then it is best to look for a more resistant variety.

Bacterial rots are common on stored tubers, but usually as secondary problems following fungal infection. They give rise to wet slimy patches which hasten the collapse of the tuber. Chemical treatment is not effective and the tuber is best destroyed.

VIRUSES

By far the most serious diseases affecting dahlias are viral. The most common is dahlia mosaic virus which causes a yellowing of the leaf veins and blister-like distortions on the leaf underside. The infected plants grow very slowly, giving rise to the name 'dahlia stunt'. Stunted plants rarely recover and should be pulled up and burned. There is no cure for this infection and propagation from diseased tubers simply transmits the virus to all the resulting plants. There are growers who believe that plants will sometimes grow away from a virus infection, but this is not true. It is possible to confuse physiological problems, such as chlorosis or chemical damage, with virus symptoms, and plants suffering the former can grow away if the nutrient disorder is corrected. However, once stunted growth is evident, virus infection is confirmed, and plants will not recover.

Virus particles multiply in the sap of diseased plants and can then be transmitted to healthy plants in a variety of ways: via sucking insects, such as aphids and thrips, through knives used to remove cuttings, and even on fingers as the plants are stopped or disbudded. This is why it is important for all virused stock to be destroyed.

Two other viruses are known to infect dahlias: cucumber mosaic virus and tomato spotted wilt virus.

The identification of cucumber mosaic virus infection in dahlias is quite difficult. It produces light yellow leaf markings, which are not confined to the veins as in dahlia mosaic, but does not cause pronounced stunting of growth. Tomato spotted wilt virus does not cause wilting in dahlias as it does in tomatoes, but produces light green, later brown, spots or circles on the leaves. Both these viruses are comparatively rare in dahlias and are most likely to be transmitted from infected greenhouse crops by handling dahlia plants after handling cucumbers or tomatoes. A sensible precaution is to wash hands thoroughly before handling dahlia plants.

Some varieties of dahlias have been grown for many years without ever showing signs of virus infection; others seem to break down soon after release and it is difficult to find clean stock. There is some disagreement as to the reasons for this. It is clear that some varieties are very sensitive to viruses, show clear symptoms and decline rapidly in vigour; others are believed to harbour the viruses but never fall sick and are known as 'symptomless carriers'. Some people have blacklisted symptomless carriers in the belief that, as sources of infection, they should no longer be grown. Such a drastic approach would deprive us of some very attractive dahlias, for example, 'Bishop of Llandaff'. Whether these varieties are symptomless carriers or just immune to viruses is a moot point. The best way forward is to adopt a hygienic approach to propagation and prevent the introduction and spread of viruses by aphids through a regular spraying programme. Knives or razor blades used for taking cuttings should be sterilized with methylated spirits or a strong solution of trisodium-phosphate before moving to each variety. During stopping and disbudding, fingers and hands should be wiped clean and washed regularly. The need to remove and destroy infected plants cannot be overemphasized.

It would be easy to over-react to the threat of viral disease, and to imagine that we are faced with an insuperable problem. Nurseries are very sensitive to its dangers and spend much time and effort producing clean stock, and starting from clean stock gives us a head start which, when followed by good hygiene and regular spraying, will keep our plants clean and healthy.

SYMPTOMS OF ILL-HEALTH

It is important to be able to recognize the symptoms of plant ill-health through the leaves. Chlorosis and distortion of the leaves can be produced by physiological or genetic effects, by chemical damage or from virus or other diseases. The proper diagnosis of such effects is important, as otherwise-healthy material might be discarded as virus infected when, in fact, the plant is only suffering temporary physiological effects.

Chlorosis Photosynthesis requires the presence of the catalyst chlorophyll in the leaves. Chlorophyll is a mixture of four pigments: chlorophyll *a*, chlorophyll *b*, carotene, and xanthophyll. Sometimes the mechanism for producing chlorophyll is damaged by a genetic change, a chemical effect or by disease. When this happens, leaves lose their green appearance, becoming yellow if carotin is still present or white if only xanthophyll remains. Plants devoid of chlorophyll cannot survive as they are unable to photosynthesize,

but if there is chlorophyll in some of the cells, as happens in variegated leaves, the plants may survive.

Seedlings from dahlias are often variegated or totally albino. These are usually very weak and soon die. Mature plants can become chlorotic, usually because of a chemical effect. The molecules of chlorophyll *a* and *b* contain magnesium, and if magnesium is deficient, then chlorophyll is lacking and plants become very pale. This can be rectified by watering with Epsom salts (magnesium sulphate). However, chlorosis may result even if magnesium is present. This is because soil conditions have made it unavailable to the plant. Iron is also needed as a catalyst in the production of chlorophyll, so if the soil is deficient in iron or it is unavailable to the plant this can also cause chlorosis.

Viruses Viruses can also cause changes in leaf form and colour. This is due to the virus particles damaging the enzyme and hormone balance of the tissues by breaking down some of the key growth hormones. Mottling of leaves is due to chlorophyll defects sometimes caused by viruses, and in severe cases can cause necrosis of the tissue. Growth defects such as dwarfing can be a secondary effect of deficient photosynthesis. Phloem necrosis, caused by viruses and some fungi, prevents translocation of food and growth hormones, and can also cause dwarfing and stunting.

Lack of auxin Developmental defects, such as retarded growth, can be caused when the auxin supply is destroyed (see p.16). Lack of auxin prevents normal elongation and allows lateral buds to grow. The mesophyll, the tissue between the upper and lower epidermis of the leaf, can be reduced when auxin is not present in enough quantity, in severe cases resulting in very narrow leaves where the midrib dominates. In other cases, retarded vein development causes the leaf to bulge and become corrugated and contorted. These symptoms are all the result of growth-hormone destruction but can be confused with the effects of herbicide damage. There is a way to distinguish between the two: with virus damage individual plants show symptoms while neighbouring plants are healthy, whereas with herbicide damage the whole group of plants will have the same symptoms.

7

PROPAGATION

The most common form of dahlia propagation is vegetative, either by dividing tubers or by taking cuttings. As dahlias rarely come true from seed, these propagation techniques are important to preserve the variety form and characteristics. To obtain a reasonable number of new plants each year it is necessary to be prepared in advance as a field tuber left in the ground to overwinter or lifted in autumn and replanted in the spring will probably only give rise to a mass of shoots and small blooms competing with a tangle of foliage. Growers require more manageable plants and so propagate daughter plants from the parent tuber. Raisers also want to multiply their stock quickly in order to meet the likely demand for new varieties.

DIVIDING TUBERS

Dividing tubers is common among pompon growers and those who want to propagate late-flowering varieties. In America most dahlias are propagated by division. Large tuber clumps can be divided longitudinally through the stem, leaving a piece of stem attached to each tuber. A sharp knife is usually quite adequate for the task.

Dig the tubers up in the autumn and store them overwinter, as described in Chapter 6 Cultivation. In dormant tubers, the new buds are often not visible on the tissue where the tuber neck joins the old stem, so it is advisable to start the tubers into growth before trying to divide them. It is important to time the division of the tubers so that the young plants are still growing actively at planting-out time. For example, for planting in early summer, it is not necessary to start tubers into growth before mid-spring, otherwise, by planting-out time the plants will have become too large to handle easily. Moreover, if light intensity is low, the young plants will become weak and leggy, particularly if temperatures rise.

Place the old tuber clumps on a bed of peat or soil and provide gentle bottom heat – 18°C (65°F) is adequate. A soil-warming cable is ideal for the purpose. Tubers need moisture and warmth to begin growing, but there is no clear evidence that light is useful at this stage. Fertilizer should not be used for 'boxing-up', as this process is called. There are sufficient nutrients available in the tuber to get the plants started, and any additional inorganic fertilizer may burn the delicate roots as they start to grow. Should the tubers show evidence of excessive drying out and starting to shrivel then it is helpful to spray them with tepid water to help them plump up. Too much water should be avoided; a light spray for two or three days before boxing-up is all that is necessary.

After two or three weeks, buds should be visible on the collar of the stem where it joins the tubers. The clump can now be divided into pieces, each piece having a bud. The divisions are then potted up, leaving the neck of the tuber and its bud above the soil surface. The compost used should be free draining. John Innes No. 1 is ideal, but a peat-based compost can be used as long as extra sharp sand is incorporated to improve the drainage.

During the first few days after potting up, water should be applied sparingly. As the root system develops, more liberal quantities of water can be given. In two or three weeks, the divisions will need potting on into larger pots. They will make rapid shoot growth and care must be taken to ensure that they do not become pot-bound.

PLATE VI

FIMBRIATED DAHLIAS

'Belle of the Ball'

'Nenekazi'

'Jennie'

'Marlene Joy'

All flowers are shown at approximately half size

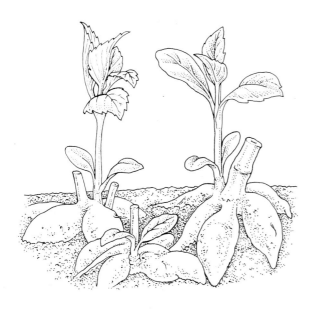

Tubers boxed up and producing shoots, which are removed with a sharp knife for propagation.

Once the plants are growing well, they can be moved to a coldframe or placed outside in the shelter of a wall or fence to harden them off. However, they will be sensitive to frost and cold winds, so protection is needed if the weather turns cold.

CHICKEN LEGS

Some growers wash all the soil from the tubers when they lift them in the autumn. They then divide them up into separate roots, commonly called 'chicken legs', each with a piece of stem attached. At this stage, tiny buds, or 'eyes', can often be seen where the tuber joins the old stem. As such divided pieces have a tendency to dry out and shrivel, they are stored upright in boxes of dry peat which will retain the lost moisture. This also means they take up much less space, and are more easily inspected for any rot that may develop. The chances of rotting are reduced if the pieces are dipped in fungicide solution and allowed to dry before storage.

Specialist growers, particularly in North America, supply customers with divided tubers in this form. As the eyes are not always visible when the tubers are divided, there is a chance that every tuber section will not always have one. However, in practice, all these chicken legs usually give at least one shoot which will then be suitable for propagation by stem cuttings. The practice of making chicken legs is thought to stimulate more eyes as each piece can develop its own bud, an advantage when you want to produce plenty of stock. With conventional tubers, once the first bud has started to develop, it releases the apical dominance hormone, which supresses the development of other buds in the same clump, at least for some time.

STEM CUTTINGS

Tubers for propagation by stem cuttings are boxed-up in peat or compost as for division. The collar where the tubers join the old stem should be above the surface level, and care should be taken to avoid getting this collar wet, at least until the tubers have started to sprout. With bottom heat, the tubers should start into growth in two weeks or so. In just a few days after plunging, fibrous roots will begin to develop, and gentle rocking of the tuber will give an indication that this has happened.

Occasionally, tubers that have rooted may show no sign of producing shoots, even after four or five weeks. These should be lifted out of the box and examined. Sometimes the active buds may be underneath the tuber and may find difficulty in reaching the surface; such tubers should be cut in half vertically to allow the shoot to emerge. However, if the tuber is still plump but shows no sign of throwing shoots, it can be cut into pieces, each with a piece of the old stem attached, and re-boxed. Eventually shoots will emerge, although in some cases it might take two or three months for something to happen. Another possibility is that the tubers may throw shoots before roots are formed. These shoots should be taken for cuttings as soon as possible in case the tuber collapses through lack of water.

PREPARATION

The rooting medium for cuttings must be free draining: some growers use pure sand, others an equal mixture of peat and sand, and yet others a compost mixture. If you are using a commercial soil-less compost, mix in equal parts of sharp sand to ensure that it drains properly, as a waterlogged rooting medium will cause the cuttings to damp off with a fungal infection. The chance of damping off is reduced if a weak solution of Cheshunt Compound is used each time the cuttings are watered. The striking compost need not contain any additional

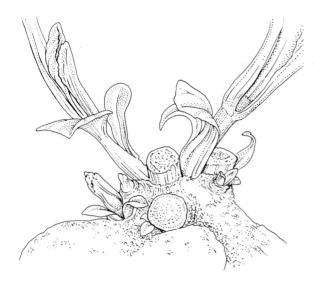

A second flush of shoots developing from the bottom node, around the site of the first cuttings taken.

nutrients, but in this case the cuttings should be potted on as soon as roots are formed. Most growers add a little balanced organic fertilizer to their composts to give their seedlings a start, but harsh inorganic fertilizers should not be used, or the roots may be damaged.

When a large number of cuttings is involved, plastic inserts in plant trays are very effective. This method reduces the quantity of compost required while allowing sufficient for rooting to take place. However, as soon as the cuttings are rooted they should be potted on into 8cm (3in) pots, otherwise they may become starved of nutrients. Cuttings are ready for taking when the shoots are about 8–10cm (3–4in) long.

TAKING CUTTINGS

A sharp knife or razor blade is used to sever the shoot from the tuber. The cut should be made just below the bottom pair of leaves so that one basal joint is left on the tuber. New buds will appear from this, usually in a week or so after the first cutting has been taken. Often four new shoots will appear, and if these are removed in the same way, another four shoots should arise in a further week or so. Thus, in three or four weeks, at least 16 cuttings may be produced from the original bud.

When taking cuttings care must be taken to avoid spreading viruses from plant to plant. The knife or razor blade should be dipped in a sterilizing solution and wiped with a cloth for each new tuber. Methylated spirits is effective for sterilizing implements, or use a saturated solution of Tri-sodium ortho phosphate.

Remove the basal pair of leaves from each cutting using a sharp knife, then dip the end of the cutting in a hormone rooting compound. Fill your pots with a suitable rooting mixture and then insert the cutting to a depth of 2–3cm (1in), and water. Label each cutting with the variety name and the date on which it is struck. Unless this is done immediately, the tendency is to forget and, in the middle of a busy propagating period, unlabelled cuttings are a disaster. Some well-known growers of old claimed to be able to recognize the variety from the leaf form, but they were invariably found out to be misled when the plant eventually bloomed.

Grow the cuttings on in a greenhouse. To prevent wilting in strong light or warm weather, shade the cuttings with newspaper or polythene. This helps reduce moisture loss until the cut ends callus over. The use of a propagator is recommended; on a commercial scale, misting equipment is used. Given bottom heat of 18°C (65°F), the cuttings should root in 14 days. Early cuttings will benefit from extra light, and a fluorescent tube suspended 60cm (24in) over the propagating bench is effective.

A well-rooted cutting that is ready for potting on.

PLATE VII

CACTUS AND SEMI-CACTUS DAHLIAS

'Banker'

'Tahiti Sunrise'

'Aloha'

'Weston
Nuggett'

'Rotterdam'

All flowers are shown at approximately half size

'Piper's Pink'

'Glenbank Twinkle'

'Kenora Sunset'

'Hayley Jane'

'Hamari Accord'

'Molly Mooney'

HEEL CUTTINGS

When only a few cuttings are needed from a tuber, heel cuttings can be taken. In this case, the young shoots are gently pulled off the tuber with a piece of crown attached. Since the actively dividing tissue is removed with the shoot, further cuttings are prevented, at least for some time. Eventually, further shoots may develop, but this cannot be relied upon. There is no real advantage in taking heel cuttings as they do not root any sooner. The only benefit in this method is that it avoids spreading viruses, through the knife or razor blade.

TIP AND LEAF CUTTINGS

Many growers buying in new and expensive varieties generate extra plants by taking out the tips of the new plants and rooting them. The tip plus a pair of leaves is cut from the young plant just above the next pair of leaves. The base of the cutting is trimmed with a sharp knife just below the node and the cut end is dipped into hormone rooting powder, then the cutting is pressed into a rooting mixture (of the same type as described under Preparation p.70) and watered in. The cuttings should be labelled and placed in a propagator, preferably with extra light.

The most rapid way of propagation is through leaf cuttings. One method is to allow the shoots arising from plunged tubers to reach 20–25cm (8–10in) long and to cut them off as before. Each shoot is then cut into lengths with about 3mm (⅛in) left each side of a node. The node is then split in half lengthways with a sharp knife, leaving a piece of node, its leaf and its axillary bud. The node is dipped into hormone compound and potted up with the leaf facing upwards. Such cuttings, given a bottom heat of 18°C (65°F) and extra light, will root in 8–10 days. They should be potted on as soon as they are well rooted.

This method can also be used on young plants with three or four pairs of leaves. After the tips have been removed, the side shoots on the remaining stem will be stimulated into growth. The tips of these side shoots can be treated similarly for more cuttings, but then the original plant will become a mass of side shoots and should be discarded.

MOTHER PLANT CUTTINGS

When a good colour sport appears, it is important to secure it by leaf or stem cuttings.

If, as is frequently the case, it is only one side shoot that is distinctly different from those on the rest of the plant, this shoot should be labelled and the bloom removed. In a few days, side shoots will start to form in the axils of the leaves and these should be removed as leaf cuttings.

If more than one branch has sported, then the whole plant can be lifted at the end of the growing season and potted into a 25cm (10in) pot or box and brought into the greenhouse. Cut off the 'normal' branches close to the main stem and label the sported branches. The main problem will be to keep this plant growing under cover throughout the winter. In order to do this, the temperature should be kept as low as possible and extra light should be provided to keep the side shoots short jointed and to prevent leggy growth. When the side shoots are 5–7cm (2–3in) long, remove them and root them in a suitable rooting medium as described above. To help the cuttings root, extra light must be provided along with a bottom heat of 18°C (65°F). Once well rooted, they should be potted on and grown in a cold greenhouse with extra light to keep them short jointed.

Keeping plants healthy and ticking over during the winter is not an easy operation and is not to be undertaken lightly. Many sports revert to the bloom colour of the mother plant during their first year. This is because the tissue in the sported branch is not uniform, and cuttings taken from mixed tissue will inevitably contain mother plant cells which tend to dominate and multiply faster than sported tissue. Cuttings from the upper part of a sported branch are more likely to stabilize as the sport than cuttings taken from lower down.

INTERNODAL AND HOLLOW CUTTINGS

The use of hormone rooting powder, along with adequate temperature, moisture and time, enables dahlia raisers to make almost any tissue form roots. There is a widespread belief that cuttings that do not have a basal node and have rooted in the internodal region produce plants which will not form tubers during their first autumn. There is some truth in this, as the mass of fibrous roots produced by internodal cuttings are not the right sort of roots to give rise to tubers. To be safe, many growers discard cuttings that have not rooted in 14 days, along with those that have rooted in the internodal region. However, such internodal-rooted cuttings can be replanted deeply enough to bury the lowest pair of leaves, and thus will have a node below ground from which the tuber-forming roots develop.

Most young shoots are solid but hollow cuttings frequently occur. This is most likely in the first shoots that arise, or in shoots that come from below ground level or have become elongated as a result of growing up from below the tuber. Hollow cuttings are difficult to root and are often discarded, but if plants of a particular variety are in short supply, it may be necessary to try to root them. In order to do this, remove the lower pair of leaves and make a cross-shaped cut into the node. Once dipped into a hormone rooting powder, these cuttings should eventually root but they may take longer to do so than normal.

GROWING ON

Cuttings grow rapidly once they are established, and in order to keep the young plants healthy the pots should be moved to cooler conditions. Cool conditions are necessary while the light intensity is low otherwise the plants become leggy. The ideal plant has short internodes and is a good green colour. Such plants can become pot-bound quite rapidly, and if allowed to remain in their pots too long, nutrients become exhausted and the stems will harden so they should be potted on as soon as the pot is full of roots, but only into the next size pot. The potting mixture should again be freely draining – soil-less composts need additional sharp sand, perlite or vermiculite for extra drainage. Further potting on into larger pots may be necessary before the plants can be planted out with safety.

POT TUBERS

Early struck cuttings may grow too tall and become too forward for planting out. Rather than continually potting on into ever larger containers, they can be left outside in 10cm (4in) pots for the whole season to produce pot tubers. This treatment causes the plants to become pot-bound and restricts the top growth. The plants should be allowed to flower in order to check that the label in the pot is correct but, having flowered, the bloom should be removed and no other blooms should be allowed to develop. Pots are best buried in the soil up to their rims to protect them from being blown over. They should be kept watered and given a high potash feed towards the end of the season. Before danger of frost, they should be cut back to within a centimetre or

two of the soil level, lifted from their bed and placed on their sides under a greenhouse bench or in a cold-frame. When the pots have dried out they can be stored until the new year when they will provide excellent propagating material. Many growers prefer to rely on pot tubers for keeping their stock over winter as they usually make better ripened tubers than excessively fed, softer field roots which can be difficult to store (see Chapter 6 Cultivation, p.57). Some varieties are almost impossible to keep through the winter as lifted field roots, and pot tubers may be the only way to ensure stock for the following season.

GRAFTING

No longer used by modern growers, grafting was popular in France during the nineteenth century and spread to England where the techniques used were modified. Grafting was used to enable new varieties with weak root systems to be grown on vigorous tubers of less attractive dahlias. It was believed that some vigorous varieties were resistant or immune to virus disease and, by grafting susceptible varieties on to such stock, strong resistant plants would be produced. As in fruit trees, grafting of taller varieties on to dwarfing stock was thought to shorten the stems of tall dahlia varieties.

In the French method, the stock tuber had the eyes removed and was partially split lengthwise. A shoot (scion) was taken from the other variety, as near to the tuber as possible, using a slanted cut. The scion was wedged into the split tuber and then the graft was planted in a small pot, 7cm (3in) below the soil surface and kept under a glass cover for 12 days. Once rooted, the tuber was lifted in its pot and put into a coldframe to harden off. In the English method, the eyes on the stock tuber were removed with a V-shaped cut. The scion from the other tuber was removed with a similar V-shaped cut and the resulting wedge-shaped piece was placed into the cut of the stock tuber and secured with a pin. These grafted tubers were again planted in small pots and grown on under glass.

The practice of grafting died out during this century, but it was tried in experiments conducted by Harold Miller of the Puget Sound Dahlia Association in Washington State, USA, in 1981. To the surprise of many members, grafting by either method proved effective, but the English method produced stronger plants that had better tubers in the autumn.

SEED

Seed saved from most varieties of dahlias does not come true to type. This is because the cultivated dahlia is a natural hybrid and is cross-pollinated. For the grower who just wants a few plants for a border and is not worried about types or colours, then this might be just the thing. Some dwarf bedding varieties like 'Coltness Gem' and 'Redskin' will come relatively true from seed, but other dahlia types, such as cactus, decorative, ball and pompon, will produce a variety of colours and flowerhead forms, many with open centres.

Dahlia seed requires some heat to germinate successfully, although a greenhouse is not essential. Propagating trays on a sunny windowsill can be used, and late sowings in a coldframe are possible. The aim is to get young plants at the correct stage of growth for transplanting outdoors in early summer. The earlier the seed is germinated, the longer the young seedlings have to be looked after and protected from frost. Ideally, seed is sown in mid-spring in shallow trays in a greenhouse.

'Figaro' (p.110) is a single-flowered dwarf bedding variety that can be grown from seed and produces a range of colours.

Heat is not essential at this time of year, but the seeds germinate more quickly at 16°C (61°F).

Use a good seed compost. Sow the seed thinly in shallow drills 5mm (¼in) deep, cover with a thin layer of compost, give a light watering and then cover the tray with a piece of glass and a sheet of newspaper. The seeds should germinate in a week or so, first producing a pair of fleshy cotyledons, and in a few days the first true leaf. At this stage the seedlings are ready for potting on into small pots using a potting compost like John Innes No. 1.

For the first few days, the young seedlings should be protected from direct sunlight and watered liberally but not allowed to become waterlogged. Before planting out, the seedlings should be hardened off in a coldframe. They can then be used in much the same way as other bedding plants.

8

RAISING NEW VARIETIES

Raising new varieties of dahlias can be a fascinating hobby. The thrill of finding a promising seedling that nobody has seen before, growing in your very own seedbed, is one that is difficult to beat. Anyone can collect a few seeds and grow them in the hope that a prize-winning variety will result; however, such a simplistic approach has as much chance of success as winning the 'Pools'. But people do win, and amateurs do raise new varieties, so how do they do it?

GENETICS AND BREEDING

Long before the science of genetics was developed to its present-day level, people were selectively breeding plants and animals, although it was a very hit-or-miss affair. Even so, breeders developed their own rules in order to avoid mistakes and so improve their chances of success. Many of these rules have since been shown to have a scientific basis, and together with our more recent understanding of genetic principles, this gives us a good chance for success. *Dahlia* is a very complex genus genetically, and insufficient research has been done to give a precise blueprint for action, so a systematic approach is still needed to raise new varieties that are worth the trouble.

GENETICS

The cultivated dahlia is likely to have arisen from an interspecific hybrid. Although its parents are not known with any certainty, one parent is thought to have been *D. pinnata*, the other *D. coccinea*. It is an octoploid plant, containing 64 chromosomes – eight sets of eight – some of them being duplicates of each other. This means that some quantitative characteristics show continuous variation, for example bloom sizes, which can range from giant to miniature, and plant heights, which can range from over 2m (6ft) to less than 30cm (12in). Moreover, as there are multiple sets of chromosomes, the simple laws of segregation as set out by Mendel, which allow inheritance to be predicted to some extent, are rarely observed. In addition, the similarity between some sets of the chromosomes results in chromosomes becoming entangled during pairing and segregation and, subsequently, sticking to each other and breaking up. This gives peculiar combinations of characters in some crosses, and even during vegetative propagation some unusual variants can occur. Sports or mutants are a common feature of dahlias. One consequence of this unstable genetic structure is that relatively large numbers of progeny have to be examined before desired character combinations are likely to be found.

BREEDING OBJECTIVES

Before starting, a breeder needs to think very carefully about objectives. Bearing in mind that probably 40,000 varieties have been listed over the years, and, of these, over 700 are current in the present NDS directory, it is wise to ask what is left to be produced. In answer, probably much remains to be done, particularly since the dahlia is continuing to develop. Looking back at the range of dahlias available only thirty years ago, it is noticeable that the ideals which breeders were looking for have changed considerably. On the showbench, this is even more the case. The quest for perfect form, strong and non-fading colours, reliability, plant habit and stems and disease resistance will always go on.

The objective of a breeding programme must be to improve on current varieties and so, as a first step, it is important to be aware of the strengths and limitations of these current varieties. Potential new dahlias must be compared with the best of those already in existence and only released if they are obviously superior. It is unfortunate that this important point seems to be being ignored by many amateur raisers: a deluge of 'new' varieties is constantly flowing, but few of these are better than what we already have.

CHOOSING PARENTS

Collecting seed willy-nilly from any variety is unlikely to produce satisfactory results; the basic rule is that a poor variety rarely gives rise to anything worthwhile. The plant habit, size and form of a dahlia seems to be inherited directly from the seed parent without much variation in the first generation, and it is not until the second generation that different characters appear. The reason for this is that many of the genes controlling these attributes appear to be present in the dominant form, so that recessive (and thus different) forms do not become apparent until the second generation. Thus, it is unlikely that a giant-flowered form will arise in the first generation from anything other than a giant parent. Similarly, an attempt to raise a pompon must start with a pompon as seed parent.

Most cultivated varieties do not set seed from their own pollen. Moreover, because this is a genetic

mechanism, many varieties will not set seed with pollen from a closely related variety as they are likely to contain common sterility genes which engender infertility when they come together. So it is essential to choose a seed parent that not only has the plant habit and flowerhead form that one is intending to raise, but that is also likely to provide adequate seed. This knowledge of potential seed parents only comes with experience. Breeders are very secretive about which varieties are self sterile and which are not.

The pollen parent also needs to be chosen carefully if systematic results are to be obtained. Some varieties make good pollen parents as well as seed parents, while others produce little useful pollen. Again, experience counts for a great deal.

Perhaps the most important single thing in breeding is to keep detailed records. It is then possible to look back over these and draw important conclusions to help in the future. For example, the fact observed by W.J.C. Lawrence (p.11) that single blooms are dominant to fully double blooms indicates that single bloom varieties should not be grown near double exhibition varieties, or all the progeny will be semi-double. (I discovered this to my cost when a few collerette dahlias were grown near some plants which I was using as seed parents.) As another example, the gene for the more formal decorative type is recessive, so any informal decorative types nearby will dominate the seedlings unless pollinated blooms are protected from insects.

A feature that I have noticed is that the progeny tend to reflect the habit of the seed parent, so that a seed parent with weak stems tends to pass this character on to its seedlings. Moreover, some seed parents will give rise to a large proportion of albino or pale-coloured and weak seedlings. Although plants with flowerheads of good form may be produced by such seedlings, they rarely produce adequate tubers and often propagate poorly. Although this fact is well known to some experienced breeders, it is not well publicised. One way around the problem is to reverse the cross – to use the pollen parent as the seed parent and vice versa. So, pick your seed parents with care.

Dr Keith Hammett, writing in the NDS *Dahlia Annual* of 1989, describes some work he did using

'Piperoo', with its intriguing striped petals, is an interesting plant for garden display.

miniature decorative dahlias. He produced a mixture of natural F1 hybrids from a planting of six carefully tested parents that were raised in total isolation from other dahlias. The seed these F1 hybrids produced gave rise to a very high percentage of fully double miniature decorative varieties covering a wide colour range. The production of such 'polycross' seed is a well-known technique that is used by commercial vegetable breeders and is repeated each year to produce the new season's seed crop. Unfortunately, a seed firm obtained some of Dr Hammett's seed without his permission and it was simply multiplied up under open pollination and sold at F1 prices: the ensuing seed was F2 generation and had lost the original characteristics. However, the polycross method, in a modified form, is used by some raisers as a simplified breeding technique.

MAKING THE CROSS

Having selected the parents, it is best to carry out controlled pollination. The first step is to prepare the flowerheads of the seed parent. With most fully double show varieties, the disc florets (the most fertile part of the flowerhead) do not become visible until the bloom is past its normal cutting time. Even under relatively dry conditions, the back petals become soggy and mouldy as the bloom ages. This can set up rotting and the whole bloom can end up a slimy mess. Such a catastrophe is avoided by removing the older florets as the bloom passes its best. As the centre of the flowerhead begins to become visible, more and more florets are removed until all that are left are the disc florets bearing rudimentary 'petals'.

When the disc florets are ready for pollination, the stigmas emerge. This happens from the outside of the disc inwards with the stigmas emerging on successive days until there are no more left.

Pollen can be collected from a pollen parent using a fine paintbrush which is then brushed over the open stigmas of the seed parent. Alternatively, an open bloom from the pollen parent can be dusted over the open stigmas of the seed parent. Stigmas close up an hour or two after pollination. The following day, the next rows of stigmas will open and the pollination process is repeated, and so on until all the stigmas are pollinated. The bloom can be covered between pollinations with a polythene or muslin bag to prevent stray bees introducing different pollen.

Although there may be fifty or more disc florets available for pollination, it is rare for more than twenty or so seeds to be produced. The outermost rings of florets are the most likely to set seed; after these have been pollinated some raisers reduce the chance of further insect pollination by sterilizing the remaining florets. This can be done by painting the unopened disk florets with methylated spirits.

A good pollen parent is capable of producing far more pollen than can be used in a single cross. Such pollen can retain its viability for many days, and it can be collected and stored in glass vials or small plastic bags and kept in a refrigerator until needed.

When the cross has been made, the head should be labelled with the details of the parents and the date, and the information should also be entered into a notebook. Small white tags, such as those on thread that are used to label jewellery, are useful for marking crosses.

SEEDHEAD DEVELOPMENT

When all the stigmas have been pollinated, the fleshy calyx and bracts start to close up and eventually a pointed seedhead is formed. This is a critical stage for seed development. Moisture in the seedhead can cause rotting, so it is helpful to squeeze the developing heads gently to express any excess. In two or three weeks, the heads start to dry off, and when this happens, some breeders cut the heads and hang them up in the greenhouse to dry completely. Others wait until the heads dry completely on the plant before removing them. To a large extent, weather conditions will determine when the heads should be removed. A very wet and cold period as the heads are drying off may give rise to mildew and consequent rotting of the seedheads. If this happens, the heads must be removed and dried artificially to stop it spreading further.

Crosses made late in the season may not develop proper seedheads if left outdoors. Therefore, two or three weeks after pollination, it is advisable to cut off the developing seedheads, along with a length of stem, and stand the stem in water in a bottle or vase. The seeds will continue their development, but care must be taken to avoid damping-off. The water must be changed regularly, and a dry atmosphere maintained in order to avoid the development of mildew.

When the seedheads are fully ripe, the bracts become thin and papery. The heads start to open up and this means that the seed inside is fully ripe. Pull the seed-head off the stem and gently rotate it between the fingers. The old calyx and bracts will break off from the dried receptacle, and the seeds will fall out.

Seed may be removed from the seedheads before it is fully ripe, but this is a more difficult process and residual moisture from the bracts may spread on to the seeds. If this is the case, the seeds should be laid out to dry on absorbent paper for a few hours. As long as the seeds are black or purple in colour, they should be viable. Any that are still pale green are unlikely to ripen properly. They may shrivel up and if so they will not germinate. Unless the seed is completely dry when it is packeted, it will develop mildew and will not survive.

Seed is best stored in paper packets – small wage packets are ideal; plastic packets should be avoided as any moisture will be trapped inside and the seeds will rot. Seed must be stored over the winter in a dry atmosphere but not at too high a temperature, or germination will be reduced. Dry seed stored at 5°C (41°F) will retain its viability for two or three years; after this period, its capacity for germination will fall.

SEED SOWING

I find that the best time to sow dahlia seed is during early April. First I prepare the seed trays. Shallow trays are best as the seedlings will not remain long in them. The seed compost should be freely draining: a suitable mix is two parts of soilless compost to one part of sharp sand, well combined before use in a bucket or similar container.

Seed is best sown in shallow drills about 1cm (½in) deep. A standard seed tray can accommodate nine drills. I sow one drill of seeds from each cross; if some crosses have been rather prolific, then I spread the seed along two drills. It is important that the drills are labelled with the reference code of the cross immediately the seed is sown as mistakes can easily occur. After labelling, cover the drills with a layer of seed compost, and when the box is full water it well with a fine rose on the watering can.

Tap water is preferable to rainwater, as water taken from a butt is likely to contain bacteria or fungal spores, which can decimate young seedlings. Rainwater can be made safer by adding Cheshunt Compound, which is a mixture of ammonium carbonate and copper sulphate.

This should be dissolved in a little warm water and made up to volume with cold water at the rate of 28g (1oz) to 9 litres (2 gallons). Alternatively, a stock solution of four times the normal strength can be prepared and diluted appropriately for use. Cheshunt solution attacks metal containers so plastic vessels must always be used.

Cheshunt Compound prevents damping off so the seed trays should be watered with this solution after seedling emergence and after potting on.

GERMINATION

A temperature of 15°C (59°F) is adequate for germination and this is best provided as bottom heat. The seed trays should be covered with a sheet of glass or plastic or placed in a propagator so that the compost does not dry out. Germination usually takes about four or five days, but some crosses may take twice as long as this. As

The dwarf variety 'Reddy' (p.126) is useful for growing in containers and garden borders.

soon as the bulk of the seed has germinated, the seed tray is best removed from the propagator, or any covering should be removed.

The seed germination may be quite uniform in some crosses, but in others it may be quite erratic. Sometimes, the old seed cases are stuck to the cotyledons. They should be removed very gently, otherwise one cotyledon may break off. Any pale, misshapen or even albino seedlings may survive for some weeks, or may even grow into mature plants, but they rarely make good specimens. It is best to ignore such weak seedlings when pricking out. Should a high proportion of such seedlings occur in a particular cross, then try reversing the cross next time (ie using the pollen parent as the seed parent and vice versa).

PRICKING OUT

As soon as the seedlings are big enough to handle, they should be pricked out into small pots. Hold the seedlings by the cotyledons when pricking out, not by their stems as these will be fragile and even the slightest damage will allow damping off fungi to invade.

A similar freely draining compost as was used for seed compost is needed for the young seedlings as they are prone to root rots at this stage. Although using Cheshunt Compound will reduce the risk of root rot, a cold wet soil can do considerable damage to the seedlings. However, as soon as the seedlings are established, they must be moved into cooler conditions since light levels are still low at this time of year and they will become drawn and leggy in a warm greenhouse.

Holding the seedlings back until it is safe to plant them out is likely to be a problem, and it may be that some will have to be potted on into slightly larger containers until the risk of frost is over. Before planting out, the seedlings will have to be hardened off in a coldframe or in a sheltered spot in the garden against a wall or fence.

PLANTING OUT

First year seedlings can be planted quite close together because as they come into flower those that do not make the grade will be pulled out and thrown away. It is rare for more than ten per cent of seedlings to remain in the seedbed at the end of a season. I usually plant seedlings 15cm (6in) apart both ways so that at the end of the season one plant is left in a block 45cm (18in) square. The blocks should not be too large or, before thinning, it may be difficult to get close enough to the seedlings for a careful examination of each.

Seedlings are watered with a liquid feed before planting out and no more fertilizer is given until the end of the season. The strategy is to encourage the seedlings to flower but not to put on vegetative growth. By planting close together in blocks, individual canes are not required. Instead, place a cane at each corner and run a string around the block. This will be sufficient to hold the plants relatively upright.

My seedlings are planted into coldframes that have had the lids removed. These give them some protection, and a nearby fence also helps to prevent them from being blown about.

SELECTING SEEDLINGS

Each year I aim to plant about 300 seedlings from which I expect to have retained about 30 by the end of the season. Each cross is labelled and a record of the number of seedlings planted out is kept in a notebook. The first seedlings to flower may do so in midsummer. They are not stopped, as one would exhibition blooms, but are allowed to flower on the crown bud. I mark any unusual seedling with a little white tag and make special note of it as the season progresses. Plants to be discarded are uprooted, care being taken to remove all of the tuber at the same time. At the end of the season all that should be left are the tubers of the selected seedlings for propagation next year.

Always bear in mind the objective of the cross while examining the seedlings for quality. Immediately discard any plants that produce blooms with open centres, unless, of course, you are breeding for collerettes or single types. With experience, the bud shape can be interpreted as an indication of open-centred bloom, such buds being pointed in contrast to the more flattened buds of fully double blooms. When the flowerheads open, their size and formation can be studied in detail. Although it takes some skill and experience to judge the flowerheads that open from a crown bud, as they are rather coarser than those that open from side shoots, it is vital to be ruthless in rooting out substandard blooms, otherwise you will be overwhelmed with material the following year. Potential varieties rarely improve in subsequent years.

By late summer, most of the plants for next year should have been chosen. Those plants that have not flowered by this time are likely to be late-flowering types and a decision should be made about whether the selection process should cease or whether it should continue for another week or so. Occasionally, good plants with a promising bud could be allowed to flower, but this must be balanced against the possibility of the resulting selection proving to be late flowering. By the third week in August, I have usually decided to uproot all the remaining unflowered plants, particularly if I already have enough selections for next year.

LIFTING AND STORING SEEDLINGS

By mid-autumn the only plants left in the seedling bed will be those selected for growing on next year. Now, a liquid feed of a high potash fertilizer is in order so that the tubers plump up and ripen off. It is too much of a risk to wait until a frost has cut back the top growth before lifting the tubers, so I prefer to lift seedlings a couple of weeks later. Each tuber is carefully lifted, the top growth cut back, and the white tag removed from the foliage. I then tie this tag around the stem of the tuber and add a plastic label with the cross number as well. The information on the tag is cross checked with that in the notebook and the record confirmed.

The lifted tubers are laid out on the bench in the greenhouse so that all surface moisture dries off. This should only take a few days and, because the tubers may not be fully ripe, care should be taken to inspect them each day to check that they have not shrivelled.

Storing such immature tubers can be a problem. They are best trimmed up and placed in a box of dry peat or compost with their crowns exposed. The boxes should be stored in as low a temperature as possible without the risk of them becoming frosted; 5°C (41°F) is ideal. To avoid the risk of fungal infection, the tubers can be dusted with flowers of sulphur.

GROWING ON SELECTIONS

During their second season, the selected plants will undergo a rigorous evaluation. The selected tubers are grown on to produce plants similar to show or garden display plants. I normally start my selected tubers at the same time as I start tubers of show varieties by giving them some bottom heat and watering sparingly until the eyes break into growth.

For evaluation, I grow a maximum of four plants by taking four cuttings from each tuber, but I like to have a few spares, which, if not required to replace evaluation plants, I grow on as pot tubers. Care must be taken to avoid overpropagation of young tubers, as the health and vigour of intensively propagated plants may suffer. At the same time, every precaution must be taken to avoid virus infection getting into the precious new stock. It is also important to note the way in which the tubers propagate. Some new varieties may lack vigour and propagate poorly. While enthusiasts may be willing to struggle with this, the majority of growers do not want such difficult plants, and commercial nurseries will also be reluctant to handle them.

Evaluation plants need to be treated exactly as one would treat existing varieties – plant them at the same time and at the same spacing. A note should be made of the planting date, stopping date, and the number of branches grown up to flowering. Flowering date should also be noted; hopefully, no late-flowering types will be present.

Remember, the objectives of the cross must be kept in mind when evaluating the plants, and a change in objectives is to be avoided. For example, a cross intended to produce a small-flowered decorative should be evaluated as such. If the resulting blooms do not come up to size, the plant should be discarded, not grown for a second year in an attempt to evaluate it as a miniature decorative, particularly as the blooms are likely to go oversize when treated as a miniature. Similarly, a cross intended as a ball dahlia should be discarded if the formation of the bloom tends towards decorative form. There are too many varieties already in existence with indeterminate formation without adding to the problem!

At the end of the season, it would be surprising if more than one or two promising varieties are left out of the 20–30 selected from the first year. For these outstanding varieties, it is worth getting a second opinion, and so plans should be made to find a friend or an expert to grow a few plants during the next season. This stage is vital: unless others have a chance to evaluate your new plant, you may find that your swans turn out to be other people's geese.

DAHLIA SPORTS

Not all new varieties of dahlias are the result of hybridization. The octoploid nature of the cultivated dahlia means that it is genetically unstable. During cell division, chromosome 'stickiness' and breakage can cause genetic changes. Mostly these are not visible, except by close investigation. However, changes in flower colour are often evident, and frequently occur only in part of the plant. Dahlias produced through this type of obvious genetic change are known as sports. The changes can be unstable and the changed sector of the plant may revert to the original colour. Changes in flowerhead formation are less often seen. One famous example is the collerette form. This arose in Lyons, France in 1899, and was fixed and propagated to give rise to the collerettes of today.

Sports are eagerly sought in Britain because of the many multi-vase classes popular in shows. For example,

'White Klankstad' is a sport of the small cactus dahlia 'Klankstad Kerkrade' (p.117).

a class calling for three vases of different varieties are easier to match and stage with three different colour sports of one variety. Irradiation treatment, chemical mutagens and high temperatures are known to give rise to sports and some varieties are more prone to produce them than others. Why they arise in nature is not clear. Varieties with blended colours are more prone to give rise to sports, some difficult to distinguish from the parent, but often giving pink or yellow forms, and then cream and/or white.

In order to preserve and propagate the sport, side shoots arising from the leaf axils of the sporting shoot must be removed and rooted. Natural sports tend to arise late in the growing season and the problem is to keep the young cuttings growing through the winter. Normally, extra light is needed in order to keep them growing well. The rooted cuttings are grown the following season, and if they remain true to type, then they can be further propagated.

One problem has been seen recently in Britain due to a number of identical sports having arisen simultaneously in different parts of the country. Confusion has been caused because these have been given different names by their various raisers.

9

EXHIBITING DAHLIAS

Visit any horticultural show during late summer and early autumn and you will find dahlias on display, either in floral arrangements or in special classes. They provide a most spectacular centrepiece; no flower show is complete without them. In addition to general flower shows, dahlia societies stage shows catering only for dahlias.

Perhaps the leading specialist dahlia exhibition in the world is the National Dahlia Society Show held in early September each year. It used to be held in Westminster, London, and is now at Shepton Mallet in Somerset. This is closely followed by the Northern Dahlia Show at Harrogate in Yorkshire. In Britain, there are also many regional dahlia society exhibitions spanning the months of August and September, and local dahlia societies combine with other specialist societies to hold shows in their own areas. Well over 1,000 local societies are affiliated to the National Dahlia Society, primarily so that they can stage specialist dahlia classes judged by national judges and offering NDS Affiliated Society Medals.

If National Dahlia Society medals are to be awarded then qualified NDS judges must be engaged to judge the classes and a statement needs to be made in the schedule that the dahlia classes will be judged according to the current NDS *Classified Directory and Judging Rules*, which lists most of the current show varieties and the classes in which they can be exhibited. A variety shown in the incorrect class will be disqualified, as will any variety of a size that is wrong for the class. The implication of NDS judging rules should be carefully

considered by any schedule maker, and any NDS judge will be glad to advise on this.

During judging, anomalies or failures to abide by the rules often arise. In such cases, the judge will draw these to the attention of the steward; a good judge will encourage the steward to make the appropriate correction or ask that the show organisers are brought in to make a decision, otherwise the exhibit may have to be disqualified. This means that the dreaded NAS (Not According to Schedule) will appear on the entry card, and no judge likes to see a good exhibit disqualified through lack of foresight during the hustle and bustle of staging. Even at national shows, exhibits without an entry card or those staged in the wrong class do occur and if the stewards can put this right before judging then this is good for the show. At judging, the only people allowed near the exhibits are the judges and stewards, and the public should be excluded from the hall.

GROWING FOR SHOW

The consistency with which some growers feature in the medal lists has nothing to do with luck, and indicates an above-average level of expertise. What is the difference between what an ordinary gardener does and what a show grower does? At NDS Annual Conferences experts talk about how they do it, but one still wonders whether there are any hidden secrets.

First you need to read potential show schedules, decide what varieties, and how many plants of each, to grow and where they will be planted.

SOIL AND RAINFALL

It may rain most days in a wet summer, but the total rainfall is still much less than the dahlia needs. Soil

'Periton' is a miniature ball with excellent formation and good stems. It is suitable for exhibition.

conditions also determine the effectiveness of rainfall: heavy clay retains water whereas on light sandy soil it will soon drain away. Dahlias do best on free-draining, light soil, but if your soil is very sandy, then you will need to be prepared to put on the equivalent of 750mm (30in) of rain during the growing season.

Commonsense dictates a compromise. All growers should consider adding plenty of organic matter to the soil to retain water and help make it open-textured and well-drained. Winter digging to incorporate the previous season's vegetation together with loads of manure is a theme that runs through the operations of all top growers. Some even grow an autumn crop of green manure to be turned in during spring just to build up organic matter in the soil.

FEEDING

When dahlias are grown from rooted cuttings, some fertilizer is necessary to develop the plant framework to carry show blooms. Dahlia growers generally believe that no artificial fertilizer should be applied at planting out as this could damage the delicate roots, giving the plants a set-back from which they might never recover. Fertilizer applied in the autumn, or bonemeal applied at 2.25kg (5lb) per 100sq m/ft some weeks before planting is acceptable. A week or two after planting, a handful per plant of a balanced general fertilizer can be given, preferably watered in if no rain has fallen. Some growers prefer to use sheep or chicken manure diluted in water. This is prepared by suspending a sack of the manure in a drum of water, and it is fed at the rate of 4½ litres (1 UK gallon) per plant every evening if no rain has fallen. An alternative is to dissolve two teaspoons of calcium nitrate in 4½ litres (1 UK gallon) of water, per plant until they are growing away well. No more fertilizer is then needed until flower buds are formed. As long as the plant has a good framework only water is then required for good show blooms. Fertilizer makes foliage and water makes blooms is the motto of the old dahlia growers. More problems are caused by overfeeding than underfeeding, and if growing plants need feed it should be in liquid form, not solid.

RAISING PLANTS

It takes between 70 and 140 days for a dahlia tuber to flower from planting, depending on the variety. Counting back from the main show date will give the ideal date for planting out. Thus, for a show like the National held in the first week in September, early varieties need to be planted out by June 23rd, while late varieties should have been planted by April 14th.

SPLIT TUBERS

To get early blooms from late-flowering varieties, start tuber clumps into growth in moist peat three weeks before the planting out date. A week before planting out cut the clumps into pieces consisting of a single tuber, each with a section of stem bearing an eye or small shoot. In North America, it is common practice to plant divided tubers (chicken legs, see p.72), and to take the crown bud of the main stem up to flowering to give the largest possible specimen bloom. This technique is geared to the typical North American show, where single blooms of all types are normally called for and maximum size is the objective. In contrast, most shows in Britain call for vases of 3 or 5 blooms of the same variety (except for giant and large classes), and the oversize rule demands that blooms do not exceed the size limit. This calls for a different method, namely that of using rooted cuttings. Very late varieties are difficult to time accurately, and so most modern show varieties grown in the British Isles tend to be early to mid-season. Even so, in the pom and also the giant sections, where some good show varieties are late-flowering, many growers use the divided tuber approach to help time their show blooms.

CUTTINGS

Tubers for cuttings need to be started into growth earlier than for split tubers because of the time taken for cuttings to root (normally 10–14 days). Rooted cuttings should be growing strongly with at least three pairs of leaves by the time of planting out, after the risk of frost is over. Thus if the date for the last frost is taken to be the last week of May, cuttings should be rooted by the May 1st, and therefore should be taken by mid-April. In order to have a set of identical cuttings of the same age, these are ideally second-flush cuttings, so first-flush cuttings are taken at the beginning of April. Many top growers believe that April-struck cuttings are ideal and the above sequence of events bears this out. However, it pays to know your varieties, as later-flowering varieties need to be timed two or three weeks earlier than this. To fit in with the above calendar of

A view of the National Dahlia Show in the RHS hall at Westminster, London.

events, most exhibitors would start their tubers off in January and discard the first, and sometimes the second flush of cuttings, or keep them for growing on as pot tubers. Clearly, careful planning is essential for good results.

The arguments over how deep dahlias should be planted are dealt with on pp.48–49. The case for deep planting is that it encourages four or six shoots to grow from below the soil surface and these will give rise to more roots. The giant 'Hamari Gold' appears to respond well to this treatment under British conditions.

TIMING BLOOMING
DISBUDDING AND STOPPING

Records kept over many years by top growers indicate that the average time from disbudding and securing the bloom (selecting the potential show bloom) to full flower is 30 days. This can vary between 20 and 50 days according to variety and season. Miniature and small varieties tend to vary 3–4 days around a mean of 20, medium varieties around 30 days, and giant and large varieties around 40 days.

The North American technique using chicken legs, assumes that the crown bud of the main shoot will give a show bloom, and each shoot is disbudded down to ground level. However, this method gives little control over timing of the blooms. Some American growers improve their timing by pinching out the main shoot in about the third week in June to leave 4–8 side shoots. These are then stripped down to four shoots, one at each pair of leaves, to give staggered flowering over approximately four weeks. In the British Isles, imposing such restrictions on small and miniature varieties would result in oversize blooms, as it also would on many medium varieties.

The average stopping date in Britain appears to be around June 16th, with a spread of a week or two each side of this. However, in some seasons in the north of England, planting in the first week in June does not allow enough time for sufficient breaks (shoots) to be produced if plants are then stopped a week or so later. Thus earlier planting, with frost protection, may be necessary to get blooms for early shows. If early blooms are needed on giant varieties, they are often stopped when they are planted out.

KNOCKING BACK

Some top growers have developed elaborate techniques for controlling the development of blooms to meet particular show dates. One such is the 'knock back' method. This is based on early stopping of the main shoot to produce the breaks, and then 'knocking back' the tips of each lateral until 25 days before the show.

For example, the early-flowering small decorative 'Ruskin Diane' takes about 25 days to develop a fully opened bloom from a pea-sized bud. Thus, for a show on, say, August 30th, laterals should not have the crown bud or side buds visible until 25 days before (August 5th). In order to achieve this, the plants need to be stopped four weeks beforehand (July 7th). However, the British weather is unreliable – a cold spell after stopping will delay flowering and a hot dry spell

may mature flowers too quickly – so, to take this into account, plants are actually stopped two weeks earlier (June 22nd). If the weather is hot and dry the first buds will appear in mid-July and the flowerheads will be fully open in mid-August. However, if it is cold and wet bloom development may be nearer the show date. Thus, from mid-July, the laterals are inspected daily and if the crown bud appears too soon, it is removed together with the side buds. The next side shoot will start to develop and its crown bud will be examined regularly. Again, if it becomes visible more than 25 days before the show, then the side shoot is removed, and so on, until a side shoot with a crown bud is visible 25 days before the show date.

Most top exhibitors will be growing 20 or so plants of a winning variety like 'Ruskin Diane' and planning for eight laterals per plant in order to provide enough blooms to cover the main three-week show season. Most shows require five blooms of identical maturity in a vase, and most blooms will be at their best for only one or two days, thus every three days at least five blooms will be needed, and over a three-week show period at least five successive sets of five blooms will be needed. After August 5th, any laterals not knocked back can be allowed to develop naturally.

Top growers will have detailed records of how long buds of each variety take to develop into fully-opened blooms and a timetable of stopping and disbudding is prepared for each variety. Medium-sized varieties will take longer for their buds to mature, and so also will large-flowered varieties. Giant-flowered varieties are not adapted to the 'knock-back method' since their blooms take a long time to mature and the main problem will be to get them flowering early enough and not to delay flowering.

POMPONS

To get accurate control of pompon flowering and flowerhead size, sufficient branches need to be developed on the plant. This is achieved by double stopping. After three pairs of leaves have developed, rooted cuttings are stopped while still in the pot. This will give rise to six branches. These branches are then stopped a second time (mid-June), after each has developed a further three pairs of leaves. Four to six weeks later (mid/end July), each plant will have 36 branches, and terminal buds can be secured by removing the wing buds on all 36 branches. It will take 18–20 days for the secured buds to flower and then bloom size can be checked. If the blooms are below size then extra side shoots can be removed to make the next flush of bloom larger. If they are oversize, the wing buds can be left on for an extra week or so to produce more, and therefore slightly smaller flowers in the second flush.

Variety is crucial with pompons: some, such as 'Moor Place' and 'Willo's Violet', tend to throw oversize blooms at first but quickly settle down. Others, such as 'Hallmark' may need extra disbudding to bring them up to size. One technique used by pompon growers is to remove the crown bud and let the wing buds take over, the final show blooms being fully open two or three days later than the crown bud. A decision as to which wing bud is taken for show is left until the last minute. However, this results in a slightly bent flower stem which requires considerable skill to disguise at staging.

GIANTS AND LARGE VARIETIES

The timing of giant and large varieties is different again because size is of the essence. Some growers rely on the crown bud, while others pinch out very early, plant deep and restrict growth to two or three branches, in each case stripping side shoots right down to the ground. But here, variety is the key variable, and experience is needed to come up with a system that suits one's own ground.

SPREADING AND DELAYING BLOOMING

During very hot weather, blooms may be over in a day, while in cool, moist conditions they can hold their form for three or four days. In order to spread the timing as much as possible, some growers start securing blooms 45 days before the show date. They disbud the first shoot 45 days before the show, the second shoot seven days later, the third shoot a further seven days later, and so on. Flowering can be delayed by a few days by rubbing out the crown bud on a shoot and securing a side bud. A delay of over a week can be achieved by removing the tip and selecting a lower bud.

BLOOM SIZE

If flower buds about the size of a pea are taken and dissected under a microscope, they can be seen to be fully developed. Petal number is already established at this stage and all the cells are present. When the potential exhibition bloom is secured as a pea-sized bud, water is essential to achieve maximum size and no amount of feeding will make any difference. On the contrary, feed supplied at this stage will go to produce more foliage, which also needs water and will reduce the water available for developing buds. Any feed supplied must be dilute and quick-acting, its purpose being to develop second- and third-flush blooms, rather than to increase the size of existing flowerheads. A foliar feed when the first buds are secured will only benefit later blooms, and can only really be justified if the first flush of blooms is too early for the key show. However, as colour is influenced by trace elements, a weak foliar feed at this stage can help produce stronger shades. Magnesium sulphate (Epsom Salts) at the rate of 50gm (2oz, or a tablespoon) per 9 litres (2 UK gallons) of water, to each plant will give extra brilliance to the colours.

Even in cold, wet summers, only about 40mm (1½in) of rain falls during mid- and late summer. Despite cool but moist conditions, water availability is low and plants become stressed, and bloom size suffers, when the sun does occasionally appear.

North American growers are used to hot and dry conditions during the show season and tend to apply far more water than British gardeners, using vast quantities during the late evening and night. Moreover, they are also good at conserving what water may be available in the soil by heavy mulches: I was fascinated by a picture of a plot that looked more like a carpet warehouse than a garden, with strips of old carpet carefully covering all the ground between the plants. Expert growers in Britain have learned to follow this example. Some of them have plots that look like hydroponic factories with water plumbed to all areas. Many of us are not able to contemplate supplying water in this quantity, especially those who have to carry it all in watering cans. In this case it is best to concentrate on getting the soil into such a condition that it retains water and covering the surface with a thick mulch.

THE NUMBER OF FLOWER-BEARING STEMS

Size of blooms is also influenced by the number of flowers that the plant is expected to support at any one time. For giants and large types it is usual to restrict the number of flower-bearing stems to 3–4 per plant; for mediums, one would normally restrict the number to 6–8; and for small types 8–10. Miniatures will need 10–12 flower-bearing shoots. To achieve this, 'double stopping' may have to be used. This means an early stop (pinching out the main tip) in early June or while the plant is still in the pot, followed by a second stop of each side shoot at the end of June. Exhibitors tend to use jargon such as 3-up, 6-up or 12-up to denote the number of stems allowed to grow for exhibition blooms.

CUTTING FOR SHOW

Dahlia blooms are very prone to wilting, particularly if cut during the heat of the day. Growers of cut flowers have experimented in reviving wilted blooms and extending the life of cut flowers. The general view seems to be that dahlias that have wilted can be revived by making a slanted cut at the base of the flower stem while it is under water and standing it in deep cool water in the dark. Plunging the cut stem into boiling water first does not appear to help in reviving wilted blooms, neither does adding chemicals to the water. As long as the flowerheads are kept in the dark and the water is changed every day, they can be kept in good condition for four or five days.

For the cut-flower trade, the quality of such revived blooms seems to be adequate. On the showbench, I doubt whether these flowerheads can compare with those that are freshly cut, but in an emergency it may be the only solution.

Many top exhibitors cut their blooms during the evening of the day before a show, and some will even cut two days before if they have a cool dark place for storage. But beware, blooms stored in water will continue to increase in size; small cactus blooms have been known to increase by a couple of centimetres or so following this treatment. One advantage of storing blooms in water before a show is that once put on the showbench, they are unlikely to increase much more in size. Conversely, freshly cut blooms sitting on a show-bench overnight could exceed the size limit by the time they are judged in the morning. Cutting pompons two days before a show and storing them in water is likely to ensure that they do not go oversize after staging. There is a story of one champion grower of large cactus dahlias who worked on a dairy farm. He used to store his cut blooms in water in the cold milk room for days

before a show. He also recovered prize-winning blooms from one show, took them home to the milk room and restaged them at a second show a few days later, winning another first prize with them.

COVERING

Some experts maintain that top-class exhibition blooms cannot be grown without covers, but uncovered blooms do win silver medals. With giant or large dahlias, covering of some kind is essential, if only to prevent the blooms filling up with rain and collapsing under the extra weight. Covering also reduces the risk of strong colours fading under bright sun. This is less of a problem in Britain than in North America, which can experience very hot summers. On the contrary, covering blooms in the British Isles can lead to paler colours and, in cool wet summers, encourages the spread of mildew on the foliage and marking on the backs of blooms.

Easy to grow and good for exhibition, 'Wanda's Capella' (p.131) is a giant decorative variety.

Some growers erect vast structures over their blooms on which portable covers are fixed just before a show. Others use portable paper cones or umbrellas to cover individual blooms when needed. Cloth or plastic mesh has been very popular in North America and is proving useful in the British Isles, although enclosing the whole plot with such material cuts down air movement, with a subsequent increased risk of mildew. High winds often occur during show time in Britain, so whatever the covering, it must be secure or disaster may result.

It would be reasonable to ask why bother to cover at all as the dangers could outweigh any benefits. The answer is that growers want to ensure that they will be able to put up high-quality blooms at all the shows they plan to enter and, as such, covering is part of the overall approach; however, their true secret is flexibility and a willingness to adapt to whatever weather conditions are prevalent.

JUDGING

So what are British judges looking for?

As stressed in the judging section of the NDS *Classified Directory and Judging Rules*, quality must override mere size. Quality is defined as formation, centre, freshness, colour and strong flower stems. Formation and size, as given in the directory, are an indication of the performance of the variety as grown under reasonably good conditions. Plants grown for exhibition using superior cultivation techniques, may produce larger blooms, and the rules for judging provide for some leeway in size before disqualification is required. However, this has given rise to the view, held by some exhibitors and judges, that blooms which do not reach the size limit imposed by the measuring rings are undergrown and should be marked down. So, unless the philosophy that quality must override mere size is rigidly adhered to, many potential varieties will never be released. Instead, raisers will offer poorer types that are capable of meeting the ring sizes. This is most clearly evident in the medium decorative group, where many excellent formal types never make the grade for size against the more informal types like 'B.J. Beauty'. Those formal types that make the size limits are often, in reality, large types which need to be undergrown to make the medium ring. A similar problem exists with the miniature and small ball groups. In this case, the upper size grouping suffers from a lack of good show varieties.

In North America, size seems to be the main criterion for judging all groups from small to giant. However, there is a school of thought that miniature blooms should be smaller than is allowed in Britain, and of good formation. There is no disqualification for oversize blooms, but some enthusiasts consider that pompons and miniatures should be restricted in size. The debate continues.

SHOWING BLOOMS

With the emphasis in the British Isles on quality and freshness for show, getting the blooms to the show-bench without marking the petals or inflicting even more serious damage is an operation that requires careful planning. The days when it was possible to pack

'Nenekazi' (p.121), from South Africa, has made its mark all over the world as an exhibition variety.

blooms in flower boxes for transport to a show have long since gone. Today's exhibitors rely on drums containing water, milk or beer crates with cut-down plastic bottles, or specially constructed boxes or racks to carry the blooms. A stem of at least 60cm (24in) is required on most show blooms, so headroom in the transporting vehicle is important.

In order to hold it firmly for transport over long distances, each bloom should have a thin cane tied to its stem using three pieces of plastic-coated wire, one below the bloom, one at the base and one in the middle. The cane is then securely tied to the rim of the drum or a framework above the container.

Bearing in mind the requirement for most British show classes of three or five blooms of each variety, it is important to cut and transport some spares. Thus for a class requiring three vases of five blooms per vase, a total of twenty blooms may be needed to cover against accidents and to select the best matched set. To achieve this number of blooms, a top grower will probably grow five varieties and 20 plants of each variety, simply to cover one class. If a total of five different size and form classifications is required then a total of five

hundred plants will need to be grown. This is a major operation and one not to be undertaken lightly.

STAGING

Most larger shows supply vases to exhibitors; these are usually plastic 'bikini'-type vases. The show schedule must be read carefully and interpreted correctly, otherwise the exhibit may be judged NAS. The rules for judging in British shows are laid out in the NDS *Classified Directory and Judging Rules*. Judges are looking for blooms that meet the requirements for shape and form, are held on good stems and have no damage or defects. Disqualification occurs if they exceed the size limit specified, if they are artificially supported above the top of the vase, if the number of blooms is incorrect for the class, and if they are exhibited in the wrong class.

No marks are awarded for staging, but the impact of a well-staged vase of blooms on the judges should not be underestimated. Blooms should face the judge, they should be well-matched for size, colour and angle of presentation, and the exhibit should be appealing to the eye. Medium and large varieties are usually staged three to a vase, small and miniature varieties are staged five to a vase, and pompons five or six to a vase. Giants are usually staged singly. If slight differences in size exist between blooms, this can be disguised to some extent by staging the larger blooms to the back of the vase and smaller blooms to the front. Slightly bent stems and wrongly angled blooms can also be disguised by clever staging, although in most cases judges will know what has been done and take this into account. It is important to look at how the top exhibitors deal with staging. They are usually very helpful if approached by a novice who wants to learn how it is done.

Blooms need to be firmly held in the vase because judges will take down the vases and move them about in order to examine them more closely. It is unfortunate if the blooms then swing about in the vase or the exhibit collapses. The stems of the blooms are usually packed with newspaper to hold them firm, but recently 'oasis', used for many years by flower arrangers, has become popular with top showmen.

In Britain, exhibits are required to have some dahlia foliage, preferably on the flower stem, but if it is damaged or diseased, then there is nothing to prevent the poor leaves being removed and substituted with healthy ones.

CONCLUSION

To become a top exhibitor takes many years of experience. The way forward is to gain that experience by trying different growing methods and entering the resulting blooms in local shows. Take note of what wins in your local shows and this will reveal which varieties do well in your local conditions.

The NDS *Dahlia Winter Bulletin* gives variety analyses for the main shows. Compare these with what seems to succeed locally. For example, the top variety

'Kenora Challenger' (p.116) is a semi-cactus dahlia which produces well-formed blooms that are superb for exhibition.

at London (now Shepton Mallet) and Harrogate since 1992 is 'Kiwi Gloria', but this variety is difficult to grow well and may not suit your ground and growing conditions. So be prepared to experiment and concentrate on one or two varieties for a few seasons to find out how to grow them well.

Know your ground and know your varieties!

10

A–Z OF DAHLIAS IN CULTIVATION

The cultivars described are mainly of *D. × variabilis*, which is a convenient label to define cultivated forms of dahlia. (For information about dahlia species which are being grown by some enthusiasts see Chapter 4.) The descriptions include cultivars grown in Europe and America and in many other parts of the world. The names used here are registered in some countries, but sometimes the same names are used for different plants in different countries, which can cause confusion. Where possible, these are pointed out.

The cultivar name is followed by the name of the raiser or introducer and the date the cultivar was released or registered. The classification is described, but sometimes varies slightly from country to country, and the expected height of the cultivar under normal cultivation conditions is also provided. Cultivars grown in different conditions, such as in the shade of trees or near a wall or hedge may prove to be rather taller.

Most of the plants described are relatively easily obtained from specialist nurseries, but some of the older cultivars may be more difficult to find. In Britain they may be traced through the National Collection.

Abbreviations: H = height; AGM = Award of Garden Merit. Plants that receive this award from the RHS have been judged to be valuable for garden use. AM = Award of Merit. This award is made to plants that are excellent for exhibition. Judgement is usually made of cut material in a vase but may occasionally be of specimen plants. Details of other awards are given in Chapter 12 pp.147–148.

'Tender Moon' (p.130) is a small decorative of waterlily form that is ideal for garden display and cutting.

Abridge Ben (J. Kinns 1986) A miniature decorative with purple blooms held on strong stems. Can give exhibition-quality blooms. Excellent for cut flowers and garden decoration. H to about 1m (3ft).

Abridge Taffy (J. Kinns 1978) This miniature decorative has white blooms of classic formation on strong stems. Although over twenty years old, it is still an excellent exhibition variety and continues to win prizes on the showbench. For exhibition, it needs to be grown '12 up' and well disbudded to make top size for its class. A strong grower, it is excellent for garden decoration and its good stems make it useful as a cut flower. H to 1.2m (4ft).

Akita (Y. Konishi 1988) An unusual variety from Japan, this is classified as miscellaneous and has large, chrysanthemum-like blooms. The flowerheads are in red-yellow blends, with tips of the petals folded in at the end like a chrysanthemum. This is a tall grower. H 1.2m (4ft).

Alan Melville (M. Roberts 1993) AGM 1996 Collerette bearing red blooms with yellow collars. Ideal for garden decoration. H to 75cm (30in).

Alfred C (J. Almand 1968) A giant-flowered semi-cactus with massive orange-bronze blooms. Introduced from California, it was a leading show variety of the 1980s, but is not easily available today.

Allan Sparkes (J. Crutchfield 1991) AGM 1996 A waterlily dahlia with lavender-lilac flowerheads. Good for cut flowers and garden decoration. H1.4m (4½ft).

Alloway Cottage (J. Stitt 1970) This medium decorative, which came from New Zealand, was a leading show variety during the 1970s and is still found on the showbench today. The flowerheads are yellow and pink blends and are held on strong stems. H1.1m (3½ft).

Alltami Corsair (H. Williams 1975) Dark red, medium semi-cactus flowerheads are well formed and of exhibition quality. Makes an attractive spot plant in the border. H to 1.2m (4ft).

Almand's Climax (J. Almand 1968) An American giant decorative that has been a leading show variety for many years. Its lilac and white blended blooms are of excellent formation and are held on strong stems. A sport of 'Kidd's Climax', it matches its parent well for multi-vase classes. H to 1.2m (4ft).

Alva's Doris (V. Frost 1965) AGM 1993 This New Zealand variety has red small cactus blooms. No longer able to compete with more recent varieties on the showbench, it is excellent for garden display. H to about 1m (3ft).

'Alltami Corsair' is a medium semi-cactus that is good for garden display.

Alva's Supreme (V. Frost 1956) AGM 1994 This giant decorative from New Zealand is still one of the leading exhibition varieties. Its formal giant bright yellow blooms on strong stems make it easy to stage on the showbench. It also makes an excellent garden plant if grown unrestricted at '6 up', but it still needs to be disbudded to produce a good flower stem and raise the blooms above the foliage. It has given rise to two sports: 'Cream Alvas' (E. Machin 1990), AGM 1995, AM, a cream variety of the same form and 'White Alvas' (J. Mills 1979) AGM 1997, AM. H 1.4m (4½ft).

Amberglow (C. Geerlings 1994) A well-formed orange-amber miniature ball, excellent for garden decoration. It can be exhibited but has a tendency for hard centres, so must be well grown to produce quality blooms. H to about 1m (3ft).

Amelisweert (Bruidegom 1962) One of the classic medium semi-cactus varieties to come out of Holland during the 1960s and one of the leading show varieties at the time. The bronze blooms of excellent formation are held on strong stems. No longer easily available. H1.2m (4ft).

Amgard Coronet (D. Bates 1985) A miniature decorative with flowerheads of pink and yellow blends. Plants will produce exhibition-quality blooms, but the blended coloration can vary and makes them difficult to match. However, it does win on the showbench and is useful for multi-vase exhibits. H1.2m (4ft).

Amgard Delicate (D. Bates 1994) Large decorative exhibition variety. Its blooms of pink and yellow blends easily make the 25cm (10in) size when grown '4 up' and well disbudded. There has been an increasing number of large decorative exhibition varieties on the market in recent years, and 'Amgard Delicate' is a welcome addition. H to about 1.1m (3½ft).

Amira (C. Geerlings 1997) A recent introduction from Holland, 'Amira' has deep purple blooms of ball formation on strong stems. In America it would be regarded as a small ball, but in Britain its blooms will make the miniature classification. Easy to grow and does well as a garden plant. H to about 1.1m (3½ft).

Ananta Patel (J. Crutchfield 1988) A miniature decorative bearing flame and yellow blooms. It can be grown as a dwarf bedder or, when not disbudded, makes an excellent border plant. H75cm (30in).

Andrew Lockwood (A. Lockwood 1961) This lavender pompon of classic form is good for exhibition. It has been around for over thirty years and is still found on the showbench. H to about 1m (3ft).

Andrew Magson (W. Mark 1994) AGM 1996 A small semi-cactus with dark red blooms of excellent form. Even grown unrestricted, the flowerheads often exceed the size limit for the class so it has to be under-grown for showing. Its sport 'Jackie Magson' is described below. All the Magson family are useful for garden decoration. H all to about 1.2m (4ft).

Andrew Mitchell (L. Nickerson 1996) A medium semi-cactus of excellent formation. Its sparkling red

blooms are of exhibition quality. Best grown '7–8 up' for the best-quality blooms. H usually 1.4m (4½ft).

Andries' Orange (Andries 1936) The orange miniature semi-cactus blooms of this dahlia are much prized by flower arrangers for autumn displays. It makes a fine display in the border and is useful for cutting. Not readily available, but well worth looking for. Medium height, H 1.1m (3½ft).

Andries' Wonder (Andries) An unusual variety bearing large golden-peach-blended flowerheads with petals that roll over at the tip, somewhat like those of a chrysanthemum. Classified as miscellaneous, it is now rarely seen. Similar to more recent introductions from Japan such as 'Akita'.

Anglian Water (N. Lewis 1991) A purple miniature decorative of good formation. This dahlia will produce show-quality blooms and makes a useful border plant. It is also ideal for cutting and flower arranging. H to 1.1m (3½ft).

Angora (C. Piper 1961) A white small decorative, unusual in that its decorative petals are split at the ends making the bloom look like a powder puff. One of the earliest fimbriated (laciniated) decorative varieties to be introduced. Makes a most unusual border plant. H to 1m (3ft).

Anja Doc (F. Docherty 1996) A lavender medium semi-cactus with fine formation and an unusual colour. A good show variety. Rather tall, H 1.4m (4½ft).

Anniversary Ball (G. Rowlands 1992) A miniature ball with tightly formed blooms of pink blends. Originally called 'Brookfield Enid', it was renamed by the public at various show venues around the country to celebrate Aylett's nurseries fortieth anniversary, and was released under its new name. It is excellent for garden decoration. It has to be restricted to 7 or 8 stems and heavily disbudded to make the exhibition bench. H 90cm (3ft).

Apache (Bruidegom 1960) Although classified as a medium semi-cactus, 'Apache' is more like a large small semi-cactus. Its red blooms are fimbriated (laciniated). Not seen a great deal today. An attractive border variety. H to 1.1m (3½ft).

Apricot Beauty (C. Geerlings 1996) A recently introduced golden-pink medium semi-cactus of exhibition quality. It received a Bronze Certificate at the NDS Northern Trials, Leeds, in 1997. H 1.2m (4ft).

Apricot Jewel (raiser not known 1995) A small decorative with peach-apricot blooms. Makes a good garden plant and is suitable for cutting. H to 1.2m (4ft).

Arab Queen (F. Rossack 1949) An old Australian variety, 'Arab Queen' dominated the show scene in the 1960s, but is no longer readily available. A giant semi-cactus with orange-yellow blooms. H 1.35m (4½ft).

Arranger's Delight (E. Richards 1967) A small waterlily with red petals shading to a yellow centre. It is ideal for cut blooms and flower arranging. Rather tall for garden display, H to 1.5m (5ft).

Arthur Hills (A. Hills 1985) AGM 1994 A bronze small cactus which will provide show blooms, but makes an excellent garden plant and can be used for cutting. H to about 1.2m (4ft).

Athalie (W. Dawes 1974) A small cactus with pink and bronze blends, until recently the leading small cactus exhibition variety. Its widespread use has led to a large number of sports: 'Lavender Athalie' in 1981, 'Majestic Athalie' (pink/yellow blends) in 1982, 'Peach Athalie' in 1986 and 'Salmon Athalie'. All make excellent cut flowers with strong stems, but are rather unmanageable in the garden except for dedicated exhibitors. H all reach about 1.5m (5ft).

Aurora's Kiss (W. Holland 1997) A recent introduction from America, this has dark red miniature ball blooms on strong stems. H 1.1m (3½ft).

Autumn Fire (Dobbie 1960) A dazzling dahlia in red and gold, this is classified as a medium semi-cactus. It won many prizes on the showbench but, sadly, has been superseded by more recent varieties. Makes a very attractive garden display. Suffered health problems and not now generally available. H to 1.1m (3½ft).

Autumn Lustre (R. Aylett 1991) AGM 1994 A robust small waterlily dahlia with orange-red blooms on strong stems. Makes an excellent garden plant. H to about 1.2m (4ft).

Babette (C. Geerlings 1998) A rich beautiful dark purple small ball introduced from Holland. A good exhibition variety. H to 1m (3ft).

Banker (Bruidegom 1970) This red medium cactus and its amber sport, 'Amber Banker' (P. Tivey 1982), are two of the best true medium cactus varieties available. Their refined formation makes them ideal for showing. They are also excellent in the garden. H to 1.2m (4ft).

Barbarry Ball (B. Davies 1991) An orange small ball of excellent form. It is good both as an exhibition variety and in the garden. H to 1.2m (4ft).

Barbarry Banker (B. Davies 1988) An exhibition-quality pink miniature decorative that is also good as a garden variety. Needs disbudding early to make longer stems. A low grower, H 90cm (3ft).

Barbarry Bluebird (B. Davies 1996) A violet-purple miniature decorative, awarded a Bronze Certificate at the NDS Northern Trials, Leeds, in 1997. H 1.1m (3½ft).

Barbarry Gem (B. Davies 1990) A miniature ball with tightly formed purple blooms, 'Barbarry Gem' has excellent exhibition form, but is on the small side for exhibition in Britain. However, it does extremely well on the exhibition bench in North America, where the classification size limits are different and comparable with the large pom (or 'Dutch pom') of old. It is ideal for garden decoration and for cutting. H 1.1–1.2m (3½–4ft).

Barbarry Oracle (B. Davies 1991) A red small decorative of exhibition quality. H to 1.2m (4ft).

Barbarry Snowball (B. Davies 1995) A small ball of exhibition quality with well-formed white blooms. Definitely a small in America but with careful growing could make a miniature ball in Britain. H to 1.2m (4ft).

Baret Joy (J. Joyce 1994) A large semi-cactus with quality white blooms on strong stems. An outstanding exhibition variety. H to 1.2m (4ft).

Beatrice (C. Geerlings 1997) An orange-bronze miniature decorative from Holland with exhibition potential. Medium height.

Belle of the Ball (R. Surber 1995) This large semi-cactus, with fimbriated (laciniated) petals in lavender, produces show-quality blooms when grown '5 up' and is not to be confused with the pink large semi-cactus released by Bruidegom in 1957. H to about 1.2m (4ft).

Ben Huston (E. Huston 1985) A Canadian giant decorative with huge, prize-winning blooms of orange blends. Later-flowering than many giant decoratives. This is an exhibitor's variety and not suitable for gardens as it is rather tall. H often exceeding 1.5m (5ft).

Bernard C. Hayes (Boore 1962) This is a pure lavender sport from the deep purple 'Reverend Colwyn Vale'. Classified as a small ball, it has difficulty competing for size with more recent introductions on the showbench. Rather tall for gardens. H to 1.5m (5ft).

'B. J. Beauty' is a medium decorative that frequently takes prizes on the showbench.

Berwick Wood (R. Turrell 1989) Purple-pink medium decorative blooms on strong stems. Exhibition quality. A good grower making a strong plant. H 1.35m (4½ft).

Bishop of Llandaff (I. Treseder 1928) AGM 1995 An old variety still in great demand for garden decoration. Its small red peony-type blooms are set off by the bronze foliage. H to 90cm (3ft).

B. J. Beauty (T. Clarke 1976) The leading medium decorative variety for exhibition today. Its white well-formed, easy to match blooms and good habit make it the exhibitor's ideal. H to 1.2m (4ft).

Black Fire (E. Richards 1974) A very dark red small decorative. Ideal for cut flowers and for garden decoration. H to 1.2m (4ft).

Bloom's Wildwood (Bloom 1998) A bright yellow true cactus. Its small blooms will make the showbench, and its continuous flowering habit makes it excellent for the border.

'Bon Esperance' is good for growing as a patio plant.

Bonaventure (B. Simon 1982) One of the biggest giant decoratives ever produced. The huge formal bronze blooms are borne on strong stems making them easy to stage. The plants are tall and need extra firm staking and some form of covering to produce exhibition blooms. Not suitable for garden decoration and needs special treatment by exhibitors. H 1.5m (5ft).

Bon Esperance (Topsvoort 1951) Pink single blooms are borne on dwarf plants, ideal for growing in pots or containers on patios. It is early to flower and will continue flowering throughout the season provided that the dead heads are removed. Youngsters should be stopped after three pairs of leaves have been produced so as to make short bushy plants. This variety is often sold in plastic bags at garden centres. H rarely exceeding 40cm (16in).

Bonny Blue (Archer 1920) Sometimes called 'Blue Danube', this dahlia was at one time considered to be the nearest to a true blue but, unfortunately, it is not blue but a rich lavender. A leading ball dahlia for exhibition before the First World War, it is now virtually unobtainable. However, the National Dahlia Collection still lists it.

Border Prince (D. Maarse 1960) A dwarf bedding variety with rose-pink cactus blooms on dainty bushes. Not easily found today. H to about 60cm (24in).

Border Princess (Lammerse 1964) This dwarf bedder with pink small cactus flowerheads was extremely popular in public parks and gardens, when it was grown so close together in beds that it needed little or no staking. H 1m (3ft).

Bracken Ballerina (Naumann 1988) This Australian variety is a small waterlily with pale-centred pink blooms. Excellent for cut flowers and for borders. H to 1m (3ft).

Bracken Tribune (Naumann 1997) Yellow-bronze small waterlily blooms are held on strong stems making this ideal for cut flowers. It flowers early and profusely. H 1.1m (3½ft).

Brackenhill Flame (E. Furness 1995) A flame-coloured small decorative that received a Bronze Certificate at the NDS Northern Trials, Leeds, in 1996. Makes a fine garden plant and is also suitable for cutting. H to 1m (3ft).

Brandaris (Topsvoort 1950) A medium semi-cactus with flame and yellow blended blooms. Great for garden display. H to 1.2m (4ft).

Brandysnap (origin unknown) AGM 1995 An orange-yellow small decorative with dark green foliage. Ideal for garden decoration and cut flowers. H to 1.35m (4½ft).

Breckland Joy (Greenbury) A bronze medium decorative that ruled the showbench in the 1960s, but is no longer seen at shows. Its pink sport 'Pink Breckland Joy' may still be found. Medium height, 90cm (3ft).

Bridge View Aloha (M. Giesert 1986) AGM 1996 A medium semi-cactus from North America producing flowerheads with yellow petals tipped with red. As with many bicoloured varieties, the disinction between the colours becomes less obvious as the flowerheads age, the petals developing a more general flame blend coloration. The strong stems hold the blooms clear of the foliage. It is not really regarded as an exhibition variety, but its colour makes it stand out in the garden. Its name was changed from 'Aloha' as this had already been registered for a decorative variety released by Bruidegom in Holland in 1938. However, this is no longer in cultivation. H to 1.2m (4ft).

Brookfield Deirdre (G. Rowlands 1982) A yellow miniature ball, released as a replacement for 'Nettie' when it suffered health problems. A good exhibition variety. H to 1.2m (4ft).

Butterball (A. Lister 1960) AGM 1993 A dwarf bedding miniature decorative with yellow blooms borne in great profusion on compact plants. H to 50cm (20in).

Cameo (W. Tapley 1986) A small waterlily from Australia. The flowerheads are cream on a yellow base. Ideal for cut flowers and also for garden decoration. H 90cm (3ft).

Can-Can (J. Crutchfield 1960) A collerette with white-collared lilac blooms, this old variety is no longer easily available. H 90cm (3ft).

Carolina Moon (C.W. Welch 1990) A small waterlily bearing white blooms tipped with lilac. Ideal for cut flowers and for garden decoration. H to 90cm (3ft).

Carstone Cobblers (J. Kidd 1982) A small ball with lemon-yellow blooms. Good exhibition variety. H to 1.1m (3½ft).

Carstone Ruby (J. Kidd 1996) Bearing ruby-red blooms of classical formation, this was released as a small decorative but may be better grown as a miniature decorative. Grown '12 up', it will make an exhibition miniature decorative; it will also make an ideal plant for garden display. 'Carstone Ruby' won the Harry Howarth Memorial Medal in 1996 at the NDS Northern Trials, Leeds. It has also also won awards as the best seedling at shows. H to 1.2m (4ft).

Charles Dickens (D. Maarse 1974) A small ball with purple-lilac blooms. It did well on the showbench in the 1970s but is not often seen today. Medium height, H 1.1m (3½ft).

The medium decorative 'Charlie Two' is suitable for exhibition use.

Charlie Kenwood (C. Kenwood 1991) A miniature decorative with flowerheads of pink blends. It can produce exhibition blooms, and is useful for cutting and for garden display. H to 1m (3ft).

Charlie Two (E. Fuller 1989) A medium decorative with yellow blooms, 'Charlie Two' is a consistent winner on the showbench, easily makes top size and is easy to match for colour. It is virtually indistinguishable from 'Mascot Maya'. H 1.2m (4ft).

Cheerio (J. Barwise 1953) A small semi-cactus bearing cherry-red blooms with silver tips. A leading bicolour

The recent introduction 'Cindy' is suitable for showing as a miniature decorative.

of forty years ago, much in demand for garden display and cutting. H to 1.1m (3½ft).

Cherida (J. Crutchfield 1966) A lavender and buff miniature ball, much prized by flower arrangers. Medium height, H 90cm (3ft).

Cherwell Goldcrest (J. Davies 1996) A yellow small semi-cactus for exhibition. Also does well for garden decoration. H 1.1m (3½ft).

Chic (Ballego 1958) A purple miniature ball that was a leading exhibition variety in its day. H about 90cm (3ft).

Chimborazo (J. Crutchfield) A collerette with red ray florets and a yellow collar. One of the leading show varieties and an outstanding garden dahlia, making an eye-catching focus in any display. H to 90cm (3ft).

Choh (Ishii 1974) A lilliput collerette producing tiny flowerheads that are purple with a white collar. Ideal for patio containers. Often found only in the plastic bag racks in garden centres. Popular in America. H 30–35cm (12–14in).

Christmas Carol (L. Connell 1988) A collerette dahlia with red blooms and a red and yellow collar.

Christopher Nickerson (L.J. Nickerson 1991) AGM 1995 A medium semi-cactus with gold-tipped yellow flowerheads. Ideal for garden decoration and will produce show blooms. H to 1.2m (4ft).

Christopher Taylor (C. Taylor 1980) A waterlily dahlia with striking dark velvety red flowerheads. Good for cutting and for garden display. H 1.2m (4ft).

Cindy (C. Geerlings 1997) A yellow miniature decorative with a ball formation, this is suitable for garden decoration and may make a show variety if well grown. H to 1.1m (3½ft).

Claire de Lune (Bruidegom 1946) A lemon-yellow collerette with a yellow collar. A strong grower. Ideal for cutting and flower arranging. H to 1m (3ft).

Classic A1 (L. Connell 1995) A medium cactus of classic form bearing orange blooms on strong stems. A good exhibition variety, it is also suitable for garden display and cutting. H to 90cm (3ft).

Coltness Gem, syn. Coltness Hybrids (Purdie 1922) The large single flowerheads are usually red with a yellow centre. One of the few dahlias to come true from seed, except for the flower colour. H 45cm (18in).

Comet (N.J. van Oostens 1952) 'Comet' and its sport 'Scarlet Comet' are anemone-flowered dahlias with red ray florets surrounding a dense group of red tubular florets in the centre. They are useful for garden decoration and for cut flowers. H to 1m (3ft).

Connie Bartlam (T. Mantle 1987) A medium decorative with salmon-pink flowerheads tipped with gold. It will make exhibition-quality blooms. Good grower. H 1.35m (4½ft).

Connoisseur's Choice (Bruidegom 1967) A red miniature ball that was a leading show variety in its day. A useful garden plant. H 90cm (3ft).

Conway (N. Weekes 1986) AGM 1993 This is a small semi-cactus with blooms of pink blends. It makes a good exhibition variety and is excellent for garden display. H to 1m (3ft).

Cornel (C. Geerling 1995) A red miniature ball in Britain; a small ball in North America. An excellent show variety, and useful in gardens. H to 1m (3ft).

Corona (Westwell) A dwarf bedder with small semi-cactus blooms in vermilion on a yellow base. Ideal for garden bedding. H to about 60cm (24in).

Croydon Masterpiece (H. Brand 1948) One of the top exhibition giant decoratives of the post-war period. Its blooms are buff overlaid with orange-red and are of good size on strong stems. When it arrived from Australia it was regarded as the best, but now has strong competition from more recent American introductions. H to about 1.2m (4ft).

Cryfield Bryn (F. Wilson 1973) A bright yellow small semi-cactus. Strictly a show dahlia, it suffered from health problems and is now rarely seen. A tall grower. H 1.2m (4ft).

Cryfield Max (F. Wilson 1973) A pale yellow small true cactus. Another show variety. Now difficult to find. H 1.1m (3½ft).

Curiosity (Bruidegom 1954) This collerette has red ray florets with bronze tipping, and white collar petaloids. Great for show and garden. H to 90cm (3ft).

Daddy's Choice, syn. Daddies Choice (E. Richards 1978) A yellow small semi-cactus with fimbriated (laciniated) petals. H to 1.2m (4ft).

Daleko Jupiter (G. Krzywycki 1979) The leading giant semi-cactus show variety. Produces huge blooms with red and yellow blends. 'Pink Jupiter' (K. Hardham 1981) is a pink sport and in turn gave rise to 'Rose Jupiter' (1986) which is pink and white. Grow them '4 up' for massive blooms or '6 up' for garden decoration. H all to 1.35m (4½ft).

Daleko Polonia (G. Krzywycki 1974) Orange and yellow giant semi-cactus show variety. Now superseded by 'Daleko Jupiter' and its sports. H to about 1.5m (5ft).

'Daleko Jupiter' is a giant semi-cactus of exhibition form and has produced a number of sports.

Dana Alice (R. Cook 1996) A pompon with pink-flushed yellow flowerheads. It makes compact plants and will produce exhibition blooms when well grown. A useful addition to the pom scene as yellow poms are scarce. H to 1m (3ft).

Dana Frank (R. Cook 1996) Pompon with red flowerheads, gold on the reverse. A strong plant, it produces exhibition-quality blooms on strong stems. H to 1.2m (4ft).

Dana Iris (R. Cook 1977) Red small cactus, excellent for garden display, cut flowers and exhibition. H to about 1.2m (4ft).

Dark Stranger (P. Tivey 1997) AGM 1996 A dark red small semi-cactus. Makes a nice garden plant, but the blooms are rather large for small semi-cactus classes, and a bit small for medium, making it difficult to show. H to about 1.2m (4ft).

Davar Donna (J. Whitton 1988) AGM 1995 A yellow small cactus of fine form. It will produce show blooms and is excellent in the garden. H to 1.2m (4ft).

Davenport Sunlight (A. Dunlop 1980) Medium semi-cactus with deep yellow blooms of top exhibition quality. Excellent for garden display. H to 1m (3ft).

PLATE VIII
DECORATIVE DAHLIAS

'Kenora Christmas'

'Charlie Kenwood'

'Cindy'

'Kidd's Climax'

All flowers are shown at approximately half size

'Phoenix'

'Kotari Magic'

'Ruskin Diane'

'Gala Parade'

'Hamari Sunshine'

'Easter Sunday' is a collerette that is good for both garden display and cut flowers.

David Digweed (B. Davies 1995) Amber-bronze small decorative of tight formation. Good for exhibition. H to 1m (3ft).

David Howard (Howard 1965) AGM 1995 Orange-yellow miniature decorative flowerheads contrasting with blackish foliage. An excellent dahlia for garden display. H to 1m (3ft).

Dazzler (Cheal 1915) AGM 1995 as 'Aylett's Dazzler' A dwarf bedding miniature decorative with red blooms and very dark green foliage. H about 30cm (12in).

Debra Ann Craven (A. Craven 1988) A deep wine-red giant semi-cactus show variety. It bears huge blooms when grown '4 up'. H to 1.2m (4ft).

Dedham (T. Clarke 1972) One of the first formal small decoratives in lilac and white blends, this set the standard for show varieties in the 1970s. Early to flower and very prolific. Makes a fine garden plant. H to 1m (3ft).

Diana Gregory (J. Gregory 1947) Like many of the classic poms, this arrived from Australia after the war. The refined blooms in lilac blends are held on strong stems making it suitable for garden display, cutting and exhibition. H to 1m (3ft).

Doc van Hoorn (D. Maarse 1978) A large semi-cactus with pink blooms. A good exhibition variety. Rather tall for the border, but easy to grow. H 1.2m (4ft).

Don's Diana (D. Brawn 1975) A deep purple sport from 'Diana Gregory'. It is a good exhibition variety and also does well in the garden. H to 1m (3ft).

Doris Day (Weijers 1952) A bright scarlet small cactus of exhibition quality. Excellent in the garden. Its purple sport is fittingly called 'Doris Knight', and is equally good for garden display and cutting. H to 1m (3ft).

Downham Royal (J.A. Sharp 1972) A purple globular miniature ball that was an outstanding show variety. With the increased tolerance for exhibition miniature balls up to 115mm (4½in), it disappeared from the British showbench as it was much smaller than the 'Cupid' group. However, it still wins in North America where the 'Cupids' are classified as small ball. H to 90cm (3ft).

Dr Caroline Rabbett (P. Tivey 1985) AGM 1995 A small decorative with yellow and orange blooms on strong stems. Rather tall, H usually about 1.4m (4½ft).

Dr John Grainger (A. Lister 1950) Originally classified as miniature ball, this was later re-classified as miniature decorative. One of the leading show varieties of the 1960s with dark orange blooms, it makes a lovely garden plant. H to 1m (3ft).

Duet (Scott 1955) A striking bicolour of blood-red with white tips. The blooms were classified as medium decorative, but are rather small. H to 1.2m (4ft).

Easter Sunday (Bruidegom 1956) A collerette with creamy white blooms on long stems. An excellent garden plant. H to 1m (3ft).

Eastwood Moonlight (J.A. Sharp 1975) Outstanding medium semi-cactus for exhibition, bearing bright yellow blooms on strong stems. A white sport, 'White Moonlight', arose in 1984. Recently it has given rise to a number of primrose sports almost indistinguishable from each other, including 'Lauren's Moonlight' and 'Pim's Moonlight'. H to 1.1m (3½ft).

Ed Lloyd (Ballego 1969) A large decorative exhibition variety with pink blooms held on strong stems. Rather tall but strong growing. H 1.2m (4ft).

Edinburgh (Dobbie 1950) Small decorative with white-tipped purple flowerheads. Less popular than it used to be. H to 1m (3ft).

Edna C. (R.P. Comstock 1968) This yellow medium decorative from America was a sensational show-stopper when it arrived in Britain. The blooms can become too heavy for the stems. H 1.1m (3½ft).

Elizabeth Hammett (K. Hammett 1980) A New Zealand miniature decorative with lilac blooms. Excellent for exhibition. Short in stature, H 90cm (3ft).

Ella Britain (origin unknown) A dwarf bedding dahlia with single yellow-bronze blooms on compact plants. It is an old variety not often seen these days.

Ellen Huston (E. Huston 1975) AGM 1993 This miscellaneous variety, which has dark foliage, is similar to 'Bishop of Llandaff', but has more petals and is shorter. A dwarf bedding variety, it does not require staking. Received the John Brown Medal in 1995 for the best dwarf bedder at Wisley. H usually to 45cm (18in).

Elma Elizabeth (E. Redd 1993) Often abbreviated by exhibitors to 'Elma E' , this is a large decorative from America with deep pink well-formed blooms. It is slightly on the late side so well-grown plants must be planted as early as possible. Grow '4 up' to get the biggest blooms. Now joined by a lavender-pink sport, 'Vera's Elma'. Low grower, H usually 1m (3ft).

Elmdon Hank (A. Ross 1986) AGM 1996 A small decorative with purple well-formed blooms. Makes a fine garden plant. H to 90cm (3ft).

Enfield Salmon (Baynes 1954) A large decorative with rich salmon blooms. An old show variety. H to 1m (3ft).

Ernie Pitt (T. Clarke 1978) A small decorative with well-formed blooms of pink and yellow blends. It has won on the showbench. H about 1m (3ft).

The small decorative 'Edinburgh' has been around for about 50 years and makes a stunning display in the garden.

Evelyn Foster (C. Foster 1971) The finest white, reflexing, medium decorative for form. Slightly late flowering. Now being superseded by 'B.J. Beauty' for showing. H to 1.2m (4ft).

Evelyn Rumbolt (Baynes 1961) A royal-purple giant decorative, a leading exhibition variety in its day. Now rarely seen on the showbench. H 1.2m (4ft).

Evening Mail (G. Brookes 1981) AGM 1993 This giant semi-cactus exhibition variety bears yellow blooms on strong stems. H to 1.2m (4ft).

Exotic Dwarf (Nuyens 1965) A lilliput variety bearing lavender-pink single blooms with darker centres. Good for pots and containers on patios. H to 30cm (12in).

Fascination (Elsdon 1964) AGM 1994 Bearing large semi-double flowerheads of purple-pink, with black foliage, this makes an excellent dwarf bedding variety. Awarded the John Brown Medal for the best dwarf bedder at Wisley in 1996. H to 60cm (24in).

Fashion Monger (origin unknown) A cream collerette with pink stripes and a lemon collar. H to 90cm (3ft).

Fermain (N. Flint 1991) Bearing lovely white and lavender blooms on compact plants, this miniature decorative won a Silver Certificate at the NDS Northern Trials, Leeds. Attractive in gardens. H to 90cm (3ft).

Figaro (V. de Schoot 1938) A dwarf bedder, often grown from seed bearing single, or sometimes semi-double flowers, of mixed colours.

Figurine (W. Tapley 1982) AGM 1995 Small waterlily with blooms of pink and white blends. Very good for cut flowers and garden display. H 1.2m (4ft).

Finchcocks (J. Crutchfield 1994) AGM 1995 A small waterlily with unusual salmon-orange blooms. The petals have split ends but are not fully fimbriated (laciniated). H to 1.2m (4ft).

First Lady (R.P. Comstock 1956) This is an old American variety with yellow, reflexing medium decorative blooms. It is not often seen on the showbench today. H 1m (3ft).

Flutterby (J. Sharp 1963) A small waterlily with pale yellow and red bicolour blooms. H to 1.2m (4ft).

Foreman's Jubilee (Bruidegom 1967) A giant semi-cactus with cardinal-red blooms on strong stems. A striking plant. H to 1.35m (4½ft).

Formby Supreme (G. Harding 1986) A medium decorative exhibition variety with yellow blooms on strong stems. H to 1.2m (4ft).

Frank Holmes (F. Holmes 1976) This ia a classic pom-pon with blooms of lavender blends. Makes a lovely garden plant as well as being ideal for exhibition. H to 1m (3ft).

Frank Hornsey (G.J. Chester 1971) A leading show variety of the 1970s, this orange-yellow small decorative produced a number of sports: 'Pink Frank Hornsey' (1973), 'Yellow Frank Hornsey' (1977) and 'White Frank Hornsey' (1978). These varieties are no longer seen on the showbench, but can make good garden plants. H to 1.2m (4ft).

'Figurine', a waterlily type for cut flowers and garden display, can also win on the showbench.

Gaiety (origin unknown, introduced by R. Aylett) AGM 1997 This is a dwarf bedder of miscellaneous form with blooms in blends of pink. H to 45cm (18in).

Gala Parade (T. Morgan 1996) A pink small decorative from New Zealand, this strong grower makes a good show variety and is also ideal for gardens. H to 1.1m (3½ft).

Galator (1956) A sport of the medium cactus 'Tornado', 'Galator' has orange-red blooms on strong stems. It gave rise to further sports in golds and yellows, namely 'Golden Galator' and 'Yellow Galator'. H 1.2m (4ft).

Garden Festival (D. Reid 1992) Very colourful small waterlily type with red blooms tipped with orange. Excellent for garden display and cut flowers. Ideal for floral decoration. H to 1.2m (4ft).

Garden Party (V. Vlen 1961) AGM 1993 A dwarf bedding variety with orange small cactus blooms. H to 60cm (24in).

Gay Princess (E. Richards 1975) A small waterlily with blooms of lilac-pink. It has rather more petals than is usual for a waterlily type. Makes a beautiful garden plant and excellent for cut flowers. H to 1.5m (5ft).

Geerlings Indian Summer (C. Geerlings 1984) AGM 1993 A small semi-cactus with bright red blooms. An excellent garden plant and ideal for cut flowers. H to 90cm (3ft).

Geerlings Queeny (C. Geerlings 1992) AGM 1994 This is a small cactus with yellow-pink blooms. H to 90cm (3ft).

Gerrie Hoek (Hoek 1945) This small waterlily has pink blooms. A superb cut flower and good for garden display, it can also produce exhibition-quality flowerheads. H to 1m (3ft).

Gipsy Boy (A. Hayes 1981) A large decorative with dark velvet red blooms. A good exhibition variety. Also a lovely garden plant. H to 1m (3ft).

'Gala Parade' is a new small decorative from New Zealand. It is good for show and garden display.

Giraffe (Hoek 1948) An unusual flower belonging to the miscellaneous section and classified as double orchid. The blooms are yellow and bronze, variegated or striped. Much sought after for flower arrangements. The pink sport of this variety is named 'Pink Giraffe' (1961). A low grower, H 1m (3ft).

Glenbank Twinkle (Davison 1982) A miniature cactus bearing bicolour white blooms with red tips. Makes an excellent garden plant. H to 1m (3ft).

Glenvalley Kathy (1996) An American bicolour with small semi-cactus blooms of yellow with red tips. A striking garden plant. H to 1m (3ft).

Glorie van Heemstede (Bakker 1947) A small waterlily with bright yellow flowerheads on excellent stems. Ideal for cut flowers and a fine garden plant, it is also good for exhibition. H to 1m (3ft).

Go American (S. Johnson 1959) A leading giant decorative variety which has been top of the show list for forty years. Its massive blooms are in orange blends. In order to get the blooms up to size it needs to be grown

'4 up'. 'Go American' has now produced a coppery-coloured sport, 'American Copper', of a looser formation. H to 1m (3ft).

Golden Impact (G. Littlejohn 1989) A golden sport of the bronze medium semi-cactus 'Wootton Impact'. H to 1.2m (4ft).

Golden Willo (N. Williams 1961) A corn-coloured pompon from Australia which will win prizes and makes a lovely garden plant with plenty of blooms for cutting. A medium grower, H to 90cm (3ft).

Grace Rushton (C. Rushton 1994) A brilliant orange-red small waterlily. It is early to flower and keeps on producing flowerheads throughout the season. Ideal for cut flowers. H 1.1m (3½ft).

Grand Duc (C. Geerlings 1956) A striking collerette producing red blooms with yellow tips and with a yellow collar of petaloids. A good show variety and also excellent in the garden. H to 1m (3ft).

Grand Willo (N. Williams) A lilac pompon, from the Australian raiser Norman Williams. It is no longer

For many years 'Go American' has been a top giant decorative showing variety.

common, having been replaced by 'Hallmark' from the same raiser. H 1.1m (3½ft).

Grenidor Pastelle (J. Carrington 1988) A very successful medium semi-cactus exhibition variety with blooms of pink and yellow blends. 'Pink Pastelle', a pink sport, arose in 1991, and 'Gill's Pastelle', a white and pink sport, in 1996. H all to about 1.2m (4ft).

Gurtla Twilight (H. Wilkinson 1996) A pompon with a white base and pink blush. Excellent exhibition form. H to 90cm (3ft).

Hallmark (N. Williams 1960) The perfect exhibition pompon producing superb pink globular blooms on strong stems. Makes a good garden plant. 'Hallmark' often fails to make a good tuber by the end of the season, so take out insurance by growing pot tubers from spare cuttings. H to 1m (3ft).

Hamari Accord (H. Ensum 1986) AGM 1994, AM 1997 Top-quality large semi-cactus blooms of bright yellow. Excellent exhibition blooms on long stems. H to 1.2m (4ft).

Hamari Bride (H. Ensum 1968) AGM 1993 A white medium semi-cactus with well-formed blooms on strong stems. Still capable of winning prizes on the showbench. This makes a lovely garden plant. H to 1.2m (4ft).

Hamari Fiesta (H. Ensum 1962) A small decorative, bearing yellow flowerheads with red tips. Makes a striking garden plant and is also ideal for cut flowers. H to 1m (3ft).

Hamari Girl (H. Ensum 1960) A pink giant decorative of exhibition standard, 'Hamari Girl' has featured in winning exhibits for thirty years and is an easy variety for the novice to grow. H to 1m (3ft).

Hamari Gold (H. Ensum 1984) AGM 1993 AM 1996 This is a giant decorative for exhibition. Huge bronze blooms are borne on strong stems. Responds well to deep planting – remove the bottom two pairs of leaves and plant to the level of the third pair. A super garden plant. H to 1m (3ft).

Hamari Katrina (H. Ensum 1972) A large semi-cactus with well-formed pale yellow blooms. A good exhibition variety. A strong grower. The blooms tend to close up in the evening, so avoid using it for evening shows. H to 1.2m (4ft).

Hamari Rose (H. Ensum 1993) AGM 1996 AM 1997 This variety can be grown as a small or miniature ball. If the plants are stopped while still in their pots, and then given a second stop during early summer so that 15 to 18 stems are produced, then show-quality miniature ball-size blooms will be produced. Makes a fine garden plant. H to 1m (3ft).

Hamari Sunshine (H. Ensum 1994) AGM 1997 Bright yellow large decorative with somewhat pointed petal formation that can mimic a semi-cactus. Not yet classified and may remain unclassified because of its intermediate form. Its use as an exhibition variety in top shows is not advisable, but it makes an excellent garden plant. Flowers profusely for a large variety.

Awarded the Stredwick Medal by the NDS as the best garden variety at Wisley in 1997. H to 1m (3ft).

Hamilton Amanda (Hamilton 1994) AM 1994 A yellow small decorative of exhibition standard. H 1.35m (4½ft).

Happy Hanny (C. Geerlings 1985) AGM 1993 A small waterlily with dark pink blooms. It has too many petals to make a good exhibition variety but is excellent for the garden and flowers profusely. H 90cm (3ft).

Harvest Amanda (I. Butterfield 1995) AGM 1997 A lilliput variety with tiny single orange blooms that cover the plants. Excellent for pots and containers. H to about 60cm (2ft).

Harvest Samantha (I. Butterfield 1995) AGM 1996 Similar to 'Harvest Amanda' but with pink blooms. Goes well with 'Harvest Amanda' in pots and containers. Slightly shorter at H 45cm (18in).

Hayley Jane (G. Titchard 1978) A startling small semi-cactus bicolour, producing white blooms tipped with purple. Makes an eye-catching focal point in a garden. Also good for cut flowers. H 1.2m (4ft).

Highgate Robbie (W. Robinson 1967) A well-formed small ball in dark red. A top show type in its day, its stems are hardly strong enough to hold the heavy blooms. Not really a gardener's variety, but one for the specialist exhibitor. H 1m (3ft).

Highgate Torch (W. Robinson 1968) A medium semi-cactus with flame-red blooms. It used to be regarded as a show variety, but now better considered as for gardens. It won an FCC at Wisley in 1980 as the best all-round variety and would grace any garden. H 1.1m (3½ft).

Hillcrest Albino (L. Jackson 1991) AGM 1993 A white medium semi-cactus. Good exhibition variety, also super in the garden. H to 1.2m (4ft).

Hillcrest Blaze (L. Jackson 1992) AGM 1993 A yellow and red bicolour small cactus. A stunning garden plant. H to 1m (3ft).

Hillcrest Carmen (L. Jackson 1998) A small decorative with blooms of lavender blends on strong stems. This exhibition-quality plant is also lovely for gardens and cutting. H to 1m (3ft).

Hillcrest Desire (L. Jackson 1991) AGM 1995 A small cactus with pink and bronze flowerheads. It will produce exhibition blooms and makes a useful garden plant. H to 1.2m (4ft).

Hillcrest Divine (L. Jackson 1998) A miniature decorative of excellent exhibition quality bearing pink blooms on strong stems. H to 1.2m (4ft).

Hillcrest Jessica (L. Jackson 1998) A small golden-flowered decorative. An exhibition variety that also makes a nice garden plant. H to 1m (3ft).

Hillcrest Royal (L. Jackson 1991) AGM 1993 A medium cactus, that can be of exhibition quality, with well-formed purple flowerheads on strong stems. Makes a striking garden plant. H to 1.2m (4ft).

Hillcrest Suffusion (L. Jackson 1991) A small decorative of exhibition quality, having blooms of bronze and peach blends. Makes a pretty garden plant. H to 90cm (3ft).

Hillcrest Ultra (L. Jackson 1993) A small decorative with yellow-pink blooms. An exhibitor's variety. H 1.1m (3½ft).

Holland Herald (Bruidegom 1967) An old large semi-cactus with red blooms on long, strong stems. An exhibition variety in its day but also ideal for cut flowers and as a spot plant in borders. H to 1.2m (4ft).

Honey (Ballego 1956) A dwarf bedder with anemone-type flowerheads of pink and yellow blends. Ideal for pots and containers. H 30–45cm (12–18in).

Honeymoon Dress (L. Jones 1981) Another exhibition small decorative with light pink blooms borne on strong stems. H 90cm (3ft).

'Hillcrest Royal' is a medium cactus that is good for growing in gardens and for showing.

Horn of Plenty (Bruidegom 1959) A miniature decorative with flaming red blooms on wiry stems. Very free-flowering and a lovely garden plant. H to 1.2m (4ft).

Hy Fire (W. Holland 1996) A red small ball from America, which may be better grown as a miniature ball in Britain, but it has exhibition potential. H 1m (3ft).

Ice Cream Beauty (C. Geerlings 1988) AGM 1994 A pale yellow small waterlily, excellent for cut flowers and garden decoration. H 90cm (3ft).

I Lyke It (W. Mark 1996) A small semi-cactus with bright red blooms of exhibition quality. Also makes a nice garden plant. H to 1.2m (4ft).

Ina Spurs (N. Weekes 1970) A red miniature decorative that produces blooms of exhibition quality on strong stems. Its fault is that the flower stems are a little short and thus it is best flowered on the side bud. A strong garden plant. H to 1m (3ft).

Inca Dambuster (G. Brookes 1975) A giant semi-cactus with huge blooms of creamy yellow. They are of good exhibition formation on strong stems. A variety for the expert grower. On the tall side, H often 1.5m (5ft).

Inca Metropolitan (G. Brookes 1978) AGM 1993 A large decorative with yellow blooms of exhibition standard. It makes an excellent plant for the back of the border. H1.2m (4ft).

Inflammation (Ballego 1961) AGM as 'Harvest Inflammation' A lilliput variety with tiny bronze-coloured single blooms. Makes a pretty patio plant for container growing. H to 45cm (18in).

Inglebrook Jill (origin unknown 1996) A trials winner in New Zealand, this collerette has red petals and a red collar. It produces exhibition blooms on strong stems. H 1.1–1.2m (3½–4ft).

Inland Dynasty (Anselmo 1993) Giant yellow semi-cactus blooms of exhibition quality. H to 1.2m (4ft).

Iris (Mann 1974) An excellent pompon of exhibition quality. The purple blooms are of superb form on strong stems. Also makes a lovely garden plant. H to 1m (3ft).

Jackie Magson (W. Mark 1996) A golden-orange small semi-cactus with exhibition potential. Free-flowering, with blooms slightly smaller than its parent 'Andrew Magson', it received a Gold Certificate at the NDS Northern Trials, Leeds and a Bronze Award at the Welsh Trials in 1997. Its bright yellow sport 'Mary Magson' is also free-flowering. Both are good show varieties and make nice garden plants. H to 1.2m (4ft).

Jaldec Joker (D. Hewlett 1991) AGM 1995 A small semi-cactus with red and white bicoloured blooms. An interesting plant for the garden. H to 1.2m (4ft).

Jaldec Jolly (D. Hewlett 1990) AGM 1995 A small cactus with red and white bicoloured blooms. Makes an attractive garden plant. H to 1.2m (4ft).

Jean Lister (A. Lister 1945) A white miniature ball in great demand by flower arrangers during the post-war period. Not readily available today. H 1.1m (3½ft).

Jeanette Carter (E. Carter 1988) AGM 1994 This miniature decorative bears pale yellow blooms overlaid with rose-lavender. It will produce show blooms and is a useful garden dahlia. H to 1.1m (3½ft).

The lilliput variety 'Inflammation' is ideal for borders and growing in containers.

Jennie (P. Traff 1993) A medium semi-cactus from America bearing fimbriated (laciniated) blooms with a cream base and pink margins. A delightful garden plant, it will also produce show blooms for fimbriated classes. H about 1.2m (4ft).

Jescot Julie (E. Cooper 1974) A similar type of dahlia to 'Giraffe'. The double orchid blooms, in orange and purple blends, are in great demand for flower arranging. H to about 90cm (3ft).

Jessica (Hale 1988) A small semi-cactus with bright yellow bicoloured blooms tipped in red. An excellent focal plant in any garden display. H to about 1m (3ft).

Jessica Crutchfield (J. Crutchfield 1988) AGM 1995 A yellow small waterlily. Excellent for cut flowers and for garden decoration. Grows to medium height. H 1.2m (4ft).

'Kenora Sunset' is a striking bicoloured medium cactus making a fine display in the garden.

Jessie G. (J. Connell 1994) A miniature ball with well-formed purple blooms. A good exhibition variety from America, slightly small for British show requirements. H usually makes 1.4m (4½ft).

Jessie Ross (A. Lister) A miniature decorative dwarf bedder. The rose-pink blooms are held on compact plants. H to about 35cm (14in).

Jill's Delight (Dr Lester 1989) A medium-flowered decorative with pink blooms. H to 1.35cm (4½ft).

Jim Branigan (A. Branigan 1981) A large semi-cactus with bright red blooms. A good exhibition variety. H to 1.35m (4½ft).

John Street (J. Crutchfield 1977) AGM 1994 A small waterlily with bright red flowerheads on long stems. Ideal for cut flowers and, as this is a rather tall grower, it is a good plant for the back of a border. H usually about 1.5m (5ft).

Jo's Choice (J. Sharpe 1959) A red miniature decorative which was the top miniature decorative exhibition variety of its day. Also makes a beautiful garden plant. Medium height, H perhaps 1.05m (3½ft).

Jura (C. Geerlings 1988) A strong bicoloured small semi-cactus very similar to 'Hayley Jane'; white flowerheads with purple tips. H to 1.2m (4ft).

Karenglen (G. Woolcock 1990) AGM 1994 AM 1996 This is the top miniature decorative for exhibition. The well-formed scarlet blooms are produced on strong stems. Well-grown plants tend to produce oversize blooms, but the variety responds well to double stopping, when larger numbers of slightly smaller blooms will result. H to about 1.2m (4ft).

Kathleen's Alliance (K. Davison 1989) AGM This is a pink sport from the excellent small cactus 'Shirley Alliance'. A prolific flowerer. H about 1m (3ft).

Kelsae's Carla (A. Hindle 1996) A small cactus with pink exhibition-quality blooms. Received a Silver Award for exhibition potential at the Welsh Dahlia Trials in 1997 and at Leeds in 1998. A good grower.

Keltie (A.T. Barnes 1960) A small decorative with deep orange-red blooms of good formation. One of the first formal small decoratives to be raised, it is now well surpassed by a new generation and may be difficult to find these days. H 1m (3ft).

Kelvin Floodlight (McDougall 1961) One of the leading giant decoratives to come from Australia, this has huge yellow blooms with strong stems and is easy to grow. H to 1.35m (4½ft).

Kenora Challenger (G. Leroux 1991) A large semi-cactus with well-formed white blooms of superb exhibition quality – *the* semi-cactus in its class. Most exhibitors rogue their stocks to avoid those that produce short plants. H about 1.2m (4ft) tall.

Kenora Christmas (G. Leroux 1993) A small decorative with well-formed bright red blooms. A good exhibition variety, and also makes an ideal garden plant. Slightly late flowering, so well-grown plants need to be put out early to make the early shows. H to 1.3m (4¼ft).

Kenora Frills (G. Leroux 1996) A medium semi-cactus with dark pink fimbriated (laciniated) blooms on strong stems. It makes a large bush. H 1.2m (4ft).

Kenora Sunset (G. Leroux 1996) A medium semi-cactus with yellow-centred brilliant red blooms. Young flowerheads are a distinct bicolour but as they age, the red tipping suffuses along the petals blending the colours together. A spectacular garden plant that will produce blooms of show quality. H to 1.2m (4ft).

Kenora Superb (G. Leroux 1992) A large semi-cactus with orange-yellow flowerheads held on strong stems. It will produce exhibition blooms and also makes a lovely garden plant. H to 1.05m (3½ft) tall.

Kenora Valentine (G. Leroux 1990) AGM 1996 AM 1996 Classified as a large decorative, the bright red blooms of 'Kenora Valentine' will make giant size if restricted. An excellent show variety and a very good garden plant. H to 1.2m (4ft).

Kidd's Climax (Kidd 1940) AGM 1995 A giant decorative that has been a top exhibition variety for nearly sixty years. Classified as only large in America, it needs extra attention to make giant size. The form of its pink and yellow blooms is excellent for showing, and it often wins prizes against bigger but less high-quality exhibits. Makes a good garden plant. H to 1m (3ft).

King Soccer (Bruidegom 1970) A medium decorative with orange-yellow blooms. An exhibition variety, not the easiest to grow, but a winner if grown well; not recommended for a novice. H 1.1m (3½ft).

Kiwi Brother (E. Durrant 1975) A showman's variety with pink-bronze small semi-cactus blooms of excellent formation. H about 1.05m (3½ft).

Kiwi Gloria (E. Durrant 1988) The small cactus blooms of pale lavender do not stand out, but the formation is extremely fine, making this probably the best show variety of all and a regular winner of 'Best in Show' awards. However, it is an exhibitor's flower and not easy to grow to show standards. It is slightly late flowering for the garden. There are a number of sports, eagerly sought by exhibitors: 'Deborah's Kiwi' (1996) is lavender-pink and 'Trelyn Kiwi' (1997) is white with a faint lavender flush. H to 1m (3ft).

Klankstad Kerkrade (Bruidegom 1954) Together with its sports, this small cactus variety, known affectionately as 'KK', dominated shows until 'Kiwi Gloria' came along. Its pale yellow blooms of superb form can still win prizes and it makes an attractive garden plant. It has produced the following sports: 'White Klankstad' (1967), 'Majestic Kerkrade' (1973) pink and yellow, 'Pink Kerkrade' (1987) and 'Lady Kerkrade' (1987) lavender and white blends. All are similar in habit and make lovely garden plants. H to 1m (3ft).

Kotari Jackpot (P. Burrell 1996) A small semi-cactus with vivid scarlet-red blooms. Difficult to get to exhibition standard as the flowerheads are slightly small for its class. An outstanding garden plant. H to 90cm (3ft).

Kotari Magic (P. Burrell 1998) This small decorative, recently introduced from New Zealand, has blood-red blooms on strong stems and makes a good exhibition variety. H 1m (3ft).

Kung Fu (N. Lewis 1976) A red small decorative which produces exhibition-quality blooms. Rather a tall grower, H often 1.8m (6ft).

'Kenora Superb' is a large semi-cactus that is good for the garden and for exhibition.

'Kiwi Gloria' (p.117) is one of the top exhibition small cactus dahlias but needs experience to grow well.

L'Ancresse (N. Flint 1982) A white miniature ball with excellent exhibition-quality blooms. H to about 1.3m (4½ft).

La Cierva (Entrup 1939) A collerette with purple petals, tipped with white, and a white collar. A show variety that also looks effective in the garden. H 90cm (3ft).

Lady Linda (N. Lewis 1980) A small decorative with lavender-tipped, yellow blooms. Excellent for exhibition and also ideal for cut flowers. H to 1.05m (3½ft).

Lady Sunshine (Ballego 1970) A small semi-cactus with clear yellow blooms on strong stems. A good strong bush, it is a useful garden plant and is also ideal for cutting. H about 1.2m (4ft).

Laura Marie (N. Lewis 1988) This is a red miniature ball with exhibition blooms held on long stems. It is suitable for cutting and ideal for garden decoration. H to 1.2m (4ft).

Lavender Perfection (H. Johnston 1941) An old New Zealand variety with rich lavender giant decorative blooms held on strong stems. Easy to grow. H reaching 1.2m (4ft).

Lavengro (A.T. Barnes 1953) A giant decorative of somewhat loose formation with lavender and bronze blooms. Of historical rather than cultural interest, it is not seen very much on the showbench today except in multi-vase classes. H to about 1.5m (5ft).

Lemon Elegans (C. Geerlings 1988) AGM 1995 AM 1996 A pale yellow small semi-cactus capable of producing fine exhibition-quality blooms. Does well as a garden plant and has a compact habit. A cream sport 'Cream Elegans' has recently appeared. H to about 90cm (3ft).

Liberator (Harris 1941) A bright red giant decorative from Australia, originally called 'Pop Harris', after its raiser, when it first came out. A variety for the specialist giant decorative grower. H to 1.2m (4ft).

Light Music (Bruidegom 1966) A Dutch introduction in the large-flowered cactus class. Its lilac blooms are held on strong stems. Great for exhibition and cut flowers. A rather tall grower.

Linda's Chester (J. Watson 1991) A small-flowered cactus with yellow blooms tipped with orange-bronze. Good for exhibition, cut flowers and garden display. H to 1.2m (4ft).

Lismore Moonlight (W. Franklin 1998) A bright yellow pompon of exhibition quality. Awarded best in seedling class in the Scottish National Show in 1996. H to 1.05m (3½ft).

Lismore Peggy (W. Franklin 1985) A pompon with blooms in pink blends. Suitable for exhibition, cutting and garden display. H to 1.05m (3½ft).

Lismore Willie (W. Franklin 1992) A small waterlily with pale gold blooms of exhibition quality. Grows rather tall and so needs firm staking. Has strong stems and is good for cutting. H 1.5m (5ft).

Little Glenfern (raiser unknown 1980) An Australian variety with yellow well-formed blooms, classified as miniature cactus. An excellent garden plant that produces masses of blooms for cutting. Will produce show blooms. H 1.1m (3½ft).

Little Sally (J. Greggs 1961) This Australian introduction is a pompon with vivid orange-scarlet blooms and makes an excellent garden display. It was once regarded as a show bloom but has now been superseded. H to 90cm (3ft).

Little William (Bruidegom c1954) This would now be classified as a miniature ball although when originally released it would have been regarded as a medium or large pompon. It has striking blooms of reddish-purple with white tips. A low grower, it makes a useful dwarf bedding plant. H rarely exceeding 70cm (28in).

Lloyd Huston (E. Huston 1983) A bronze giant semi-cactus from Canada, this is a top show variety for the specialist. A slightly tall grower. H 1.2m (4ft).

Loretta (C. Geerlings 1996) A miniature decorative with lilac-purple blooms. Good for show. Received a Silver Certificate at the NDS Northern Trials, Leeds, in 1997. H 1.1m (3½ft).

Loud Applause (Lindhout 1993) AGM 1993 A medium semi-cactus with yellow blooms on strong stems. Lovely garden plant and excellent for cut flowers. H 1.2m (4ft).

Lula Pattie (R.P. Comstock 1960) A huge giant decorative with white informal decorative blooms. One of the biggest giants available, it lacks the form to be a top competitor in Britain, but still wins prizes in North America, where big giants are popular. H 1.1m (3½ft).

Mabel Ann (R. Adley 1995) This bronze giant decorative of good form is a seedling from the giant 'Bonaventure'. An ideal show variety. Slightly shorter than its parent, H 1.3m (4½ft).

Maisie Mooney (Mooney 1994) Classified as large decorative in America but a giant in Britain. The white informal decorative blooms of 'Maisie Mooney' have won prizes in giant classes but it needs the skills of a specialist grower to achieve its potential. H 1.1m (3½ft).

Maltby Fanfare (Cunnard 1995) A new collerette from New Zealand. It has white-tipped purple blooms

'Lula Patte' is one of the biggest giant decorative types from America.

and a white collar. They are of exhibition quality on strong stems. A good grower, making an attractive plant. H 1.2m (4ft).

Margaret Anne (T. Clarke 1977) A primrose-yellow miniature decorative. Good for exhibition and also very free-flowering, thus making a lovely garden plant. Stems are a little short for cut flowers. H to 1m (3ft).

Mariner's Light (J. Sharp 1970) AGM 1994 A small-flowered semi-cactus with yellow blooms. A good exhibition variety but also does well as a garden plant. H to 1.1m (3½ft).

Mariposa (Topsvoort 1958) A collerette bearing flowerheads with lilac-pink petals and white collars. A good show variety and useful for garden display. H 1m (3ft).

Mark Hardwick (M. Hardwick 1985) A giant decorative with yellow blooms of show quality. An exhibitor's variety needing skill to get the best results. Short and compact. H to 1m (3ft).

Marlene Joy (L. Steenfort 1989) A medium semi-cactus with white blooms tipped with pink. A true bicolour with fimbriated (laciniated) petals. The plant is good for garden display and also for cut flowers. H to about 1.2m (4ft).

Mary Partridge (C. Geerlings 1991) A small waterlily with reddish purple blooms on strong stems. Slightly shorter than most waterlily varieties. H to 1m (3ft).

Mary Pitt (E. Pitt 1991) A miniature decorative bearing white blooms with a faint pink blush. An exhibition variety, very similar to 'Abridge Taffy'. H to 1.1m (3½ft).

Mary Richards (A. Drewett 1952) An old small decorative with white blooms flushed with pink, darkening to pink tips. Seen on the showbench in the past, its informal blooms cannot compete with the modern formal types. Good for garden display and its strong stems make it ideal for cut flowers. H to 1.2m (4ft).

Mascot Maya (S. Mellen 1992) A yellow medium decorative exhibition variety. Its blooms are virtually indistinguishable from those of 'Charlie Two'. H to 1.2m (4ft).

Match (A. Hindry 1965) When this small red and white bicolour semi-cactus was first introduced from South Africa it raised quite a stir. Today there are a number of similar varieties (see 'Jura', 'Hayley Jane' and 'Glenbank Twinkle'). 'Match' is tallest. An ideal plant for the back of the border. H to 1.2m (4ft).

Minley Carol (W. Wilkins 1983) A pompon with red and yellow blends. Good for exhibition and for garden display. Has given rise to some sports, such as 'Red Carol' (1994). H 1.1m (3½ft).

Minley Linda (W. Wilkins 1983) A reddish orange pompon, ideal for exhibition and garden use. Usually needs disbudding to make full size. H to 1m (3ft).

Misthill Contessa (F. Currie 1996) A miniature decorative with orange blooms that will do well on the showbench or in the garden. Received a Bronze Certificate at the NDS Northern Trials, Leeds, in 1996. H to 1m (3ft).

Misthill Delight (F. Currie 1974) A miniature decorative bearing white blooms with a pink flush at the centre. An all-round variety that will produce exhibition blooms. H to 1.2m (4ft).

Mistral (R. Surber 1996) An unusual fimbriated (laciniated) medium cactus with purple and pale yellow blooms. H 1.1m (3½ft).

Mme. Stappers (origin unknown) A dwarf bedding variety with red single blooms. Not often seen these days, but still grown for bedding displays at Anglesey Abbey in Cambridgeshire.

Molly Mooney (Mooney 1997) A new small cactus/semi-cactus from Canada. Its well-formed yellow blooms are borne on compact plants. H to 1m (3ft).

Monkstown Diane (B. Fowler 1994) A small cactus with bright pink blooms of exhibition quality. Awarded a Bronze Certificate at the NDS Northern Trials, Leeds, in 1994. H to 1.2m (4ft).

Moonfire (origin unknown) An old dwarf bedding variety producing single blooms of deep gold with red centres and bronze foliage. H to 75cm (30in).

Moor Place (Newnham 1957) A purple pompon of perfect form, this has been a top exhibition variety since it first came out. It is slightly late to flower and hence well-grown plants should be planted out as early as frosts allow. Early blooms tend to go oversize and plants should be double stopped to produce sufficient breaks. Some exhibitors use split tubers for propagation rather than cuttings in attempt to get them into flower early. Some sports have been recorded but few differ significantly from the original; one that is sufficiently distinct is 'Wendy's Place'. H about 90cm (3ft).

Mrs A. Woods (Buckhaven 1955) An old Australian variety that was a leading exhibition dahlia in its time, but now rarely seen. A medium decorative with deep rich mauve blooms of good quality. H to 1.2m (4ft).

Mrs McDonald Quill (Douglas 1954) An old New Zealand variety, much seen at shows during its heyday. A large decorative with red-tipped white bicoloured blooms. Rather tall, H 1.4m (4½ft).

Naargold (C. Higgo 1994) An orange medium semi-cactus with fimbriated (laciniated) blooms. Does well in classes for fimbriated varieties. H 1.1m (3½ft).

Nantenan (Bruidegom 1961) A veteran show variety from Holland, 'Nantenan' set the standard for many years. Large semi-cactus bright yellow blooms are held on great stems. H to 1.2m (4ft).

Nationwide (J.H. Stanners 1980) AGM 1994 A small decorative with bronze flowerheads. Produces show blooms but also excellent for gardens. H to 1.3m (4½ft).

Nellie Birch (origin unknown) Now classified as a miniature ball, but originally a large pompon, this has very dark red blooms of excellent quality. With no large pom classes available at shows, it cannot compete with modern miniature balls and has disappeared from the show scene. Excellent as a garden plant and for cut flowers. H 1.1m (3½ft)

Nenekazi (C. Higgo 1997) A medium semi-cactus with fimbriated (laciniated) blooms. The blooms are pink with coral and red edges. A great eye-catching variety for the garden but also provides show blooms for fimbriated (laciniated) classes. A strong grower. H about 1.2m (4ft).

'Moor Place' is a very reliable exhibition pompon that has been grown all over the world for many years.

Neon City (K. Hammett 1991) A small or miniature pink decorative from New Zealand. As an in-between variety, it gives problems for exhibitors. Useful for cut flowers. H to 1.2m (4ft)

Nepos (Lombaert 1958) A small waterlily dahlia that produces white flowerheads suffused and tipped with pink. Ideal for cutting and gardens. H to 90cm (3ft).

Nettie (T. Clarke 1966) A miniature ball, once the top variety in its class. Its clear yellow blooms are held on strong stems. It is still popular in America, as is 'White Nettie', the sport it gave rise to in 1974. H to 1m (3ft).

Neveric (N. Weekes 1976) A large-flowered semi-cactus with well-formed orange-yellow blooms of exhibition quality. H 1.2m (4ft).

Newby (J. Barwise 1951) An old miniature decorative variety with orange-pink blooms on strong stems.

Introduced about 40 years ago, 'Noreen' is a good exhibition pompon type.

Good for cut flowers. It has produced a number of sports such as 'Rose Newby'. H to 1.2m (4ft).

Newchurch (J. Barwise 1959) Another old miniature decorative with salmon blooms. Very floriferous; ideal for cut flowers – an arranger's dream. H to 1m (3ft).

Nicola (T. Clarke 1968) A white-flowered small semi-cactus. Very free-flowering and an excellent garden plant. Also ideal for cut flowers. H to 1.2m (4ft).

Night Editor (Hulin 1952) This purple-flowered giant decorative is from North America where giants are big. Good stock may be difficult to find and might be most easily obtained by consulting a specialist giant decorative exhibitor.

Nijinsky (G. Flood 1970) A small ball variety with purple-cerise blooms. An exhibition dahlia, it requires some skill to produce the best blooms. A strong bushy grower. H 1.2m (4ft) tall.

Nina Chester (G.J. Chester 1974) One of the first small decoratives with the tight formation now regarded as essential for exhibition, 'Nina Chester' was a top show variety for many years. Its white blooms have a faint pink blush in the centre. It is still grown

and shown locally, but now rarely seen at national shows. H to 1m (3ft).

Noreen (J. Baggs 1962) An outstanding show variety from Australia, where many of the best pompons have originated. A pink pom with purple markings on excellent stems. Matching blooms for colour is often a problem and centres are also variable, but when it comes good it is a sure prize winner. H to about 1m (3ft).

Nunton Harvest (raiser unknown 1964) A small decorative with orange-bronze formal blooms on long, strong stems. A good exhibition variety but rather a tall grower. H 1.2m (4ft).

Omo (origin unknown) AGM 1996 One of the earliest of the lilliput types to be introduced, 'Omo' bears single white blooms with a yellow disc about 5cm (2in) in diameter. Ideal for pots or containers on the patio. H rarely more than 45cm (18in).

Opal (Allyn 1961) An Australian small ball variety with pink-white blooms. The excellent quality of the flowerheads makes it a good exhibition variety. Also ideal for cut flowers. H 1.1m (3½ft).

Orange Mullet (origin unknown) AGM 1994 This miniature decorative with its orange flowerheads first received attention in 1992 with the revival of interest in dwarf bedding types. It can be grown in borders or containers and is a reliable bloomer, flowering continuously if regularly deadheaded. H 45–60cm (18–24in).

Orel (origin unknown 1993) This collerette arrived in Britain via the Czech Republic. It has pale purple-red petals and a white collar. A good exhibition variety, it is also a fine garden plant. H to about 1m (3ft).

Oreti Duke (W. Jack 1996) A recent arrival from New Zealand, 'Oreti Duke' has already won prizes as an exhibition variety. It is a pompon with violet blooms on a white base. H to 1m (3ft).

Park Princess (D. Maarse 1959) This classic dwarf bedder, which flowers continuously until the autumn frosts, was much used in public parks and gardens where its short stature meant it needed no staking. It has small cactus blooms of a delicate pink. Parks and gardens no longer put on such displays, but the variety is still popular in domestic gardens. H 45–60cm (18–24in).

Paul Chester (G.J. Chester 1966) A small cactus with blooms of orange and yellow blends. Excellent exhibition variety. It produced a number of sports including: 'Lemon Chester', 'Yellow Chester' and 'Linda's Chester' (similar to 'Paul Chester') which in turn gave rise to 'Yellow Linda's Chester'. H to 1m (3ft).

Paul Critchley (Critchley 1961) An old British-raised large-flowered cactus with dark pink blooms held on strong stems. It used to do well as a show variety but now does not compete with the large semi-cactus varieties of today. H to about 1.2m (4ft).

Pearl of Heemstede (C. Geerlings 1990) AGM 1993 A small waterlily with silvery pink blooms on strong stems. Excellent for cut flowers and garden display. H to 90cm (3ft).

Pembroke Pattie (A.G. Davies 1996) A purple pompon with a good pedigree, as a seedling from 'Willo's Violet'. It produces a massive bush with blooms held on strong stems. An exhibition variety, also useful in the garden and for cutting. H 1.2m (4ft).

Penhill Moonrise (W. Maritz 1998) A massive new giant decorative from South Africa, this has yellow blooms but is rather a low grower. 'Penhill Moonrise' finds it difficult to compete with the many yellow giants already established and it is a variety for the specialist. Grown '7 up' it makes a lovely garden plant. H 1.1m (3½ft).

Pensford Marion (F. Newbery) A flame-coloured pompon on strong stems. It has excellent form, as would be expected from a variety raised by one of the leading pom exhibitors of our time. Its long stems make it good for cutting, but it is rather tall for the garden. H usually to 1.3m (4½ft).

Periton (T. Waddle 1991) A dark red miniature ball with good form making a useful exhibition variety. The strong plants look well in the garden. H to 1.2m (4ft).

Phill's Pink (J. Kinns 1970) AGM 1995 A small decorative with pink blooms on very good stems. Very similar to a waterlily type but with more petals. Makes an excellent cut flower and also a lovely garden plant. H 1.2m (4ft).

Phoenix (R. Turrell 1989) A medium decorative with good flowerheads held on strong stems. The colour is blends of pink and the blooms are of exhibition quality. It is a strong-growing plant. H about 1.2m (4ft).

Pineapple Lollipop (P. Traff 1991) An American variety classified as miniature decorative in America, but rather small for British shows. An in-between variety, its ball-shaped blooms would not look out of place in a ball class. Very free-flowering and thus ideal in the border. H 1.1m (3½ft).

Piperoo (origin unknown) A decorative variety with unusual pale pink blooms striped with red. Grows to about 1m (3ft).

Piper's Pink (C. Piper 1964) AGM 1993 Pink semi-cactus blooms on a strong grower. It is an excellent dwarf bedder, although slightly taller than most, and also an ideal plant for the middle of a border. H 90cm (3ft) or more in good growing conditions.

Playboy (A. Hayes 1975) A yellow giant decorative which has been winning prizes for over twenty years. An exhibitor's variety. H to 1m (3ft).

Polar Sight (D. Maarse 1960) One of the few giant true cactus varieties available. (Most of the giants of today are semi-cactus, the preferred formation for show.) The white blooms are held on long stems. Stock may be difficult to find. H 1.2m (4ft).

Polventon Supreme (C. Watkins 1992) A yellow small ball on strong stems. This is a leading exhibition variety, but it has to be grown well otherwise the blooms become big and coarse. The white sport it has recently produced complements it for multi-vase classes. H to 1m (3ft).

Polyand (T. Young 1953) From Australia, this variety made an immediate impact on the showbench. Its large

PLATE IX

POMPON DAHLIAS

'Minley Linda'

'Red Carol'

'Moor Place'

'Willo's Violet'

All flowers are shown at approximately life size

'Dana Frank'

'Frank Holmes'

'Pensford Marion'

'Noreen'

'Hallmark'

'Dana Alice'

The blackish foliage of 'Preston Park' sets off the flowers of this single-flowered dwarf bedding variety.

decorative lavender blooms of excellent form can go oversize and become coarse unless carefully grown. They also have a tendency to face downwards; serious exhibitors prop them up with cotton wool balls on small canes to achieve the correct angle for shows. This is an exhibitor's variety and is not suitable for gardens as it grows too tall. H to about 1.3m (4½ft).

Pontiac (N. J. van Oostens 1958) A small-flowered cactus with bright carmine overlaid salmon blooms. A good variety for the garden and also for cut flowers. H about 1.2m (4ft) tall.

Pop Willo (N. Williams 1971) A pompon with yellow blooms flushed orange. A show variety: one for the expert grower. H to 1m (3ft).

Porcelain (J. Crutchfield 1969) AGM 1995 A small waterlily with white-lilac blooms on strong stems. Excellent for cut flowers but a little tall for borders. H to 1.5m (5ft).

Preston Park (J. Crutchfield 1969) Scarlet single flowerheads with yellow centres, and blackish foliage, make this dwarf bedder a spectacular sight. It is also suitable for growing in containers on a patio. Named after the public park in Brighton. H 45–60cm (18–24in).

Pride of Berlin (Schwiglowski 1914) An old miniature ball with lilac blooms on strong stems. Originally called 'Stolze von Berlin'. A good garden plant and for cut flowers. H 1m (3ft).

Princess Marie Jose (West c1946) A dwarf bedder with single lilac blooms. In its day, one of the reliable bedders of public parks. H 60cm (24in).

Pwll Coch (I. Treseder 1961) A small semi-cactus with brilliant red blooms. An excellent variety for garden display. H to 1m (3ft).

Quel Diable (Bruidegom 1968) As its name implies, this Dutch variety is quite a sight with large semi-cactus blooms of flame-red on long stems. It looks particularly fine in the back of the border. A recent sport 'Gold Diable' will complement it. Both varieties are excellent for cutting. H to about 1.2m (4ft).

Red Balloon (C. Geerlings 1996) A small ball from Holland. It has excellent exhibition form with dark red blooms on strong stems. H to 1–1.1m (3–3½ft).

Red Velvet (Clark 1962) This small waterlily from Australia has red blooms with gold centres. A good garden plant, it is also ideal for cutting. H 90cm (3ft).

Reddy (origin unknown) A lilliput variety that was noticed during the early 1990s. 'Reddy' has single red blooms. Ideal for containers. H 30–45cm (12–18in).

Reginald Keene (G. Flood 1974) Classified as a large semi-cactus in Britain, but regarded as medium in the North American list. 'Reginald Keene' has show-quality blooms of orange and red blends on excellent stems. Still a top exhibition variety, it needs careful growing to achieve its full potential. Keen exhibitors rogue their stock each year because the vigour tends to reduce. It has given rise to a succession of sports, which are in great demand for use in multi-vase classes.

'Candy Keene' (1976) is slightly smaller than its parent and could have been classified as a medium. 'Salmon Keene' (1978) is slightly bigger than 'Reginald Keene'. 'Cryfield Keene' (1991) is light pink. A yellow sport 'Starlight Keene' arrived in 1995. A white sport of 'Cryfield Keene' appeared in 1995 but is no longer available. However, another white sport arose in 1995, this time from 'Salmon Keene'. This excellent sport is 'Chloe's Keene'. 'Reginald Keene' was the result of a cross between the large semi-cactus 'Quel Diable' and the medium semi-cactus 'Autumn Fire', which confirms its size as intermediate between large and medium. H varies from 1–1.2m (3–4ft).

Respectable (Ballego 1962) This orange-flowered giant semi-cactus variety ruled the showbenches for many years. Today, it does not compete with the 'Jupiters' and is thus rarely seen. H 1m (3ft).

Reverend Colwyn Vale (Parker 1954) A purple small ball that has been a leading show variety for many years. It and its lavender sport, 'Bernard C. Hayes', are rather tall. H over 1.5m (5ft) in some situations.

Rhonda (M. Rumble 1947) Another Australian pompons that has done well on the showbench. 'Rhonda' has blooms of perfect form in lilac and white blends. It may require disbudding to bring it up to size. Like many of the classic poms it often makes a poor tuber, and spare cuttings should be raised as pot tubers to ensure survival of the stock. H rarely exceeding 90cm (3ft).

Richard Marc (G.J. Chester 1968) This small cactus was a leading exhibition variety. Its yellow-pink blooms are of excellent form. A number of sports with similar excellent show qualities have arisen from it, among them 'Monk Marc' and 'Pink Marc', both pink. H to 1.1m (3½ft), 'Monk Marc' is more vigorous at about 1.2m (4ft).

Riisa (L. Connell 1996) A miniature ball with well-formed red blooms. It is very free-flowering and produces blooms of exhibition quality. H to about 1.2m (4ft).

Recently introduced from North America, the miniature ball 'Riisa' has excellent form and good exhibition potential.

Risca Miner (T. Clarke 1977) A purple small ball of good formation named after the popular Miners Show at Risca, South Wales, during the 1970s. The blooms are on the small side compared with more recent varieties; for the showbench, the stems need to be heavily disbudded. H to 1.1m (3½ft).

Rokesley Mini (A.R. Wood 1971) AGM 1995 A white miniature cactus of very fine formation, but like many miniature cactus varieties, difficult to keep below the show limit of 11.5cm (4½in). It makes an excellent garden plant. H to 1m (3ft).

Rossendale Tara (D. Kershaw 1997) A yellow miniature decorative that won awards in the NDS Northern Trials, Leeds, and the Welsh Trials in 1997. A variety for exhibitions and garden display. H to 1m (3ft).

Rothsay Reveller (A. Lister 1954) A medium decorative variety with purple blooms with a white tip. A striking spot plant in the garden, but the tipping is variable and thus does not make it easy to match blooms for exhibition. Moreover, it is not easy to make blooms of show size. H about 1.3m (4ft).

Rothsay Robin (A. Lister 1968) A small decorative with magenta blooms. When first released, it was regarded as the perfect exhibition dahlia, but it has now been displaced by the tight formal yellow small decoratives like 'Ruskin Diane'. H 1.1m (3½ft).

Rothsay Superb (A. Lister 1956) A red miniature ball, once a top show variety but nowadays considered slightly small. It makes a very good garden plant and is also in demand by flower arrangers. H to 1.2m (4ft).

Rotterdam (Bruidegom 1961) A deep velvety red medium semi-cactus. Makes an ideal spot plant in borders. Excellent for cut flowers. One of the best reds ever produced. H to about 1.3m (4½ft).

Ruby Wedding (S.C. Long 1981) A red miniature decorative type with well-formed blooms on strong stems. An all-round variety for show, garden decoration and cut flowers. H to 90 cm (3ft).

Ruskin Belle (S. Pennington 1987) A deep purplish pink medium semi-cactus. Good for show and also as a garden plant. H to 1.2m (4ft) tall.

Ruskin Diane (S. Pennington 1984) One of the top small decorative exhibition varieties. It has yellow blooms of tightly reflexing form held on strong stems. It is easy to grow and makes a compact bush. A variety with slightly paler blooms called 'Primrose Diane' has been released, but whether it is sufficiently distinct is open to question. H to 1.1m (3½ft).

Rustig (A. Hindry 1970) A yellow medium informal decorative that came from South Africa. It was a leading show variety during the 1970s but is now largely

superseded. Makes a strong plant. Its white sport 'White Rustig', which appeared in 1979, was equally popular as a show variety. H 1.2m (4ft).

Salsa (Verwer 1989) AGM 1993 A very free-flowering red miniature decorative. A good garden plant and ideal for cutting. H to 1.2m (4ft).

Sam Huston (E. Huston 1994) An orange giant decorative from America. Good for exhibition. Rather tall for garden use. H between 1.2m and 1.5m (4–5ft).

Schweitzer's Kokarde (Schweitzer 1963) A miniature decorative dahlia with orange blooms on long strong stems. Very popular with flower arrangers and for cutting. 'Scarlet Kokarde' is a red sport. Rather a tall grower, H to 1.4m (4½ft).

Senzoe Ursula (H. Zobel 1985) A small decorative once popular as an exhibition variety. It has well-formed blooms of lavender and white, but the stems are rather weak. Needs special treatment by the exhibitor to strengthen them. H to about 1.2m (4ft).

Shandy (J. Crutchfield 1972) Small-flowered semi-cactus with orange-pink blooms. An excellent garden variety, it received the Stredwick Medal at Wisley in 1989 for the best variety in the trial. H 1.05m (3¼ft).

Sherwood Titan (R. Marshall 1983) A giant decorative with huge orange-bronze blooms. An exhibition variety. H to 1.35m (4½ft).

Shirley Alliance (W.E. Hall 1977) A small-flowered cactus with well-formed orange-gold blooms. An excellent exhibition variety, also ideal for garden display. 'Pink Shirley Alliance' is a pink sport that arose in 1980. Grows slightly taller than its parent. H to 1m (3ft).

Shy Princess (K. Fleckney 1981) A white true cactus with medium blooms on long stems. A good exhibition variety, also suitable for cut flowers. Rather a tall grower. H 1.2m (4ft).

'Skipley Spot' is a striking bicolour and is excellent for growing in the garden.

Siemen Doorenbos (Ballego 1943) A dwarf bedding variety with lavender-pink anemone-type blooms. H 30–45cm (12–18in).

Silver City (Brother Simplicius 1967) A large decorative of superb exhibition form that still wins prizes on the showbench. It is rather tall for garden use, H between 1.2m and 1.5m (4–5ft).

Skipley Spot (R. Williams 1989) A small decorative with unusual coloration: the red blooms are tipped with white, making a very attractive garden plant. An American novelty. H to about 1.2m (4ft).

Small World (N. Williams 1967) Another top exhibition variety from Australia. Its perfectly formed white pompon blooms are held on excellent stems. 'Bowen' from North America is virtually indistinguishable from it. H to 1m (3ft).

Snip (W. White 1978) This bronze miniature semi-cactus from North America makes a strong bush and is

'So Dainty' is a miniature semi-cactus that is good for growing in the garden and for cutting.

an excellent garden plant. Its blooms are slightly large for the British exhibition size limit. A pink sport has recently been discovered. H about 1.2m (4ft).

Snoho Peggy (W. Bonneywell 1996) A small ball with dark pink blooms. A recently introduced North American variety, this has show-quality blooms and is a strong grower. H 1.2m (4ft).

Snowy (C. Geerlings 1997) A small ball variety with white exhibition-quality blooms. H to 1m (3ft).

So Dainty (E. Richards 1971) AGM 1993 A miniature semi-cactus with bronze-coloured blooms. A strong grower making a bush H 1.05m (3¼ft).

Suffolk Bride (G. Flood 1974) A white medium semi-cactus that produces exhibition blooms. Now not often seen on the showbench. H 1.1m (3½ft).

Suffolk Punch (G. Flood 1975) A medium decorative with wine-red blooms and bronze foliage. A lovely garden plant. H to 1.2m (4ft).

Sure Thing (Bruidegom 1966) A medium true cactus with scarlet blooms on strong stems. The flowerheads are well formed but cannot compete with the modern medium semi-cactus on the showbench. A good garden plant and super for cutting. H 1.2m (4ft).

Surprise (Baker 1955) An American introduction that made an impact on the show scene from the first. Its pink and yellow giant semi-cactus blooms are huge and they ruled giant classes across Britain. Today, however, it finds it difficult to compete with the 'Jupiters'. A specialist grower's variety. H 1.2m (4ft).

Swanvale (R. Turrell 1989) A yellow small decorative similar to 'Ruskin Diane' and rivalling it as an exhibition variety. A strong grower making a vigorous bush. It has thick stems, making the blooms difficult to stage at shows. H 1.35m (4½ft).

Sweetheart (origin unknown) A lilliput sometimes referred to as 'Topmix' (but not the same as the 'Topmix' below). The tiny white blooms are tipped with purple and grow on compact bushes. Ideal for pots or containers on a patio. H 30cm (12in).

Sylvia's Desire (G. Ormes 1996) Sport from the small cactus 'Hillcrest Desire', this has excellent blooms in salmon, orange and pink blends. H to 1m (3ft).

Symbol (Bruidegom 1958) This is one of the classics of the post-war period. Its medium semi-cactus orange- and bronze-blended blooms set the standard for its class in exhibitions for many years. Many sports have been recorded. The first was 'Salmon Symbol', with blooms of pink and orange blends, followed by the similar 'Pink Symbol' in 1975. 'Yellow Symbol' arose in 1977 and 'Lavender Symbol' in 1980. 'Cantab Symbol', in yellow and pink, came out in 1983 and 'Majjus Symbol', in yellow and orange, in 1984. The last sport to emerge was 'Golden Symbol' (1993), which is slightly darker than 'Yellow Symbol'. Many are still available and sometimes win prizes even now. No white sport has yet been recorded. H all to about 1.2m (4ft).

Tahiti Sunrise (G. Cox 1975) Despite its name, this medium semi-cactus arose in Britain. A spectacular bicolour, with yellow flowerheads tipped in dark pink, it is excellent in the garden, but cannot compete with the best exhibition varieties. Best at the back of borders. H to 1.2m (4ft).

Taratahi Lilac (J. Frater 1996) This introduction from New Zealand created a sensation in North America: however, its small semi-cactus lilac blooms do not have the refinement desired for exhibition in the British Isles. It makes a fine garden plant. H to 1.2m (4ft).

Tender Moon (origin unknown) A small decorative with white blooms pink flushed in the centre. The flowers are between decorative and waterlily in form. Not recommended for exhibition but makes a good cut flower. Also attractive for gardens. H 1.3m (4ft).

Thais (D. Maarse) This collerette came from Holland after the Second World War. Its blooms are red with a white collar tipped in purple and it has perfect form for exhibition, but needs an experienced collerette grower to produce good specimens. H to 1m (3ft).

Thalia (origin unknown) AGM 1997 as 'Freya's Thalia'. A lilliput variety with dark red single blooms. The name 'Thalia' has been used at least twice before: it was used for a dark pink pom and an anemone dwarf bedder in the early 1900s. H 30–45m (12–18in).

The Master (Australian origin) A giant decorative with bronze blooms, 'The Master' was a favourite show dahlia during the 1960s and 1970s. A variety for the specialist. H 1.2m (4ft).

Tiny Tot (origin unknown 1949) AGM 1996 as 'Harvest Tiny Tot'. A lilliput with tiny orange blooms. Ideal for containers on patios. H to 50cm (20in).

Topmix (Topsvoort) This was the forerunner of a race of lilliput single-flowered dahlias that were often grown from seed which resulted in a range of colours and formation. Some of these forms were selected and propagated vegetatively to produce named cultivars, for example 'Topmix Reddy' (Ballego 1967), which may be the same variety as 'Reddy'. 'Topmix Brookfield

Delight' is a form with dark foliage and red single flowerheads. H 30–45cm (12–18in).

Trengrove Jill (G. Woolcott 1990) Bronze-flowered medium decorative of excellent formal reflexing form, suitable for exhibition, although the flowerheads need special care to reach top size. H to about 1.2m (4ft).

Trengrove Tauranga (G. Woolcock 1990) One of a group of medium decoratives of similar bronze colour and form, released in 1990 with the prefix 'Trengrove'. To reach the size limit required for showing, they need to be restricted to 4–5 up. H to 1.2m (4ft).

Trengrove Terror (G. Woolcott 1996) Possibly a giant decorative or maybe a large decorative, this needs extra effort for its bronze blooms to make show quality and giant size. H 1.2m (4ft).

Tui Orange (B. Buckley 1990) This New Zealand small semi-cactus variety has orange-flame blooms that stand out in the garden. Although it can produce exhibition-quality blooms, it tends to go oversize for British limits, so must be grown accordingly. H 1.1m (3½ft).

Vaguely Noble (T. Clarke 1970) A rich deep purple small ball, prominent as an exhibition variety for over two decades. A pink sport 'Pink Vaguely Noble' is also found on the showbench. H to 1m (3ft).

Valerie Buller (A. Buller 1977) Rich dark red miniature ball, an exhibition variety of the late 1970s but now considered to be too small for British showing. Rather short, H to 1m (3ft) at the most.

Vantage (P. Traff 1972) An American giant semi-cactus with huge yellow blooms of rather loose formation. It won prizes during the 1970s because of its size but does not stand up to the competition of today's giant semi-cactus varieties. H 1.2m (4ft).

Vidal Tracy (Willfang 1980) A small-flowered semi-cactus with pink blooms. A showman's variety of the 1980s. H 1.1m (3½ft).

Video (Artsen 1988) AGM 1994 The red medium semi-cactus blooms of 'Video' stand out like a beacon

'Tahiti Sunrise' has brilliant bicoloured blooms of medium semi-cactus form. It is suitable for growing in the border.

in the garden. Although they are not likely to win prizes on the showbench, they are good for cutting. H to 1.35m (4½ft).

Walter Hardisty (Gentile 1975) AGM 1993 A white giant semi-cactus often featuring in giant decorative classes at shows. Makes a lovely garden plant. H to 1.2m (4ft).

Wanda's Antarctica (L. Wright 1996) A white giant decorative of show potential. H to 1.1m (3½ft).

Wanda's Capella (L. Wright 1986) An excellent yellow giant decorative for exhibition. It is a strong grower making a vigorous bush. Easy to grow and ideal for the novice looking to exhibit giant decoratives. H 1.2m (4ft).

Wandy (C. Geerlings 1988) AGM 1993 A pompon with yellowish bronze blooms. Not really in the top flight of exhibition varieties, but makes a nice garden plant. H to 90cm (3ft).

Warkton Amber (L. Walker 1998) A small decorative with well-formed amber blooms. A strong grower making a good bush. H to 1.2m (4ft).

Warkton Ann (L. Walker 1998) A small decorative with pink blooms. Making a very vigorous bush, it is probably best as a garden variety rather than for exhibition. H 1.2m (4ft).

Weston Flamingo (T. McLelland 1998) A true cactus with masses of miniature spiky blooms in flamingo-pink. Its blooms can be held to size for show classes. An outstanding variety for show and garden decoration. H 1.2m (4ft).

Weston Nuggett (T. McLelland 1995) A miniature cactus with bronze blooms raised in Britain in order to meet the bloom size restrictions of the show scene. An excellent grower, making a bush, 'Weston Nuggett' does equally well as a garden plant and for exhibition. H about 1.2m (4ft).

Weston Pirate (T. McLelland 1998) A miniature semi-cactus of rich blood-red. An excellent garden plant and will also show well. H about 1.2m (4ft).

'Wootton Cupid' is classified as a miniature ball in Britain but a small ball in North America.

White Ballet (C. Geerlings 1985) AGM 1993 A small waterlily typical of the Dutch introductions of recent years. Its white well-formed blooms on strong stems make it ideal for cut flowers and for garden display. H to about 90cm (3ft).

Willo's Night (N. Williams & S. Ogg 1960) Believed to be a sport of 'Willo's Violet', 'Willo's Night' was introduced by Stuart Ogg, but whether it was originated by him is not known. A pompon with very dark red, almost black blooms, it makes an effective contrast in the garden and is often found on the showbench. H to 1m (3ft).

Willo's Surprise (N. Williams 1964) A pompon with intense wine-red blooms. A good show variety from an impressive stable. H to 1m (3ft).

Willo's Violet (N. Williams 1937) This Australian variety has been a top exhibition pom for over fifty years. Its perfectly formed blooms, in purple blends, are borne on manageable bushes. Under some growing conditions a number of similar varieties, such as 'Birch-wood' and 'Iris', are indistinguishable from Willo's Violet'. Moreover, there are sports of 'Willo's Violet' being released that are very similar to it and other varieties: 'Aurwen's Violet' is similar to 'Iris' and 'Hilary's Violet' is similar to 'Moor Place'. 'Pembroke Pattie', a recent seedling from 'Willo's Violet', is another purple pom that could cause confusion. H to 1.1m (3½ft).

Willowfield Gill (G. Powley 1998) A small decorative with bright pillar box-red blooms. They are very tight and formal, similar to a ball. Good for exhibition but needs special care. An excellent garden plant and suitable for cut flowers. H to 1.5m (5ft).

Winkie Colonel (J. Menzel 1996) This new giant decorative from Australia has created a stir on the show scene. Its rich red blooms on excellent stems need to be grown '3 up' to make top size. H 1.1m (3½ft).

Wisemark (W. Mark 1996) This bright yellow medium semi-cactus received a Silver Certificate at the NDS Northern Trials, Leeds, in 1997. Will make a lovely garden plant. H to about 1.2m (4ft).

Witteman's Superba (L. Berbee 1991) AGM 1993 A red medium semi-cactus from Holland, this is similar to 'Video' and equally spectacular in the garden. It has strong stems making it excellent for cutting as well as garden display. H to 1.1m (3½ft).

Wootton Cupid (L. Jones 1980) Classified as a miniature ball in Britain but small ball in America, 'Wootton Cupid' has pink flowerheads of exhibition quality on compact bushes. A series of sports have occurred of different shades of pink and pink blends, some of them difficult to distinguish. In North America 'Kathryn's Cupid' in 1987, and in Britain 'Rose Cupid' and 'Candy Cupid' in 1990 and 'Peach Cupid' in 1993. All are popular among exhibitors but all tend to have hard sunken centres, particularly if cut too young in an attempt to show them within the miniature ball ring size in Britain. The 'Cupids' make wonderful garden plants and are useful for cutting. H to 1m (3ft).

Wootton Impact (L. Jones 1982) AGM 1994 AM 1996 This is a medium semi-cactus with pink-yellow

The prize winner 'Zorro' is popular in both North America and Britain.

blooms. It is good for showing and also makes an attractive garden plant. See also 'Golden Impact'. H 1.2m (4ft).

Worton Joy (I. Lewis 1966) A miniature ball variety with lavender-pink blooms on strong stems. Useful for garden display and cut flowers. H 1.2m (4ft).

Worton Sally Ann (I. Lewis) An old variety with soft mauve small cactus blooms on fine long stems. A good choice for the garden and cutting. H to 1.2m (4ft).

Yellow Hammer (origin unknown) AGM 1994 A dwarf bedder with single yellow flowerheads on compact bushes with very dark foliage. Excellent for garden display. H 60cm (24in).

Yelno Harmony (J. Sharp 1986) AGM 1994 An orange small waterlily on strong stems, suitable for cutting. Ideal for the back of the border. H to about 1.2m (4ft).

Zorro (M. Geisert 1987) AGM 1995 AM 1989 A dark red giant decorative from North America. An excellent show variety on strong stems. A sport, 'Son of Zorro', has recently appeared. It has unusual red blooms with white tips. H to 1m (3ft).

11

DAHLIAS IN NORTH AMERICA

by Martin Kral

Not long after the first pioneers left the Eastern seashore to explore and settle the vast frontier to the west, the promises of the American continent were fulfilled in copious measure. In the nineteenth century as the Europeans probed beyond the Appalachian Mountains and then pushed westward into the Great Plains, the farmer gradually displaced the frontiersman. Homesteaders' subsistence agriculture yielded to orderly crop farming and, in time, the plains were divided into neat checkerboards of grains and grass. Midwestern farms and urban homes also sported sizeable gardens containing not only the vegetables and fruit necessary for the household, but also a small selection of flowers: settlers wanted something familiar in their new landscape. In the middle of the century, a travelling journalist reported that, in rural Indiana, among other flowering plants, dahlias were to be found in many of these homestead gardens.

It is quite surprising that the dahlia, an exotic newcomer to European horticultural collections at the turn of the century, was to be found in quantity even on the American frontier a scant few decades later. A likely explanation is the rapid acceptance of the dahlia by European gardeners and a corresponding proliferation of sources for dahlia roots. Emigrants to the New World often took plants and seeds with them to enrich their new life, and dahlias were among these. Several garden catalogues from the Eastern Seaboard touted a large selection of newly hybridized dahlias. Soon the passion for raising colourful blooms would have reached frontier settlements.

'Red Velvet' is an Australian variety that is popular in North America and Britain for showing and cutting.

The North American continent exhibits an extraordinary variety of terrain, soil types and climatic conditions, often a great challenge to gardeners and all other living things. Apart from the distinct maritime climates of the East and West Coasts, the Gulf Coast states in the south experience weather extremes that force dahlia enthusiasts to make exceptional efforts to raise these flowers. The prevailing continental climate between the coastal areas directs gardeners to heed seasonal swings of temperatures (hotter in summer, colder in winter than elsewhere). Raisers in the Rocky Mountain states experience short growing seasons, and northern Canadian dahlia lovers must be the most ardent of all.

The US Department of Agriculture plant hardiness zones (according to minimum winter temperatures) may be used as rough guidelines for dahlia gardening in North America. A more refined indicator has been developed by *Sunset Magazine*. This takes into account humidity, rainfall tendencies, the length of the gardening season, and summer high temperatures. However, dahlia growers are a plucky lot, and often raise dahlias where it really ought not to be possible – such as the Yukon, the Texas coast, and even in tropical Hawaii.

Beneficial temperate climate and fertile soil are the gifts bestowed on dahlias raised in the Pacific Northwest, these days the centre of dahlia culture in North America. Other sizeable dahlia growing regions are coastal California, the Midwest, and all along the East Coast down to Piedmont. Even the Rockies prove no obstacle to the determined gardener: there is a longstanding tradition of dahlia raising in the Denver area, and Kalispell, Montana, is home to not one, but several, commercial nurseries.

THE AMERICAN DAHLIA SOCIETY

The spread of dahlia cultivation throughout North America is, in large measure, a tribute to a combination of individual enterprise and organized group effort. When a New York garden editor lamented in 1914 that as popular as the dahlia had become, there was no society supporting education, research or exhibition of dahlias, a Scottish nurseryman named Richard Vincent, Jr., offered to help arrange a meeting of interested friends in May 1915. The American Dahlia Society (ADS) was born as a result of that gathering, and Vincent would be its president for the next decade. The ADS organized its first exhibition at the Museum of Natural History in New York in 1915. It also began publishing a quarterly bulletin and made contact with dahlia clubs and commercial growers throughout the land. Soon Canadian dahlia lovers joined the fledgling organization as well.

During the 1920s, dahlia growing became a popular pastime for the country club set. They erected elaborate shade houses in their suburban estates to shield the new blooms. The annual show was often held in fashionable New York hotels and was very much a socialite's delight. Out West, Californian raisers vied in hybridizing newer and ever-larger varieties. And commercial nurseries, such as those of Warren Maytrott's Dahliadel in rural New Jersey, offered new cultivars for the unheard-of price of $12. When an outstanding pink seedling was offered by another nurseryman, William Waite, as 'Jersey's Beauty' at $25 in 1923, there were some perplexed looks but also plenty of buyers.

The ADS developed criteria to classify, judge and reward dahlias in cultivation. A number of trial gardens were established to assist in that task. As the corps of affiliated clubs grew, so did the need for more rigorous judging standards. In time, the exhibition of floral bouquets yielded to a more regimented display of individual blooms, of multiples (3-bloom, 5-bloom vases) and of formal baskets and arrangements. Trial garden evaluation was supplemented by show bench judging of new seedlings. Refinement of the scoring system ultimately led to the selection process still in place today.

The effects of a Great Depression and of the Second World War did not become apparent until the post-war years. Regrettably, these two cataclysmic events scattered and decimated the ranks of dahlia growers. Moreover, creeping urbanization in the East and in California forced nurseries to move to more rural locales or close operations altogether. It was only through extraordinary dedication that the ADS survived through those days, and has continued to grow ever since.

CLASSIFICATION AND SHOWING

Currently, the ADS has more than sixty local clubs with a total membership of around 2,500. These clubs are found in great numbers in the hotbeds of American dahlia raising: the New York–Washington corridor, the Midwest and the Pacific Northwest. However, as noted earlier, there are also active societies in states like Alabama, Colorado, Oklahoma and California. Nine Canadian societies participate in the activities of the ADS today, activities such as generating funds for virus research, outreach programs, responding to classification or bylaws requests, publishing a quarterly bulletin and awarding honours for new cultivars. The ADS administers eight trial gardens scattered throughout the USA, and encourages on-going training of qualified judges by the dahlia clubs. The ADS National Show is no longer held just in New York; instead it rotates among these local organizations.

One of the results of long-term interaction between national and local bodies is a refinement of the classification criteria by form, type, size and colour. The annually-revised *Classification and Handbook of Dahlias* separates the fecund dahlia into no fewer than 540 classes. It differentiates between formal and informal decoratives, defines straight and incurved cactuses (whose petal tips point towards the flower centre) and has opted to give laciniated (split-tipped) dahlias their own classification. (See Appendix 6 on pp.154–156 for details on American classification and a selection of cultivars.)

The popularity of laciniated dahlias in parts of America is eclipsed by the spread of the waterlily form, which appeals to the general public and dahlia enthusiasts alike. Those liking smaller blooms gravitate towards the miniature pompons and balls, or towards collerettes, singles and star-like orchid dahlias. Blooms having characteristics that do not fall into the established categories are classified as novelties. The peony form, the favourite dahlia of an earlier era, has become unpopular, though, and few new anemone dahlias are being introduced at the annual exhibitions.

'Snoho Peggy', recently arrived in Britain from North America, has potential as a show winning small ball.

While proper form, size and colour are essential for a dahlia to succeed in shows, other factors – such as uniqueness, proportionate stem length, adequate and healthy foliage, and sufficient bloom depth – are considered in awarding the ribbons and top honours that show visitors find so intriguing. Local growing conditions are allowed for, and the fact that a bloom is slightly over- or undersized does not automatically mean disqualification.

American dahlia shows revel in the display of colours: blends and bi-coloured dahlias tend to succeed here when they fail to score elsewhere. Huge dahlias have always been an American passion; at one time California-grown giants were considered the New World contribution to dahliadom. Raisers of new varieties do not disappoint. And while the carefully overlaid petals of formal decoratives also appeal to growers here, it must be admitted that the North American judges take special delight in rewarding unusual forms and colour combinations; at the same time, they insist that even the most flamboyant dahlia meets exacting classification guidelines.

Growers are also classified: they are either novices or amateurs or compete as experienced exhibitors in the open division. Special show categories include multiple-bloom entries, challenge flowers and seedling bench displays. Once prize ribbons have been awarded in the different classes, judges then determine section champions, and from these ultimately the best in show. The top entry in each section is placed on the head table (or Court of Honour at some shows). Exhibitors receive cash awards, trophies and other gift items at the conclusion of such dahlia shows. And yes, novices have won Best in Show, sometimes with some very small blooms. Figure that!

GROWING DAHLIAS IN AMERICA

Integrating dahlias into contemporary American gardens has largely been a hit-or-miss effort. Unlike European growers, American hybridizers have tended to focus on the needs of the dahlia enthusiast, and much

Along with its sports, the British-raised medium semi-cactus 'Grenidor Pastelle' does well in shows in North America.

less so on the potential market of general gardeners. While this emphasis has avoided the excesses of mass marketing of poorly-formed, but floriferous, dahlias, it also has not endeared the dahlia to home owners in zones where it does not thrive without some care. Yet proper cultivation is essential for good growth and bloom, as has been discussed in earlier chapters. Given that some understanding of the dahlia's needs goes far towards that goal, a brief summary of American growing practices is in order.

One of the most obvious differences between raising dahlias in the New World and elsewhere is that American dahlias tend to be grown from individual root sections, rather than pot roots or cuttings. The public tends to purchase individual tubers offered by garden centres, dahlia nurseries and local societies. With tubers being made available for sale as early as February, it is difficult to convince gardeners to resist the urge to plant until after the last frost. In fact, in California and some Southern states dahlias are often left in the ground year-round and lifted only for root division.

IMPROVING THE SOIL

The complexity of soil types, terrain and climate inhibit anything other than a cursory summary of soil preparation techniques. Whether the dahlia tuber rests in the alluvial soil of Western Washington or in the red-dirt country of Piedmont, the ground will benefit from rotavating or digging over, a month before

planting. Improving tilth and creating friable soil suitable for sustained growth is particularly rewarding in regions where red or grey clay dominates, or where the topsoil is shallow. The sandstone-based earth of the Southwest as well as the sandy soil found in the Upper Midwest, along the Pacific Coast, and in portions of other states and provinces is improved by addition of organic matter such as rotted manure or compost.

Since dahlias like a neutral pH (around 6.5) growers may want to check the soil with an inexpensive soil testing kit before adding fertilizers or soil improvers. Limestone predominates in much of the eastern half of the continent and the arid zones out West similarly tend to be alkaline; lowering the pH by addition of gypsum (calcium sulphate) and other acidifiers is advisable. On the other hand, areas with copious rainfall or conifer forests – such as the Northwest – tend towards acid soils. Chemical improvers for these conditions usually involve lime in some form. Along the seashore and in parts of the Western deserts, excessive salinity is a problem for gardeners. When such soil characteristics prove too daunting, the dahlia gardener should consider raised-bed cultivation as a cost-effective alternative.

PLANTING OUT

Once frost-free days have arrived (as early as April in temperate zones, but most likely by mid-May), it is time for planting. A popular approach involves digging holes 15cm (6in) deep, loosening the soil at the bottom to mix in a handful of 5:10:10 fertilizer or bonemeal. A stake is then driven into the centre, and the tuber is placed horizontally next to the stake. Most growers mark the variety name and classification on a tag affixed to the stake. The tuber is barely covered with soil, leaving most of the excavated earth in a rim around the depression. This is because growing root hairs develop more rapidly when the soil temperature is higher; the thin soil layer is quickly warmed by the spring sunshine. In time the hole will fill on its own.

Do dahlias need to be staked? In most cases, the answer is an unequivocal 'Yes'. While some short-growing varieties (often singles or pompons) may succeed without such supports, a gust of wind or an errant pet can end the dahlia season in a few moments. A dahlia bush, tied with twine every 60cm (24in), will resist even the blustery prairie winds. If individual stakes (often made from rot-resistant wood, such as Western red cedar and redwood) are deemed unsightly, consider using tomato cages. Veteran dahlia growers with large beds often rely on long bilateral runs of wire supported by crossed spreaders at regular intervals. Other raisers swear by suspended (and upwardly adjustable) mesh netting. There is no limit on the innovative spirit of American dahlia lovers.

PESTS

As the new plants emerge, care must be taken to supply water and to protect the shoots from the effects of strong sunlight and insects. At this stage, the dahlia is also very susceptible to slug and snail attack. In the West the voraciousness of the huge brown or black slug (*Arion ater*) – sometimes also the grey-spotted *Limax maximus* – is outdone by the perfidious night-time prowls of the diminutive milky slug (*Agriolimax reticulatus*). Apart from slug baits containing metaldehyde, an ecologically sound method of preventing damage involves cutting 2-litre (4-pint) soft drink bottles in half and placing the inverted halves over the young plants for the first few weeks.

A number of opportunistic caterpillars, cutworms, wireworms and borers make dahlia growing a challenging hobby in much of the American East. The use of systemic insecticides applied directly to the young plant and surrounding soil goes far towards minimizing the effects of these creatures. If topical treatment is needed, contact insecticides include sevin, and the 'organic' forms of pyrethrin are useful.

During summer the problem pests are aphids, earwigs and spider mites.

Aphids make two forays into dahlia gardens during the season and must be controlled since they may carry viruses from one plant to another.

Earwigs, like slugs, spend the day under cover and emerge at night to climb up the dahlia stalk and munch on young blossoms. Good housekeeping (removal of bark or coarse ground cover) around the dahlias goes far towards minimizing their numbers.

Towards mid-season the red spider mite may infest lower leaf surfaces if their web-building is not disturbed by watering from below. The tell-tale yellowing of foliage is an alarm signal that the tiny mites have arrived. They are particularly difficult to treat and resistant to most insecticides, since the federal author-

ities have restricted the use of kelthane, the one effective miticide available to home gardeners.

DISEASES AND VIRUSES

Apart from these pests, fungus or bacterial diseases and viruses worry the dahlia grower. The most easily controlled by far is an outbreak of powdery mildew, a common fungus disease affecting foliage to such a degree that photosynthesis becomes difficult, leading to plant decline. It is a seasonal problem wherever hot days yield to cool nights, such as along the Pacific Coast, and wherever shade is abundant and good air circulation is not.

Botrytis spores settle on buds and blooms in hot-weather zones (East and Deep South), particularly when water is allowed to remain on dahlias overnight. *Entyloma* is a soil-borne fungal disease that can disfigure foliage, but by far the most devastating to plant and gardener is *Sclerotinia*. It manifests itself at first by discoloration along leaf nodes, leading to drooping foliage and – if not immediately dealt with – by complete collapse of the bush. *Sclerotinia* spreads within the hollow stems and its black fruiting bodies fall to the ground to begin the cycle anew. For this reason alone is it important to stress that dahlia foliage should not be composted. A plant may be salvaged if the infected lateral or stem is trimmed away, and destroyed.

And then there are viruses – several strains of them. There has been considerable discussion about dahlias and viruses since the first stunted plants were examined in the early trial gardens and it was determined that neither soil nor nutrition, and certainly not the weather, could be held responsible. An argument is made that since all modern dahlias are hybrids, the probability exists that most (if not all) harbour some type of virus, or susceptibility to one. When a second virus infects the plant, then the outward symptoms confirm the diagnosis and force the gardener to take action. Some older dahlias, such as 'Gay Pride' and all the so-called chrysanthemum-flowering varieties ('Akita') exhibit the incurved inner petals typical of infected blooms and also are very susceptible to virus disease; perhaps the observation has merit. Since the American floral industry has not yet embraced dahlias as prized cut flowers – usually the impetus for long-term horticultural research – the ADS has been engaged in raising funds and is sponsoring an investigation into

PLATE X

BALL DAHLIAS

'Red Balloon'

'Babette'

'Hamari Rose'

'Anniversary Ball'

'Little William'

All flowers are shown at approximately life size

'Downham Royal'

'Cornel'

'Riisa'

'Peach Cupid'

'Brookfield Deirdre'

dahlia viruses at Washington State University in Pullman, Washington.

Adequate water and shade help maintain the health of dahlia plants during the growing season. While overhead sprinklers (oscillating or rotary) are commonly used by commercial and long-time growers, they may be impractical elsewhere and may encourage fungus diseases. In water-starved parts of California and even in the reputedly wet Northwest, gardeners have embraced drip irrigation technology. Others have opted for soaker hoses (leaky pipes), linked to a distribution network of PVC piping, to ensure adequate nourishment.

Growers also often feed plants during summer with liquid fertilizer. To prevent sunlight from burning foliage and scorching blooms, fine-mesh shade cloth (20–50%, depending on light intensity and duration) should be installed over plants in the sun-drenched parts of the continent. Many exhibitors swear by their clothhouse dahlia plots, without which they would be unable to follow their passion. Even in the cloud-rich regions west of the Cascades, growers use umbrellas (here called bumbershoots) to shade individual blooms for show.

LIFTING TUBERS

Comes the fall, and the American dahlia grower makes preparations for digging, harvesting, dividing and storing the prized plants. Since frost comes early to Montana and the Northeast, dahlias are dug there as early as late September. In the Pacific Northwest growers reach for the spade anytime before mid-November. And the Californians may not need to lift tubers at all (but conscientious growers do). First, the stalks are cut at a solidly filled leaf node a few inches above ground. After a couple of days of rest, it is time for harvest. Spades and shovels are preferred to forks since the latter may pierce and damage a tuber irreparably, while the former make a clean cut. After lifting, some growers allow the root ball to dry overnight before washing off any soil still clinging to the tubers. The variety name or number is then marked on individual tubers with an ink pencil or indelible marker while the root ball is still whole. The weak root hairs ('rat tails') and broken tubers are trimmed off to prevent rotting. Since root division is easier in fall than spring, good growers then spend hours with sharp hawksbill or pruning knives, separating viable tubers. Gardeners not wishing to lift and divide every year are encouraged – admonished even – to make at least a coarse tuber division every two years.

The most popular storage medium for dahlias is garden vermiculite. It is inert, insulates (it was once used for home insulation) and – most important – it is light, consistently ensuring healthy tuber survival. Often the cut tubers are placed into plastic bags, covered with vermiculite, and then stored in cardboard boxes and crates. Other growers swear by storage in sand, peatmoss (which turns tubers dark), under newspaper layers and even in sawdust or wood chips. However, it is the storage conditions, not necessarily the medium, that are crucial: dahlias need to be stored at temperatures above freezing but below 7°C (45°F) to prevent disease.

PROPAGATION

Commercial growers and exhibitors take tubers out of storage early in the New Year to pot them up for taking cuttings. Dahlia roots are placed into seed trays and barely covered with potting soil. The trays are set up in a heated greenhouse or indoors under neon lighting with heat cables and capillary mats providing a perfect micro-climate to encourage sprouting. As the tuber responds, the 5–7cm (2–3in) long cuttings are dipped in a rooting compound and then potted up in trays or Jiffy-pots until well-rooted.

In this manner, a $20 tuber becomes a worthwhile investment. American growers excel at raising new varieties in great profusion. Some endure, while others are popular at exhibitions and then disappear, succumbing to disease, poor habit or the fickleness of dahlia experts. And there are many new dahlias that, frankly, do not make good garden or cut flowers and so never experience broad distribution. Despite the existence of nearly a hundred dahlia nurseries, American gardeners by and large purchase Dutch-grown roots and only occasionally come into contact with that other dahlia world.

THE FUTURE

Things are about to change, though. Lately, the trend towards marketing fully grown annuals as late as August has reached the dahlia. Gardening may be America's number one hobby, but Americans seem to have too little time to raise anything from seed. Instant lawns came first, but now instant gardens with blooming plants in jumbo-trays ready to plant have taken the trend a generation further. At many nurseries and supermarkets one can now purchase containerized 90cm (3ft) tall dahlias in full bloom for less than $10. Garden magazines grow effusive over the landscaping possibilities of dark-foliaged dahlias. Regrettably, the dahlia raisers have not yet picked up on that trend, resulting in the desperate search by millions for just one more 'Bishop of Llandaff'. Laciniated dahlias of every hue have become the rage, even among those people who garden where the finely-quilled tips wilt in the relentless summer heat. And fetching colour combinations – the stripes of 'Camano Shadows', the variegated petals of 'Nonette' and the striking bicolours and flames – enthrall the public.

NEW DAHLIAS

Good raisers of new dahlias are legion: in the Northwest, Wayne Holland, Earle Huston, the Ambroses of 'Camano' fame, Les Connell, and the largest dahlia grower on the continent, the Gitts family of Swan Island Dahlias, are just several who have reliably introduced prized varieties for years. In Montana, the 'Alpen', 'Lupin' and 'Mingus' lines find favour among growers who need small, fast-developing dahlias suited to short summers.

The ADS classification book lists more than 2,000 winning varieties and their originators. This work is updated every year; some dahlias are dropped while other varieties are added. Both the quarterly *ADS Bulletin* and the yearbook *Dahlias of Today* of the Puget Sound Dahlia Association in Western Washington provide sources for new dahlias and old favourites. Two nurseries (Connell and Swan Island) offer richly illustrated colour catalogues, while others will send price lists. And for those fortunate enough to live near a dahlia nursery, there is no better way to compare and select than by wandering among the panoply of blooms, catalogue in hand.

Some growers even send abroad for their new dahlias. So long as the tubers sent are free of soil and insects, the US Department of Agriculture has no objections to such imports. Not so the Canadian authorities; it is virtually impossible to import tubers

'Kidd's Climax' is a leading show variety, regarded as a large decorative in America and a giant in Britain.

legally without providing a phytosanitary certificate and allowing the customs officials to place the package under quarantine. As for export, the USDA has a benign policy, while the Canadian government regulates export by requiring phytosanitary inspection before shipping. American growers have developed good contacts with their friends in Australia, New Zealand, South Africa and Great Britain, though, and seeds or tubers manage to slip through the controls. They are also in communication with commercial growers in Japan, Germany, France, Austria, the Czech Republic and, of course, the Netherlands.

In short, there is no end in sight for the dahlia in the New World. There is an active corps of apostles, a vibrant and growing commercial interest in dahlias, and improvements in mass communications – just to mention the Internet web sites devoted to dahlias in passing. These, coupled with a continuing trend towards public acknow-ledgement of gardens as the essential refuge in this dynamically-evolving technological age, all augur good fortune for America's dahlias in the new millennium.

12

DAHLIA SOCIETIES AND TRIALS

The British National Dahlia Society (NDS) was formed in 1891. It organizes a National Dahlia Show in Shepton Mallet, Somerset, each year, normally in September, and a Northern Show in conjunction with the Northern Great Autumn Show at Harrogate, also in September. An annual National Conference is held in March and a Northern Conference a few weeks later. The large number of regional and local societies hold regular meetings and produce newsletters and bulletins for members.

The NDS publishes the *Dahlia Annual* in July and the *Winter Bulletin* in January. New members also receive a free guide to growing dahlias. The *Classified Directory and Judging Rules* is published every two years; the 25th Edition was published in January 1999. The NDS also offers numerous other services to individual members and affiliated societies, including lists of qualified judges, a classification service and advice where varieties may be obtained.

The Secretary of the National Dahlia Society can be contacted at 19 Sunnybank, Marlow, Buckinghamshire SL7 3BL.

BELGIUM
The Société Royal Belge du Dahlia is similar in aims to the French society. It can be contacted at Avenue de l'Exposition 418/27, B.1090 Bruxelles.

DENMARK
The Dansk Dahlia Selskab is an informal group of enthusiasts. They hold a dahlia show near Copenhagen

'Salmon Athalie' is a small cactus that is good for garden display as well as being an exhibition variety.

at the end of August each year. The society may be contacted through A. Bjerggard, Deg's Konsulent Kontor, PO Box 3073, 1508 Copenhagen, Denmark.

FRANCE
The Société Française du Dahlia was founded in 1928 in Biarritz when the Jardin du Dahlia (Garden of the Dahlia) was created at Migron near Biarritz. Gardens featuring dahlias in Paris are the Parc Floral du Bois de Vincennes, Jardin des Plantes, Parc de la Cournève and Neuilly-Plaisance. There is an annual display of dahlias in the Parc Floral de la Source in Orléans. Other cities where dahlias can be seen include the Parc de la Beaujoire et Jardin des Plantes in Nantes, Selestat, which has a floral festival during August, and the Jardin Andreas Dahl in Arles. Recently, the society has sponsored a dahlia display at the botanic garden of the Lycée Agricole et Horticole of Coutances, which is open to the public during September. The society is dedicated to growing, rather than showing, dahlias. Its exhibitions feature massed displays in public parks and gardens. Contact the President of the society Georges Clenet at Société Française du Dahlia, 6 rue du Carpiquet, 50250 La-Haye-du-Puits, France.

GERMANY
The national dahlia society in Germany reached its centenary in 1997. It concentrates on dahlias for garden display and assists in large plantings in public parks. It runs its own trial gardens at Mainau, on the German–Swiss border at the Bodensee (Lake Constance), and also at Hamburg. The plantings are judged by the public throughout the season. Every year, 20,000 tubers of more than 200 cultivars are planted.

The Secretary of the German Dahlia, Fuchsia and Gladiolus Society is Elisabeth Göring, Drachenfelsstrasse 9a, D 53177 Bonn, Germany.

NETHERLANDS

In the Netherlands the dahlia society is primarily composed of professional nurserymen. A national show is held each year, and every ten years the society organizes a dahlia garden and special show as part of the Dutch Floriade.

In many other European countries, there are groups of dahlia enthusiasts, and an informal network is developing. For example, in Eastern Europe, Czech, Polish and Hungarian groups interact, and are slowly developing contacts with the rest of Europe via Germany.

NORTH AMERICA

The American Dahlia Society (ADS) was established in 1913 and forms a focus for the many regional societies. It publishes four bulletins a year, together with an annual *Classification and Handbook of Dahlias*. It also publishes a judging manual and a growing guide. Some regional societies publish regular bulletins and annuals, many of which can be obtained direct or via the NDS.

There are seven major regional groups in the American Dahlia Society: Eastern States, Midwest Conference, North Atlantic Conference, Pacific Northwest Conference, Southern States Conference, and the Federation of Northwest Dahlia Growers. Every region has a number of local dahlia societies.

One feature of the American scene is the regional Trial Gardens, which promote dahlias, evaluate new varieties and demonstrate how a new variety will grow in different areas.

The Membership Secretary is Alan A. Fisher, 1 Rock Falls Ct, Rockville, MD 2085. email: Afisher@ftc.gov.

AUSTRALIA

A great many outstanding dahlias have been raised in Australia. The doyen of Australian raisers was Norman Williams who bred many of the best pompons now grown worldwide. This tradition is continuing with Nev Naumann of Queensland (the Bracken varieties) and Bill Tapley from South Australia. There are no dahlia trial grounds in Australia so, to prove themselves, varieties have to do well on the showbench.

The strong legislation regarding phytosanitary certificates for plant material makes it difficult to import foreign-grown dahlias into Australia.

The size of Australia precludes an effective national society, but there are strong dahlia societies in each state. Exhibitions are largely composed of single bloom or single vase classes, as in America.

NEW ZEALAND

New Zealand has a National Dahlia Society. Each year, a national show is held in the North and South Islands. Dahlia trials are also held annually and many of the winners regularly appear in Britain and America. Contact the society via the Secretary Mrs. P. Burrell, 78 Cameron Roat Te Puice, Bay of Plenty, New Zealand.

JAPAN

Yusaku Konishi is a leading Japanese dahlia specialist. He speaks and writes English and acts as an international window for Japan. His large list of dahlias includes many he has raised himself.

SOUTH AFRICA

The National Dahlia Society of South Africa was founded in 1955 and issued its own classification list of dahlias in South Africa. However, by 1970 it had dissolved and nothing has taken its place. The centre of dahlia growing in South Africa is still the Transvaal. For more information on South African dahlias, contact Wallace Maritz, Dahlia Garden, Erf 160, Kingfisher Road, Penhill 7100, South Africa.

INDIA

The Dahlia Society of India was only established in 1985 although dahlias have been grown in India ever since it was a British colony. The first recorded double dahlia in India is documented as 1838, but single-flowered dahlias were exhibited at the first show of the Agri-Horticultural Society of India in 1820.

The main dahlia-growing region in India is centred on Calcutta, although dahlias thrive in the hill areas. One Indian speciality is growing giant cultivars in large flower pots. The pots are 25cm (10in) in diameter and contain a single plant. The plant is flowered on the crown bud, all other buds and sideshoots having been removed. Blooms 35cm (14in) in diameter are achieved and take four months to develop. The

secretary of the Dahlia Society of India is Shri Kanailal Samadder, 4 Thakur Ramakrishna Park Row, Calcutta, West Bengal, Pin - 700 068 India.

German Dahlia Shows concentrate on flamboyant massed displays as this show at Mainau demonstrates.

DAHLIA TRIALS

All over the world national and regional dahlia societies run dahlia trials where new varieties are assessed for their potential. Often standard, well-tried varieties are grown alongside for comparison. A visit to such trials during the flowering season is recommended. Many commercial nurseries open their growing areas during the flowering period and welcome visitors. Before embarking on a visit to a trial ground, it is worth stopping for a moment to consider what you are looking for. Are the varieties intended for showing cut blooms? Is your objective garden decoration or are the blooms intended for cutting for the home or in flower arrangements? Each use will require particular attributes such as height of plant, length of stem and so on. You should also consider where you are going to grow the dahlias. For example, varieties to be planted near a fence or trees will grow taller in those protected sites than they will in an open nursery field; those to be grown in a windy spot will need to be short and compact otherwise

they may not withstand the wind no matter how well they are supported. It is also important to ensure that the trial will have varieties suitable for your purposes. For example, is it intended to assess show potential or the suitability for garden decoration?

RHS, WISLEY

Perhaps the biggest dahlia trials in the world are held annually at Wisley by the RHS and the NDS. The Joint Dahlia Committee is responsible for the organization and judging of the trials and consists of eight representatives each from the RHS and the NDS. The secretary to the committee is supplied by the RHS together with the trials staff. New cultivars are selected for trial after submission of cut blooms to the Joint Committee at one of its meetings at the various dahlia shows. Approximately 200 cultivars are featured each year. These are grouped according to classification, and both bedding varieties and show varieties are judged. All varieties are named, together with awards which they may have achieved.

Raisers or introducers of cultivars selected for trial are requested to supply five well-rooted cuttings grown in 7cm (3in) pots. The health of newly supplied material is checked regularly and any suspect material is destroyed. Normally, three plants of each cultivar are planted in the trial in early June, and three further plants are grown as pot tubers. Cultivars are retained in the trial for three years after which time, if no award has been received, the variety may be removed. Cultivars having received awards are retained for comparison with new cultivars. Judging takes place by the full committee on a number of occasions each season and, if necessary, additional inspections by a sub-committee are also held.

Since 1992, the primary award is the Award of Garden Merit (AGM), which is given to plants of outstanding excellence for garden decoration. The Award of Merit (AM) is also available to plants of outstanding excellence for exhibition. Each year, the outstanding dahlia variety at Wisley is awarded the Stredwick Medal by the NDS.

NDS, GOLDEN ACRE PARK, LEEDS

In contrast to Wisley, where garden merit is the main criterion, the NDS runs trials for exhibition potential at the Golden Acre Park, Leeds. The trials are organized and run by a sub-committee of the NDS consisting of four members representing the Executive Council of the NDS and four members representing the Northern Committee of the NDS. The trials, which are open to the public from August to October, are managed by staff of the trials and NDS.

Approximately 50 new cultivars intended for exhibition use are included each year. Six well-rooted cuttings are requested from introducers of the new varieties: three are planted in the open trial area, one is grown under cover and the remaining two plants are kept as spares.

The trials are inspected on at least three occasions during the flowering period and awards are based on the performance of the dahlias during the trial period. Gold, silver, and bronze certificates are awarded to outstanding varieties with exhibition potential, and the best variety in the trial is given the Harry Haworth Memorial Medal. Some varieties are grown on for a second year if they did not achieve their potential during the first year.

WDS, PENCOED COLLEGE

The Welsh Dahlia Society organizes trials at the Pencoed College of Horticulture near Bridgend in South Wales. The format of the trials is similar to that of the NDS Leeds trials with awards to the best new varieties.

COMMERCIAL TRIALS

At one time, the Horticultural Trade Association ran regional trials of dahlia varieties, but these have not been held for some years. Instead, individual nurseries run their own trials in which new releases are grown alongside established varieties. Foremost among these is Ayletts Nurseries (St Albans) which holds a Dahlia Festival each September. Other nurseries specializing in dahlias open their trial grounds to visitors, in particular Halls of Heddon (near Newcastle), Oscrofts (at Doncaster and Solihull) and Tivey (Leicester).

TRIALS WORLDWIDE
GEERLINGS, NETHERLANDS

In the Netherlands, Geerlings of Heemstede and Lindhout-Ornata of Noordwijk open their nurseries to visitors during September, and when the Dutch Floriade is held during September and October, extensive displays of dahlias are a feature.

ADS, NORTH AMERICA

In many countries national and regional dahlia trials are held. In North America trials are run by the American Dahlia Society in conjunction with regional associations. Among the foremost trial gardens are the Pacific Coast Trial Garden, in Lakeside Park in Oakland, and the Pacific North West Trial Garden, near Tacoma. There is also a large number of commercial nurseries which open their trial gardens to visitors including Pennypack Dahlias (Pennsylvania), Comstock Dahlia Gardens (Solano Beach, California), White Dahlia Gardens (Milwaukee), Phil Traff Dahlias (Washington), Blue Dahlia Gardens (San Jose, Illinois), and Almand's Dahlia Gardens (San Leandro, California).

NDS, NEW ZEALAND

In New Zealand, the National Dahlia Society runs trial gardens in both North and South Islands, and results are reported locally and also in the official publications of dahlia societies in other countries.

APPENDICES

GLOSSARY

Auxin A plant growth hormone.

Axil The point where the leaf meets the stem, from which side shoots or flowers develop.

Baby A popular term for the **lilliput** or tiny bloom type of dahlia.

Bicoloured A flower with two distinct colours on the petals: usually the tip of the petal is a different colour.

Black rot A common name for a fungus that attacks stored tubers; sometimes a seedling root rot.

Blend Two or more colours that gradually merge on the bloom.

Bloom angle Position of the flower at the apex of the flower stem. The ideal for most types is at 45 degrees to the vertical during judging, except for pompons where the bloom should be on top of the stem like a drumstick.

Chlorosis Loss of green colouring in the leaves due to chlorophyll deficiency. Often caused by a lack of nutrients but can also be a physiological effect or, in seedlings, a genetic defect.

Clamp An earth heap used for overwintering dahlia tubers.

Cross-pollination The transference of pollen from one plant to another.

Cultivar A cultivated variety.

De-branching Removal of side shoots in order to channel the plant's energies into the selected blooms and thus improve bloom quality for show purposes.

Disbudding Removal of side buds to enable the terminal bud on each stem to develop to its full potential. It also enhances stem development.

Double A bloom that has many rows of ray florets and no visible disc when in its prime state.

Dwarf bedder Varieties that do not normally exceed 60cm (24in) in height.

Fancy-type dahlia The Victorian name for multi-coloured ball dahlias specifically for showing.

Feeder roots The fine web of roots developing near the soil surface when flowers start to form.

Field tuber A tuber produced in the open garden after the growing season is over.

Fimbriated (laciniated) Describes split petal ends.

Florets The individual flowers on a flowerhead. Disc florets are at the centre of the bloom, ray florets are on the outside.

Globe The Victorian name for some ball dahlias.

Growth eyes Growing points on the collar of a dahlia tuber that give rise to shoots that can be used for cuttings.

Hormone rooting powder A chemical that assists speedier rooting of cuttings. It often contains a fungicide to prevent root rot.

Hybrid A plant resulting from crossing of two distinct types. Hybrid dahlias do not normally breed true from seed.

Hybridizing The act of cross-pollinating to create a new type.

Incurving Petals that curve inwards towards the centre of the bloom.

Inulin A carbohydrate storage material similar to starch.

Involute Petals that have margins which roll inwards along their longitudinal axis.

Lifting The digging up of tubers from the soil for winter storage.

Lilliput Very dwarf dahlias, rarely more than 30cm (12in) tall, usually with very small blooms.

Mulching Covering the soil surface with a suitable material, such as bark chippings or gravel, to retain moisture and suppress weeds.

Open-centred A normally **double** bloom that has visible disc **florets**.

Oversize An exhibition bloom that is larger than the allowed diameter for a particular show class.

Petaloids Small petals sometimes found among normal ray florets or attached to each ray petal in collerette types.

Pot tubers Cuttings grown on in small pots in order to make tubers for better overwintering.

Recurving Petals that curve back towards the stem.

Reflexing As in **recurving**, where petals curve back to the stem.

Revolute Describes the rolling backwards of a petal along its length.

Securing By **disbudding** the grower secures a selected bloom to develop for show.

Self-colour A bloom of a single uniform colour.

Show-type dahlia A Victorian term used to describe self-coloured ball dahlias.

Single-flowered Variety producing flowerheads with a single row of ray petals and a pronounced disc.

Sport A vegetative mutation from a given parent.

Stopping Removal of the growing point on a plant to promote bushiness.

Suffusion Two or more colours intermingling in a bloom.

Tuber crown The point where the old stem meets the tuber clump.

Variegated Two or more distinct colours on the petals arranged in dots, flecks, splashes, stripes or narrow lines.

APPENDIX II
WHERE TO BUY DAHLIAS

Many specialist dahlia nurseries tend to concentrate on recent releases and top exhibition varieties. Older varieties may be found in the *The RHS Plant Finder* (published annually) which also lists some dahlia species. Many of the older varieties are also sold in garden centres and supermarkets.

The National Dahlia Collection in Cornwall may be able to help locate the oldest varieties. The National Dahlia Society (NDS) Classification Committee has a database of varieties and their suppliers, and the secretary David J Bates (88 Purnells Way, Knowle, Solihull, West Midlands, B93 9EE) will do a search for NDS members; non-members may be charged a fee for the service. The Trials Office at the RHS Garden, Wisley, has records going back for many years and may be able to identify the introducer of a particular variety. The RHS also holds the International Dahlia Register which includes information on the raisers and introducers of varieties.

Many dahlia nurseries will offer a mail order service, but some only supply to personal callers.

The main specialist dahlia nurseries are listed below.

BRITAIN

Aylett Nurseries Ltd., North Orbital Rd, St Albans AL2 1DH

George S Beatty (Dahlias), 186 Mayor's Walk, Peterborough PE3 6HQ

Ian Butterfield, The Nursery, Harvest Hill, Bourne End SL8 5JJ

J & I Cruickshanks, Ridgeview Nursery, Longridge, Bathgate, Scotland EH47 9AB

Halls of Heddon, Heddon on the Wall, Newcastle upon Tyne NE15 0JS

Hillcrest Dahlias, 79 Cant Cres, Upperby CA2 4JJ

Lochend Nursery, Lochend Rd, Gartosh, Glasgow G69 8BE

Oscroft's Dahlias, Sprotbrough Rd, Doncaster DN5 8BE

Oscroft's Dahlias, 'Woodside', Warwick Rd, Chadwick End B93 0BP

Porter's Dahlias, 58 Stanley Rd, Halstead CO9 1LA

Scott's Nurseries, 'Capri', Denaby Lane, Old Denaby, Doncaster DN12 4LD

Dave Spencer's Dahlias, Field View, High Rd, Fobbing SS17 9HG

Surrey Dahlias, 28 Longdyke Merrow, Guildford GU1 2UD

Taylor's Dahlias, 12 Shawbury Grove, Sale M33 4DF

Philip Tivey & Sons, 28 Wanlip Rd, Syston, Leicester LE7 1PA

THE REST OF EUROPE

Gartenbaubetrieb Engelhardt, Guterbahnhofstr, 53 D-01809 Heidenau bei Dresden, Germany

Geerlings Dahlias, Kadijk 38, 2104 AA Heemstede, Netherlands

Lindhout-Ornata, Herenweg 105 2201, AE Noordwijk, Netherlands

Wirth Dahlien, Leschetitzkygasse, 11 A-1100 Wien, Austria

Graines à Dahlias Baumaux, 21 Allee des Grands Paquis, 54180 Heyllecourt Nancy, France

Elite Clause, 91220 Bretigny-sur-Orge, France

Oxadis/Vilmorin, 38291 La Veyrilliere, France

Ets Georges Truffaut, 21 Rue de Vineuil, 41350 Vineuil, France

Ets Ernest Turc, B.P. 315, 49003 Angers cedex 01, France

NORTH AMERICA

Almand Dahlia Gardens, 2451 West Ave, 133rd San Leandro, CA 94577

Alpen Gardens, 173 Lawrence Lane, Kalispell, MT 59901-4633

B & D Dahlias, 19857 Marine View Drive, SW Seattle, WA 98166

Bridge View Dahlia Gardens, 1876 Maple St, North Bend, OR 97459

Campobello Dahlia Farm, 1085 Prison Camp Rd, Campobello, SC 29322

Canadahlia Gardens, 82 Clifton Downs Road, Hamilton, Ontario, Canada L9G 2P3

Caproz Dahlias, 4510 174th St, SE Mill Creek, WA 98012

Clack's Dahlia Patch, 5585 North Myrtle Rd, Myrtle Creek, OR 97457

Connell's Dahlia, 10616 Waller Rd, East Tacoma, WA 98446

Creekside Dahlias, Brian Killingsworth Route 4, Ellijay, GA 30540

Dahlia Dandies, 1717 South Woodland Drive, Kalispell, MT 59901

Dan's Dahlias, 994 South Bank Rd, Oakville, WA 98568

Echo Valley Farms, 3338 Echo Valley Rd, North Bend, OR 97459

Emerald Valley Farm, 88589 Chukar Lane, Veneta, OR 97487

Farmer Creek Gardens, 27850 Hwy 101 South, Cloverdale, OR 97112

Frey's Dahlias, 12854 Brick Rd, Turner, OR 97392

Garden Valley Dahlias, 406 Lower Garden Valley Rd, Roseburg, OR 97470

Golden Rule Dahlia Farm, PO Box 266, 1220 Xenia Ave, Yellow Springs, Ohio 45387

Helen's Dahlias, 6813 NE 139th Street, Vancouver, WA 98686

Hilltop Dahlias, Route 1, 1010 Antelope Basin, WY 82410

Homestead Gardens, 125 Homestead Road, Kallispell, MT 59901

JT Dahlias, PO Box 20967, Greenfield, WI 53220

Kutschara's Dahlias, 2807 Echo Lane, Eugene, OR 97470-5437

La Conner Dahlias, PO Box 329, La Conner, WA 98257

Lakewood Dahlia Garden, 312 Beach Road, Wolcott, CT 06716

Mingus Dahlias, 7407 NE 139th Street, Vancouver, WA 98662

Mohawk Dahlia Gardens, PO Box 898, Marcola, OR 97454

Morning Sun Dahlia Garden, 7191 Morning Sun Road, Oxford, Ohio 45056

OHG Bulbs, Old House Gardens, 536 Third St, Ann Arbour, MI 48103-44957

Pioneer Dahlias, 1606 Highway 20, Burlington, WA 98233

Pleasant View Gardens, 50 Pleasant View Dr, Kalispell, MT 59901

Reynolds Dahlias, 37800 Sodaville Cutoff, Lebanon, OR 97355

Swan Island Dahlias, PO Box 700 AMD, Canby, OR 97013

TLC Gardens, 332 Parliament Drive, Kalispell, MT 59901

Windhaven Dahlias, 20 East Windhaven Rd, Pittsburgh, PA 15205

APPENDIX III
WHERE TO SEE DAHLIAS

The Victorians and Edwardians loved massed beds of dahlias which were lovingly tended by armies of gardeners. Gone are the days when every public park or garden had its dahlia border. Those that exist today are few and far between. Some of the larger public parks use bedding dahlias, but the displays vary from year to year. Hyde Park in London often has large dahlia plantings; Nottingham also features dahlias in its city parks.

In Europe, dahlias are used in many public parks and, in many European countries, so-called dahlia 'shows' are display gardens. Below is a list of some of the places in the British Isles where dahlias can be seen in a garden situation. (NT = National Trust)

Anglesey Abbey, Lode, Cambridgeshire (NT) has a long dahlia border and also features dahlias in beds.

Biddulph Grange Garden, Biddulph, Stoke-on-Trent, Staffordshire (NT) has a dahlia walk.

Calke Abbey, Derbyshire (NT) features dahlias.

Winchester Growers Limited, Penzance, Cornwall has the National Collection of dahlia varieties, which comprises nearly two thousand different dahlia species and varieties. The collection display garden is open to the public. Tubers and plants are available.

For details of opening times contact David Brown, Winchester Growers, Varfell Farm, Long Rock, Penzance, Cornwall TR20 8AQ. Tel. 01736 711271. email. varfell-winchester@btinternet.com

Golden Acre Park, Bramhope, Leeds, West Yorkshire is the location of the NDS trials of dahlia varieties for exhibition potential (see below). Trials are open to the public during park opening hours.

Pencoed College of Horticulture, Bridgend, South Wales holds the Welsh Dahlia trials. These are open to the public.

Valley Gardens, Harrogate, Yorkshire plants a long dahlia border each year. All the varieties are labelled.

Wisley Gardens (RHS), Woking, Surrey has a fine herbaceous border where some dahlias are to be found. Each year a magnificent *Dahlia imperialis* is planted out near the greenhouses and is lifted and overwintered indoors. The Joint RHS/NDS Dahlia Trials are held at Wisley annually (see p.147). The trials are open to the public during normal garden opening hours.

APPENDIX IV
DAHLIAS ON THE INTERNET

The internet contains plenty of information about dahlias. A quick search made on the keyword 'dahlia' resulted in 2,139 entries.

The RHS has a website at www.rhs.org.uk and Aylett Nurseries can be contacted at Aylett_Nurseries@compuserve.com. There are also number of private dahlia enthusiasts in the British Isles who are on the internet.

Many American dahlia nurseries can be emailed for catalogues and orders. Some also have websites. The key website is http://www.dahlia.com and the email address info@dahlia.com. The website contains general information, details on the American Dahlia

Society, ADS classification (the classification handbook has a web page at http://www.snm.com/ADS) and a discussion group. It has links to specialist growers including Dale Bishop, Wayne Holland, Stumble Falls Dahlia Garden, Cal's Dahlia Page, and Frey's Dahlia Garden.

Others can be contacted direct:
Alpen Gardens: mccl@cyberport.net
Scott Kunst: OHGBulbs @aol.com
Frey's: http://www/gardeners-advantage.com
Caproz: DahliaIdy@aol.com
Sea-Tac Gardens: MDVG64@prodigy.com

APPENDIX V
SELECTED BRITISH VARIETIES

The dahlias listed below are those I consider to be good garden varieties; they have also won awards at Wisley or elsewhere or are top exhibition varieties in Britain. They are grouped by flower shape, and the country of origin and year of introduction are given where known.

More details about the flower definitions are given in Chapter 3 pages 23–35. The abbreviations used here have been taken from the NDS classified directory. Fim denotes a fimbriated type, where the ray florets are split at the ends. An indication of height is given by the codes Dw.B and Lil. Dw.B means dwarf bedder; such varieties usually do not exceed 60cm (24in) in height. Lil indicates a lilliput variety, usually not exceeding 30cm (12in) in height. As mentioned elsewhere, height is influenced by soil conditions, cultivation and aspect. Aus = Australia, Can = Canada, Ger = Germany, N = Netherlands, NZ = New Zealand, SA = South Africa, UK = United Kingdom.

Group 1 Single-flowered
Bonne Esperance (Lil.; N 1951)
Coltness Gem (Dw.B.; ?UK 1922)
Moonfire (Dw.B.)
Omo (Lil.)
Preston Park (Dw.B.; UK 1969)
Reddy (Lil.)
Sweetheart (Lil.)
Yellow Hammer (Dw.B.)

Group 2 Anemone-flowered
Comet (N 1952)

Group 3 Collerette
Chimborazo (UK)
Curiosity (N 1954)
Grand Duc (N 1956)
Orel (1993)
Thais (N)

Group 4d Small Waterlily
Figurine (Aus 1982)
Garden Festival (UK 1992)
Gerrie Hoek (N 1945)
Glorie van Heemstede (N 1947)
John Street (UK 1977)
Lismore Willie (UK 1992)
Yelno Harmony (UK)

Group 5a Giant Decorative
Alva's Supreme (NZ 1956)
Ben Huston (Can 1985)
Bonaventure (USA 1982)
Go American (USA 1959)
Hamari Gold (UK 1984)
Kidd's Climax (NZ 1940)
Lavengro (UK 1953)
Liberator (Aus 1941)
Lula Pattie (USA 1960)

Mabel Ann (UK 1995)
Maisey Mooney (Can 1994)
Night Editor (USA 1952)
Sam Huston (Can 1994)
Wanda's Capella (UK 1986)
Zorro (USA 1987)

Group 5b Large Decorative
Amgard Delicate (UK 1994)
Elma E (USA 1993)
Kenora Valentine (USA 1990)
Polyand (Aus 1953)
Silver City (UK 1967)

Group 5c Medium Decorative
B.J. Beauty (UK 1976)
Charlie Two (UK 1989)
Evelyn Foster (UK 1971)
Rustig (SA 1970)
Trengrove Tauranga (UK 1990)

Group 5d Small Decorative
Carstone Ruby (UK 1997)
Edinburgh (UK 1950)
Hillcrest Ultra (UK 1993)
Honeymoon Dress (UK 1981)
Nina Chester (UK 1974)
Ruskin Diane (UK 1984)
Senzoe Ursula (UK 1985)
Swanvale (UK 1989)

Group 5e Miniature Decorative
Abridge Taffy (UK 1978)
Amgard Coronet (UK 1985)
David Howard (UK 1965)
Fermain (UK 1991)
Jeanette Carter (UK 1988)
Karenglen (UK 1990)
Orange Mullet (Dw.B.; 1992)

Group 6a Small Ball
Barbarry Ball (UK 1991)
Hamari Rose (UK 1997)
Polventon Supreme (UK 1992)
Risca Miner (UK 1977)

Group 6b Miniature Ball
Anniversary Ball (UK 1992)
Barbarry Gem (UK 1990)
Brookfield Deirdre (UK 1982)
Wootton Cupid (UK 1980)

Group 7 Pompon
Andrew Lockwood (UK 1961)
Diana Gregory (Aus 1947)
Frank Holmes (UK 1976)
Hallmark (Aus 1960)
Iris (Ger 1974)
Minley Linda (UK 1983)
Moor Place (UK 1957)
Noreen (Aus 1962)
Pensford Marion (UK)
Rhonda (Aus 1947)
Small World (Aus 1967)
Willo's Violet (Aus 1937)

Group 8a Giant Cactus
Polar Sight (N 1960)

Group 8c Medium Cactus
Banker (N 1970)

Group 8d Small Cactus
Athalie (UK 1974)
Border Princess (Dw.B.; N 1964)
Dana Iris (UK 1977)
Kiwi Gloria (UK 1988)
Klankstad Kerkrade (N 1954)
Park Princess (Dw.B.; N 1959)

Group 8e Miniature Cactus
Rokesley Mini (UK 1971)
Weston Nuggett (UK 1995)

Group 9a Giant Semi-cactus
Daleko Jupiter (UK 1979)
Inca Dambuster (UK 1975)
Inland Dynasty (USA 1993)
Lloyd Huston (Can 1983)
Vantage (USA 1972)

Group 9b Large Semi-cactus
Hamari Accord (UK 1986)
Kenora Challenger (USA 1991)
Quel Diable (N 1968)
Reginald Keene (UK 1974)

Group 9c Medium Semi-cactus
Aloha (USA 1986)
Davenport Sunlight (UK 1980)
Eastwood Moonlight (UK 1975)
Golden Impact (UK 1989)
Grenidor Pastelle (UK 1988)
Kenora Sunset (USA 1996)
Marlene Joy (Fim.; USA 1989)
Suffolk Bride (UK 1974)
Symbol (N 1958)
Tahiti Sunrise (UK 1975)
Video (N 1988)
Wootton Impact (UK 1982)

Group 9d Small Semi-cactus
Hayley Jane (UK 1978)
I Lyke It (UK 1996)

Jessica (USA 1988)
Jura (N 1988)
Lemon Elegans (N 1988)
Match (SA 1961)
Piper's Pink (UK 1964)
Tui Orange (NZ 1990)

Group 9e Miniature Semi-cactus
Snip (USA 1978)

Group 10 Miscellaneous
Bishop of Llandaff (UK 1928)
Ellen Huston (Dw.B.; Can 1975)
Fascination (Dw.B.; UK 1964)
Giraffe (double orchid; N 1948)
Jescot Julie (double orchid; UK 1974)

APPENDIX VI
SELECTED AMERICAN VARIETIES

Each year the American Dahlia Society publishes a list of the most popular dahlia varieties in North America, based on awards made during the show season. In 1997, the top varieties (96 in all) were those receiving at least fifty awards. The awards are mainly from shows, but nevertheless, a wide range of types is included.

The selection on page 156 is based on The Fabulous Fifty, a list of the top American varieties, published by the American Dahlia Society in 1997.

CLASSIFICATION SYSTEM

There are more than 40,000 named varieties of dahlias, a large proportion of which are still available. This huge quantity presents problems to those trying to choose which variety to grow. In order to guide growers, the ADS has devised a classification system based on groups of letters, which refer to flower size and type, and numbers with three digits, relating to flower size, flower type and flower colour respectively (see also on the internet http://www.dahlia.com/guide/class.html).

The groups of letters and their meanings are listed on page 155 (top) and are straightforward. The groups of numbers need some explanation. The first digit defines the size of most of the common types of dahlias, thus 0 for giant (or AA), 1 for large (A), 2 for medium (B), 3 for small (BB), 4 for miniature (M). Numbers begin-

ning with 5 cover balls, miniature balls or poms, those beginning with 6 and 7 cover the eight other types, so for example waterlilies are between 600–615, peonies 621–635, and mignon singles 721–735. The second and third digits in the classification refer to type and colour. Thus, the number 123 refers to a large informal decorative with orange blooms. This could also be written in short as A (large) ID (informal decorative) OR (orange). Most serious exhibitors would instantly recognize A ID but usually have to look up 3, or OR. This classification allows growers to seek, for example, a similar but giant type by looking for varieties coded 023 or a similar but smaller type by looking at codes 223.

Other examples: 002 is the code for a giant formal decorative with yellow blooms. 042 is the code for a giant semi-cactus with yellow blooms. 666 is the code for a collerette with red blooms. And specific dahlias: 'Alloway Candy' is a pink novelty dahlia, code 764. 'Kidd's Climax' is a large formal decorative with light blended colours, code 110. 'Moorplace' is a dark red pompon, code 547. 'Snoho Peggy' is a dark pink ball dahlia, code 505.

Country codes for the selected list: A Australia, B Britain, BE Belgium, C Canada, F France, G Germany, H Holland, I Ireland, J Japan, NZ New Zealand, SC Scotland, US United States.

ADS CLASSIFICATION CODES

Size or Type Codes
(vertical column below)
AA Giant
A Large
B Medium
BB Small
M Miniature
BA Ball
MB Miniature Ball
P Pompon
WL Waterlily
PE Peony-flowered
AN Anemone-flower
CO Collerette
S Single
MS Mignon Single
O Orchid-flowered
N Novelty

Additional Type Codes
(horizontal column below)
FD Formal Decorative
ID Informal Decorative
SC Semi-cactus
C Cactus
LC Laciniated

Flower Type Numbers
001–015 Formal decorative
021–035 Informal decorative
041–055 Semi-cactus
061–075 Straight cactus
061–075 Incurved cactus
081–095 Laciniated dahlias
501–515 Ball dahlias
521–535 Miniature ball dahlias
541–555 Pompon dahlias
601–615 Waterlily dahlias
621–635 Peony dahlias
641–655 Anemone dahlias
661–675 Collerette dahlias
701–715 Single dahlias
721–735 Mignon single dahlias
741–755 Orchid dahlias
761–775 Novelty dahlias

ADS CLASSIFICATION CHART

Size and Type		Form and Colour					
		FD BA WL S	ID MB PE MS	SC P AN O	C CO N	LC	
AA	001 to 095	01	21	41	61	81	White
A	101 to 195	02	22	42	62	82	Yellow
B	201 to 295	03	23	43	63	83	Orange
BB	301 to 395	04	24	44	64	84	Pink
M	401 to 495	05	25	45	65	85	Dark Pink
BA	501 to 515	06	26	46	66	86	Red
MB	521 to 535	07	27	47	67	87	Dark Red
P	541 to 555	08	28	48	68	88	Lavender
WL	601 to 615	09	29	49	69	89	Purple
PE	621 to 635	10	30	50	70	90	Light Blend
AN	641 to 655	11	31	51	71	91	Bronze
CO	661 to 675	12	32	52	72	92	Flame Blend
S	701 to 715	13	33	53	73	93	Dark Blend
MS	721 to 735	14	34	54	74	94	Variegated
O	741 to 755	15	35	55	75	95	Bicolour
N	761 to 775						

ADS SELECTED LIST

Giant Decorative
Bonaventure (011; US)
Walter Hardisty (021; US)
Zorro (027; US)

Giant Semi-cactus
Kenora Clyde (041; US)
Inland Dynasty (042; US)
Creve Coeur (046; US)
Wildman (046; US)
Irene's Pride (051; US)

Giant Cactus
Clara Huston (063; C)

Large Decorative
Elma Elizabeth (108; US)
Kidd's Climax (110; NZ)
Maisie Mooney (121; C)
Elsie Huston (124; C)
Islander (125; US)
Kenora Wildfire (126; US)
Spartacus (127; US)

Large Semi-cactus
Verda (141; US)

Large Cactus
Camano Messenger (170; US)
Stellyvonne (182; SA)
Fidalgo Climax (182; US)

Medium Decorative
Edna C (202; US)
Kenora Lisa (204; US)
Formby Perfection (208; A)
April Dawn (230; US)

Medium Semi-cactus
Magic Moment (241; US)
Hamari Accord (242; B)
Kenora Sunset (252; US)

Medium Cactus
Juanita (267; SA)
Alfred Grille (270; G)
Camano Shadows (273; US)
Nita (274 US)

Nicola Higgo (290, laciniated; SA)
Nenekazi (290; SA)
Jennie (290; US)
Nargold (292; SA)

Small Decorative
Ruskin Diane (302; B)
Hamilton Lilian (303; C)
Hy Clown (310; C)
Skipley Spot (315; US)
Kenora Moonbeam (322; US)
Goldilocks (322; US)
Chilson's Pride (330; US)
Santa Claus (335; US)

Small Semi-cactus
Camano Cloud (344; US)
Just Peachy (350; US)

Small Cactus
Brookside Cheri (365; US)
Camano Thunder (369; US)
Kiwi Gloria (370; B)
Taratahi Lilac (370; NZ)
Jessica (375; US)

Miniature Decorative
Mary Hammett (401; NZ)
Pineapple Lollipop (402; US)
Rose Toscano (403; US)
Rebecca Lynn (405; US)
Elizabeth Hammett (408; NZ)
Brookside J Cooley (422; US)

Miniature Semi-cactus
Mary Jo (444; US)

Miniature Cactus
Alpen Snowflake (461; US)
Nicole C (463; US)
Glenbank Twinkle (470; A)

Ball
Brookside Snowball (501; US)
L'Ancresse (501; B)
Snoho Peggy (505; US)
Kenora Fireball (506; US)
Cornel (507; H)

Jessie G (509; US)
Crichton Honey (511; B)
Robin Hood (513; B)

Miniature Ball
Pocrates (521; US)
Nettie (522; B)
Riisa (526; US)
Ruddy (526; US)
Barbarry Gem (527; B)
Robann Royal (528; US)
Downham Royal (529; B)

Pompon
Yellow Baby (542; H)
Poppet (543; H)
Mi Wong (545; B)
Moorplace (547; B)
Glenplace (549; ?)

Waterlily
Porcelain (601; B)
Cameo (602; A)
Figurine (604; A)
Wildwood Marie (605; US)
Red Velvet (606; A)

Peony
Powder Gull (624; US)

Anemone
Alpen Fury (646; US)

Collerette
Alpen Cherub (661; US)
Christmas Star (666; US)

Mignon Single
Inflammation (723; H)
Rembrandt (727; US)
Matthew Juul (733; US)

Orchid
Juul's Star (741; US)
Honka (742; US)
Marie Schnugg (746; US)

Novelty
Alloway Candy (764; NZ)

APPENDIX VII
READING ABOUT DAHLIAS

...of the books in this list are ...of print, but may be found in ...lic libraries.

Barnes, A. T. *The Dahlia Grower's Treasury* (2nd Revised Edition) W. H. & L. Collingridge Ltd., London, 1966. 168pp.

Clénet, Georges *Les Dahlias Culture, Utilisations, Variétés* Editions Rustica, Paris, 1995. 96pp.

Damp, Philip *Growing Dahlias* Croom Helm Ltd., London, 1981. 139pp.

Damp, Philip *Growing & Showing Dahlias* David & Charles, England, 1985. 68pp.

Damp, Philip *Dahlias: The Complete Guide* The Crowood Press, England, 1995. 157pp.

Damp, P. & Peskett, P. *Dahlia 100 (Centenary Booklet)*, The National Dahlia Society, England, 1981. 82pp.

Drayson, G. F. *Dahlias* Ward, Lock & Co., 1958. 160pp.

Drayson, G. F. *How to Grow the Dahlia* (Revised Edition), The National Dahlia Society, England, 1970. 32pp.

Hammet, Keith *The World of Dahlias* Reed Ltd., New Zealand, 1980. 142pp.

Lawrence, W. J. C. 'The Genetics and Cytology of *Dahlia variabilis*' *Journal of Genetics*, Vol. 24: 257–306, 1931.

Lawrence, W. J. C. 'The Evolution and History of the Dahlia' *The Dahlia Annual 1970*, pp.16–24. The National Dahlia Society, England.

Sorensen, Paul D. 'Revision of the Genus Dahlia' *Rhodara*, USA. Vol. 71 (786) pp.309–365 and Vol. 71 (787) pp.367–416, 1969.

Sorensen, Paul D. 'The Dahlia: An Early History' *Arnoldia*, USA. Vol. 30 (4) pp.121–138, 1970.

Swami Vinayananda *Dahlia Growing* Associated Publishing Co., New Delhi, 1985. 104pp.

Swami Vinayananda *Dahlia Breeding* National Horticulture Board & Dahlia Society of India, 1993. 80pp.

Many of the national societies regularly publish information for growers, primarily for their members, but most publications are also available to the general public. Contact should be made with the relevant National Secretary. Examples include:

Dahlia Annual. The National Dahlia Society, England.

The Bulletin of the American Dahlia Society Inc.

The Indian Dahlia Annual The Dahlia Society Of India.

Regional societies and associations also publish bulletins and newsletters, for example:

Dahlias of Today Puget Sound Dahlia Association (USA).

Dahlia Society of South Australia The National Dahlia Society of Victoria (Australia).

Other publications include:

Dahlias Classified Directory and Judging Rules The National Dahlia Society, England, published every two years.

Classification & Handbook of Dahlias The American Dahlia Society Inc.

Guide to Growing & Caring for Dahlias The American Dahlia Society Inc.

Judging and Registration The Dahlia Society of India.

Award of Garden Merit Plants The Royal Horticultural Society, England.

The RHS Plant Finder The Royal Horticultural Society and Dorling Kindersley, England.

INDEX

Page numbers in *italics* refer to illustrations

Acocotli 17
Anemone-flowered dahlias 24, 28, 153, 155, 156
Aster 14
Ball dahlias 28, 30, 32, 140, 155, 156
Cactus dahlias 12, 25, 28, 31, 74, 153, 154, 155, 156
Charm dahlias 13
Chrysanthemum 14
Chrysanthemum dahlias 27
Cocoxochitl 17
Collerette dahlias 12, 24, 28, 32, 62, 153, 155, 156
Coreopsis 14
Cosmos 14, 40
Cosmos diversifolius 41
Crocosmia 44
Dahlias:
D. 'Abridge Ben' 97
D. 'Abridge Taffy' 30, 97
D. 'Acme of Perfection' 12
D. 'Akita No Hikari' 34, 97, 139
D. 'Alan Melville' 97
D. 'Alan Sparkes' 97
D. 'Alfred C' 33, 97
D. 'Alfred Grille' 156
D. 'Alloway Candy' 156
D. 'Alloway Cottage' 98
D. 'Alltami Corsair' *98*, 98
D. 'Almand's Climax' 98
D. 'Aloha' ('Bridge View Aloha') 74, 102, 154
D. 'Alpen Cherub' 156
D. 'Alpen Fury' 156
D. 'Alpen Snowflake' 156
D. 'Alva's Doris' 98
D. 'Alva's Supreme' 29, 98, 153
D. 'Amber Banker' 100
D. 'Amberglow' 98
D. 'Amelisweert' 98
D. 'Amgard Coronet' 99, 153
D. 'Amgard Delicate' 99, 153
D. 'Amira' 99
D. 'Ananta Patel' 99
D. 'Andrew Lockwood' 99, 153
D. 'Andrew Magson' 99
D. 'Andrew Mitchell' 99
D. 'Andries Orange' 34, 99
D. 'Andries Wonder' 99
D. 'Anglia Water' 30, 99

D. 'Angora' 99
D. 'Anja Doc' 99
D. 'Anniversary Ball' *18*, 99, *140*, 153
D. 'Apache' 99
D. *apiculata* 38
D. 'Apricot Beauty' 100
D. 'Apricot Jewel' 100
D. 'April Dawn' 156
D. 'Arab Queen' 33, 100
D. 'Arranger's Delight' 100
D. 'Arthur Hills' 100
D. 'Athalie' 31, 100, 153
D. *atropurpurea* 38
D. 'Aurora's Kiss' 100
D. *australis* 38, 40
D. 'Autumn Fire' 100, 127
D. 'Autumn Lustre' 100
D. 'Aylett's Dazzler' *see* 'Dazzler'
D. 'B.J. Beauty' 29, *101*, 101, 153
D. 'Babette' 100, *140*
D. 'Banker' *25*, 31, *74*, 100, 153
D. 'Barbary Ball' 100, 153
D. 'Barbary Banker' 100
D. 'Barbary Bluebird' 100
D. 'Barbary Gem' 100, 153, 156
D. 'Barbary Oracle' 100
D. 'Barbary Snowball' 100
D. 'Baret Joy' 101
D. *barkerae* 38, 40
D. 'Beatrice' 101
D. 'Beauty of Brentwood' 12
D. 'Belle of the Ball' *71*, 101
D. 'Ben Huston' 101,153
D. 'Bernard C. Hayes' 101
D. 'Berwick Wood' 101
D. 'Bishop of Llandaff' *2*, 34, 39, 44, *52*, *58*, 101, 143, 154
D. 'Bizet' 33
D. 'Black Fire' 101
D. 'Blazdon Red' *2*, 44
D. 'Bloom's Wildwood' 101
D. 'Bon Esperance' *53*, 102, 153
D. 'Bonaventure' 29, 102, 153, 156
D. 'Bonny Blue' 102
D. 'Border Prince' 102
D. 'Border Princess' 102
D. 'Bracken Ballerina' 102

D. 'Bracken Tribune' 102
D. 'Brackenhill Flame' 102
D. 'Brandaris' 102
D. 'Brandysnap' 102
D. 'Breckland Joy' 102
D. *brevis* 38
D. 'Bridge View Aloha' (*see* 'Aloha')
D. 'Brookfield Deirdre' 103, *141*, 153
D. 'Brookfield Delight' *53*
D. 'Brookfield Enid' *see* 'Anniversary Ball'
D. 'Brookside Cheri' 156
D. 'Brookside J. Cooley' 156
D. 'Brookside Snowball' 156
D. 'Butterball' 103
D. 'Camano Cloud' 156
D. 'Camano Messenger' 156
D. 'Camano Shadows' 143, 156
D. 'Camano Thunder' 156
D. 'Cameo' 103, 156
D. 'Can-Can' 103
D. 'Candy Keene' 127
D. *cardiophylla* 38
D. 'Carolina Moon' 103
D. 'Carstone Cobblers' 103
D. 'Carstone Ruby' 103, 153
D. *cervantessii* 41
D. 'Charles Dickens' 103
D. 'Charlie Kenwood' *32*, 103, *106*
D. 'Charlie Two' *103*, 103, 153
D. 'Cheerio' 103
D. 'Cherida' 104
D. 'Cherwell Goldcrest' 104
D. 'Chic' 104
D. 'Chilson's Pride' 156
D. 'Chimborazo' *32*, *62*, 104, 153
D. 'Chloe's Keene' 127
D. 'Choh' 24, 104
D. 'Christmas Carol' 104
D. 'Christmas Star' 156
D. 'Christopher Nickerson' 104
D. 'Christopher Taylor' 104
D. 'Cindy' *55*, 104, *106*
D. 'Clair de Lune' 104
D. 'Clara Huston' 156
D. 'Classic A1' 104
D. *coccinea* 9, 10, 14, 15, 37, 38, 39, 40, 41, 79

D. 'Coltness Gem' 13, 78, 104, 153
D. 'Comet' 24, 104, 153
D. 'Commander-in-Chief' 11
D. 'Connie Bartlam' 104
D. 'Connoisseur's Choice' 104
D. 'Conway' 34, 104
D. 'Cornel' *32*, *59*, 105, *141*, 156
D. 'Corona' 105
D. *coronata* 41
D. 'Cream Alvas' 98
D. 'Creve Coeur' 156
D. 'Crichton Honey' 156
D. *crocata* 41
D. 'Croydon Masterpiece' 105
D. 'Cryfield Bryn' 34, 105
D. 'Cryfield Keene' 127
D. 'Cryfield Max' 105
D. 'Curiosity' 105, 153
D. 'Daddy's Choice' 105
D. 'Daleko Jupiter' 33, 105, 154
D. 'Daleko Polonia' 105
D. 'Dana Alice' 105, *125*
D. 'Dana Frank' *1*, 105, *125*
D. 'Dana Iris' 105, 153
D. 'Dark Stranger' 105
D. 'Davar Donna' 105
D. 'Davenport Sunlight' 105, 154
D. 'David Digweed' 108
D. 'David Howard' *51*, 108, 153
D. 'Dazzler' 108
D. 'Debra Ann Craven' 108
D. 'Dedham' 29, 108
D. 'Diana Gregory' 108, 153
D. *dissecta* 13, 38, 39
D. 'Doc van Horn' 108
D. 'Don's Diana' 108
D. 'Doris Day' 108
D. 'Downham Royal' *32*, 108, *141*, 156
D. 'Dr Caroline Rabbitt' 108
D. 'Dr John Grainger' 108
D. 'Duet' *32*, 108
D. 'Easter Sunday' *108*, 108
D. 'Eastwood Moonlight' 33, 108, 154
D. 'Ed Lloyd' 109
D. 'Edinburgh' *32*, *109*, 109, 153
D. 'Edna C' 109, 156

D. 'Elizabeth Hammett' 30, 109
D. 'Ella Britain' 46, 47, 109
D. 'Ellen Huston' 109, 154
D. 'Elma Elizabeth (syn. 'Elma E') 109, 153
D. 'Elmdon Hank' 109
D. 'Elsie Huston' 156
D. 'Enfield Salmon' 109
D. 'Ernie Pitt' 16, 109
D. 'Evelyn Foster' 29, 109, 153
D. 'Evelyn Rumbold' 109
D. 'Evening Mail' 109
D. excelsa 38, 39
D. 'Exotic Dwarf' 109
D. 'Fascination' 109, 154
D. 'Fashion Monger' 109
D. 'Fermain' 109, 153
D. 'Fidalgo Climax' 156
D. 'Figaro' 78, 110
D. 'Figurine' 110, 110, 153, 156
D. 'Finchcocks' 110
D. 'First Lady' 110
D. 'Flutterby' 110
D. foeniculifolia 38
D. 'Foreman's Jubilee' 110
D. 'Formby Perfection' 156
D. 'Formby Supreme' 110
D. 'Frank Holmes' 110, 125, 153
D. 'Frank Hornsey' 30, 110
D. fulgens 41
D. 'Gaiety' 110
D. 'Gala Parade' 32, 107, 111, 111
D. 'Galator' 111
D. 'Garden Festival' 111, 153
D. 'Garden Party' 111
D. 'Gay Pride' 139
D. 'Gay Princess' 111
D. 'Geerlings Indian Summer' 111
D. 'Geerlings Queeny' 111
D. gentryi 41
D. 'Gerrie Hoek' 26, 45, 111, 153
D. 'Gipsy Boy' 111
D. 'Giraffe' 13, 34, 111, 154
D. glabrata 40
D. 'Glenbank Twinkle' 75, 111, 156
D. 'Glenplace' 156
D. 'Glenvalley Kathy' 111
D. 'Glorie van Heemstede' 26, 26, 111, 153
D. 'Go American' 111, 112, 153
D. 'Golden Impact' 33, 112, 154
D. 'Golden Willo' 112
D. 'Goldilocks' 156
D. 'Grace Rushton' 112
D. gracilis
D. 'Grand Duc' 112, 153

D. 'Grand Willo' 112
D. 'Grenidor Pastelle' 33, 112, 138, 154
D. 'Gurtla Twighlight' 112
D. 'Hallmark' 31, 32, 112, 125, 153
D. 'Hamari Accord' 25, 75, 112, 154, 156
D. 'Hamari Bride' 33, 113
D. 'Hamari Fiesta' 113
D. 'Hamari Girl' 113
D. 'Hamari Gold' 113, 153
D. 'Hamari Katrina' 33, 113
D. 'Hamari Rose' 32, 113, 140, 153
D. 'Hamari Sunshine' 32, 107, 113
D. 'Hamilton Amanda' 113
D. 'Hamilton Lillian' 156
D. 'Happy Hanny' 113
D. 'Harvest Amanda' 113
D. 'Harvest Samantha' 113
D. 'Hayley Jane' 34, 75, 113, 154
D. 'Highgate Robbie' 113
D. 'Highgate Torch' 113
D. 'Hillcrest Albino' 113
D. 'Hillcrest Blaze' 113
D. 'Hillcrest Carmen' 114
D. 'Hillcrest Desire' 114
D. 'Hillcrest Divine' 114
D. 'Hillcrest Jessica' 114
D. 'Hillcrest Royal' 31, 114, 114
D. 'Hillcrest Suffusion' 114
D. 'Hillcrest Ultra' 114, 153
D. hintonii 38
D. 'Holland Herald' 114
D. 'Honey' 24, 53, 114
D. 'Honeymoon Dress' 114, 153
D. 'Honka' 156
D. 'Horn of Plenty' 114
D. hortensis 15
D. 'Hy Clown' 156
D. 'Hy Fire' 114
D. 'Ice Cream Beauty' 114
D. 'I Lyke It' 114, 154
D. imperialis 14, 38, 39, 152
D. 'Ina Spurs' 114
D. 'Inca Dambuster' 33, 114, 154
D. 'Inca Metropolitan' 29, 115
D. 'Inflammation' 115, 115, 156
D. 'Inglebrook Jill' 62, 115
D. 'Inimitable' 12
D. 'Inland Dynasty' 115, 154, 156
D. 'Irene's Pride' 156
D. 'Iris' 115, 153
D. 'Islander' 156
D. 'Jackie Magson' 115

D. 'Jaldec Joker' 115
D. 'Jaldec Jolly' 115
D. 'Jean Lister' 115
D. 'Jeanette Carter' 30, 115, 153
D. 'Jescot Julie' 34, 115, 154
D. 'Jessica Crutchfield' 115
D. 'Jessica' 25, 115, 154, 156
D. 'Jessie G' 55, 115, 156
D. 'Jessie Ross' 115
D. 'Jill's Delight' 116
D. 'Jim Branigan' 116
D. 'Jo's Choice' 116
D. 'John Street' 116, 153
D. 'Juanita' 156
D. juarezii 12, 41
D. 'Jura' 34, 116, 154
D. 'Just Peachy' 156
D. 'Juul's Star' 156
D. 'Karenglen' 30, 66, 116, 153
D. 'Kathleen's Alliance' 48, 116
D. 'Kelsae's Carla' 116
D. 'Keltie' 29, 116
D. 'Kelvin Floodlight' 116
D. 'Kenora Challenger' 33, 95, 116, 154
D. 'Kenora Christmas' 106, 116
D. 'Kenora Clyde' 156
D. 'Kenora Fireball' 156
D. 'Kenora Frills' 116
D. 'Kenora Lisa' 156
D. 'Kenora Moonbeam' 156
D. 'Kenora Sunset' 25, 75, 116, 117, 154 , 156
D. 'Kenora Superb' 117, 117
D. 'Kenora Valentine' 29, 117, 153
D. 'Kenora Wildfire' 156
D. 'Keynes' White' 12
D. 'Kidd's Climax' 32, 98, 106, 117, 143, 153, 156
D. 'King Soccer' 117
D. 'Kiwi Brother' 117
D. 'Kiwi Gloria' 25, 31, 35, 95, 117, 118, 153, 156
D. 'Klankstad Kerkrade' 31, 85, 117, 153
D. 'Kotari Jackpot' 117
D. 'Kotari Magic' 32, 107, 117
D. 'Kung Fu' 117
D. 'L'Ancresse' 118, 156
D. 'La Cierva' 63, 118
D. 'laciniata purpurea' 13, 41
D. 'Lady Kerkrade' 117
D. 'Lady Linda' 118
D. 'Lady Sunshine' 118
D. 'Laura Marie' 30, 30, 118
D. 'Lauren's Moonlight' 108
D. 'Lavender Athalie' 25, 100
D. 'Lavender Perfection' 118
D. 'Lavengro' 7, 118, 153

D. 'Lemon Elegans' 34, 118, 154
D. 'Liberator' 118, 153
D. 'Light Music' 31,118
D. 'Linda's Chester' 118, 122
D. linearis 38
D. 'Lismore Moonlight' 118
D. 'Lismore Peggy' 118
D. 'Lismore Willie' 118, 153
D. 'Little Glenfern' 118
D. 'Little Sally' 119
D. 'Little William' 119, 140
D. 'Lloyd Huston' 119, 154
D. 'Loretta' 119
D. 'Loud Applause' 119
D. 'Lucifer' 13, 39
D. 'Lula Pattie' 114, 119, 153
D. 'Mabel Ann' 119, 153
D. macdougalii 38, 39
D. 'Magic Moment' 156
D. 'Maisey Mooney' 119, 153, 156
D. 'Majestic Athalie' 100
D. 'Maltby Fanfare' 62, 119
D. 'Margaret Anne' 36, 119
D. 'Marie Schnugg' 156
D. 'Mariner's Light' 119
D. 'Mariposa' 119
D. 'Mark Hardwick' 119
D. 'Marlene Joy' 71, 119, 154
D. 'Mary Hammett' 156
D. 'Mary Jo' 156
D. 'Mary Partridge' 120
D. 'Mary Pitt' 120
D. 'Mary Richards' 120
D. 'Mascot Maya' 120
D. 'Match' 34, 120, 154
D. 'Matthew Juul' 156
D. merckii 14, 38, 39, 40
D. 'Mi Wong' 156
D. 'Mignon Silver' 53
D. 'Minley Carol' 120
D. 'Minley Linda' 120, 124, 153
D. 'Misthill Contessa' 120
D. 'Misthill Delight' 120
D. 'Mistral' 120
D. 'Mme. Stappers' 46,47, 120
D. 'Molly Mooney' 75, 120
D. mollis 38
D. 'Monk Marc' 127
D. 'Monkstown Diane' 120
D. 'Moonfire' 15, 120, 153
D. moorei 38
D. 'Moor Place' 31, 120, 121, 124, 153, 156
D. 'Mrs A. Woods' 120
D. 'Mrs McDonald Quill' 12
D. 'Naargold' (syn. 'Nargold') 120, 156
D. 'Nantenan' 33, 121
D. 'Nationwide' 121
D. 'Nellie Birch' 121

D. 'Nenekazi' 71, 94, 121, 156
D. 'Neon City' 121
D. 'Nepos' 121
D. 'Nettie' 121, 156
D. 'Neveric' 121
D. 'Newby' 121
D. 'Newchurch' 122
D. 'Nicola' 122
D. 'Nicola Higgo' 156
D. 'Nicole C' 156
D. 'Night Editor' 122, 153
D. 'Nijinsky' 122
D. 'Nina Chester' 122, 153
D. 'Nita' 156
D. 'Nonette' 143
D. 'Noreen' 122, 122, 125, 153
D. 'Nunton Harvest' 122
D. 'Omo' 122,153
D. 'Opal' 122
D. 'Orange Mullet' 122, 153
D. 'Orel' 62, 122, 153
D. 'Oreti Duke' 122
D. 'Orfeo' 31
D. 'Othello' 33
D. 'Park Delight' 31
D. 'Park Princess' 31, 122, 153
D. 'Paul Chester' 123
D. 'Paul Critchley' 123
D. 'Peace Pact' 32
D. 'Peach Athalie' 100
D. 'Peach Cupid' 133, 141
D. 'Pearl of Heemstede' 123
D. 'Pembroke Pattie' 123
D. 'Penhill Moonrise' 123
D. 'Pensford Marion' 32, 65,
   123, 125, 153
D. 'Periton' 86, 123
D. 'Phill's Pink' 123
D. 'Phoenix' 32, 107, 123
D. 'Pim's Moonlight' 108
D. 'Pineapple Lollipop' 123
D. 'Pink Jupiter' 105
D. 'Pink Kerkrade' 117
D. pinnata 9, 14, 15, 37, 38, 39,
   79
D. 'Piperoo' 80, 123
D. 'Piper's Pink' 34, 75, 123,
   144, 154
D. platylepsis 41
D. 'Playboy' 123
D. 'Pocrates' 156
D. 'Polar Sight' 31, 123, 153
D. 'Polventon Supreme' 123,
   153
D. 'Polyand' 123, 153
D. 'Pontiac' 126
D. popenovii 41
D. 'Pop Harris' see 'Liberator'
D. 'Pop Willo' 126
D. 'Poppet' 156
D. 'Porcelain' 26, 126, 156
D. 'Powder Gull' 156

D. 'Preston Park' 126, 126, 153
D. 'Pride of Berlin' 126
D. 'Pride of Holland' 131
D. 'Princess Marie Jose' 126
D. pteropoda 38
D. pubescens 13, 41
D. purpurea 40
D. purpusii 38
D. 'Pwll Coch' 126
D. 'Quel Diable' 126, 127, 154
D. 'Raiser's Pride' 31
D. 'Rebecca Lynn' 156
D. 'Red Balloon' 32, 126, 140
D. 'Red Carol' 124
D. 'Red Velvet' 32, 126, 134,
   156
D. 'Reddy' 21, 52, 83, 126, 153
D. 'Redskin' 78
D. 'Reginald Keene' 33, 126,
   154
D. 'Rembrandt' 156
D. 'Respectable' 33, 127
D. 'Reverend Colwyn Vale'
   101, 127
D. 'Rhonda' 127, 153
D. 'Richard Marc' 127
D. 'Riisa' 32, 127, 127, 141,
   156
D. 'Risca Miner' 30, 127, 153
D. 'Rita Hill' 63
D. 'Robann Royal' 156
D. 'Robin Hood' 156
D. 'Rokesley Mini' 31, 127, 154
D. rosea 9, 10, 14, 41
D. 'Rose Jupiter' 105
D. 'Rose Toscano' 156
D. 'Rossendale Tara' 127
D. 'Rothsay Reveller' 64, 127
D. 'Rothsay Robin' 127
D. 'Rothsay Superb' 128
D. 'Rotterdam' 33, 74, 128
D. 'Royal Adelaide' 10
D. 'Ruby Wedding' 128
D. 'Ruddy' 156
D. rudis 38
D. rupicola 38
D. 'Ruskin Belle' 128
D. 'Ruskin Diane' 29, 30, 107,
   128, 153, 156
D. 'Rustig' 29, 128, 153
D. 'Salmon Athalie' 25, 100, 144
D. 'Salsa' 128
D. 'Sam Huston' 128, 153
D. 'Santa Claus' 156
D. scapigera 38, 40
D. scapigeroides 38
D. 'Scarlet Comet' 6, 24, 104
D. 'Schweitzer's Kokarde' 128
D. 'Senzoe Ursula' 128, 153
D. 'Shandy' 22, 128
D. sherffii 38, 40, 41, 52
D. 'Sherwood Titan' 128

D. 'Shirley Alliance' 128
D. 'Shy Princess' 31, 128
D. 'Siemen Doorenbos' 129
D. 'Silver City' 29, 129, 153
D. 'Skilman's Hebe' 12
D. 'Skipley Spot' 128, 129, 156
D. 'Small World' 31, 129, 153
D. 'Snip' 129, 154
D. 'Snoho Peggy' 129, 137, 156
D. 'Snowy' 129
D. 'So Dainty' 34, 128, 129
D. 'Spartacus' 156
D. 'Springwood Rival' 11, 12
D. 'Starlight Keene' 127
D. 'Stellyvonne' 156
D. 'Suffolk Bride' 129, 154
D. 'Suffolk Punch' 130
D. superflua 10, 40
D. 'Sure Thing' 130
D. 'Surprise' 130
D. 'Swanvale' 30, 130, 153
D. 'Sweetheart' 53, 130, 153
D. 'Sylvia's Desire' 130
D. 'Symbol' 33, 130, 154
D. 'Tahiti Sunrise' 74, 130, 131,
   154
D. 'Tally Ho' 44, 44
D. 'Taratahi Lilac' 130, 156
D. 'Tender Moon' 3, 96, 130
D. tenuicaulis 38, 39
D. tenuis 13, 38
D. 'Thais' 26, 130, 153
D. 'Thalia' 130
D. 'The Master' 130
D. 'Tiny Tot' 130
D. 'Tohsuikyoh' 34
D. 'Tom Thumb' 130
D. 'Topmix' 130
D. 'Trelyn Kiwi' 35, 117
D. 'Trengove Jill' 131
D. 'Trengrove Tauranga' 131,
   153
D. 'Trengrove Terror' 131
D. 'Tui Orange' 131, 154
D. 'Vaguely Noble' 131
D. 'Valerie Buller' 131
D. 'Vantage' 33, 131, 154
D. × variablis 8, 15, 38, 41
D. 'Verda' 156
D. 'Vidal Tracy' 131
D. 'Video' 131, 154
D. 'Walter Hardisty' 131,
   156
D. 'Wanda's Antarctica' 131
D. 'Wanda's Capella' 92, 131,
   153
D. 'Wandy' 131
D. 'Warkton Amber' 132
D. 'Warkton Ann' 132
D. 'Warminster Rival' 12
D. 'Wendy's Place' 120
D. 'Weston Flamingo' 132

D. 'Weston Nuggett' 25, 54, 74,
   132, 154
D. 'Weston Pirate' 132
D. 'White Alvas' 98
D. 'White Ballet' 132
D. 'White Klankstad' 85, 117
D. 'White Moonlight' 108
D. 'Wildman' 156
D. 'Wildwood Marie' 156
D. 'Willo's Night' 132
D. 'Willo's Surprise' 132
D. 'Willo's Violet' 31, 31, 32,
   65, 132, 153
D. 'Willowfield Gill' 133
D. 'Winkie Colonel' 133
D. 'Wisemark' 133
D. 'Witteman's Superba' 133
D. 'Wooton Cupid' 30, 133,
   133, 153
D. 'Wooton Impact' 33, 133,
   154
D. 'Worton Joy' 133
D. 'Worton Sally Ann' 133
D. 'Yellow Baby' 156
D. 'Yellow Hammer' 133, 153
D. 'Yelnow Harmony' 133,
   153
D. zimpanii 41
D. 'Zorro' 133, 133, 153

Decorative dahlias 12, 26, 28,
   29, 32, 106, 107, 153, 155,
   156
Dwarf bedder 24, 153, 154
Dwarf dahlias 13,
Fimbriated dahlias 71, 155
Georgina 9, 15, 40
Georgina superflua 40
Helenium 'Butterpat' 44
Helianthus 14
Lacinated dahlias (see
   fimbriated dahlias)
Liatris spicata 45
Lilliput dahlias 12, 24, 153
Mignon dahlias 13, 155, 156
Miscellaneous dahlias 24, 154
Novelty dahlias 155, 156
Orchid-flowered dahlias 13,
   154, 155, 156
Peony-flowered dahlias 12, 24,
   27, 155, 156
Pompon dahlias 12, 27, 30, 32,
   124, 153, 155, 156
Rudbeckia 14, 45
Semi-cactus dahlias 24, 28, 74,
   154, 155, 156
Single-flowered dahlias 24, 28,
   153, 155, 156
Star dahlia 13, 27
Tom Thumb 13
Waterlily dahlias 13, 26, 28, 32,
   153, 155, 156